The Little SAS® Book

a p r i m e r

Lora D. Delwiche and *Susan J. Slaughter*

The correct bibliographic citation for this manual is as follows: Delwiche, Lora D., and Slaughter, Susan J., *The Little SAS Book: A Primer*, Cary, NC: SAS Institute Inc., 1995. 228 pp.

The Little SAS Book: A Primer

ISBN 1-55544-215-3

SAS Institute Inc., SAS Campus Drive, Cary, North Carolina 27513.

1st printing, June 1995

The SAS® System is an integrated system of software providing complete control over data access, management, analysis, and presentation. Base SAS software is the foundation of the SAS System. Products within the SAS System include SAS/ACCESS®, SAS/AF®, SAS/ASSIST®, SAS/CALC®, SAS/CONNECT®, SAS/CPE®, SAS/DMI®, SAS/EIS®, SAS/ENGLISH®, SAS/ETS®, SAS/FSP®, SAS/GRAPH®, SAS/IMAGE®, SAS/IML®, SAS/IMS-DL/I®, SAS/INSIGHT®, SAS/LAB®, SAS/NVISION®, SAS/OR®, SAS/PH-Clinical®, SAS/QC®, SAS/REPLAY-CICS®, SAS/SESSION®, SAS/SHARE®, SAS/STAT®, SAS/TOOLKIT®, SAS/TRADER®, SAS/TUTOR®, SAS/DB2™, SAS/GEO™, SAS/GIS™, SAS/PH-Kinetics™, SAS/SHARE*NET™, SAS/SPECTRAVIEW™, and SAS/SQL-DS™ software. Other SAS Institute products are SYSTEM 2000® Data Management Software, with basic SYSTEM 2000, CREATE™, Multi-User™, QueX™, Screen Writer™, and CICS interface software; InfoTap® software; NeoVisuals® software; JMP®, JMP IN®, JMP Serve®, and JMP *Design*® software; SAS/RTERM® software; and the SAS/C® Compiler and the SAS/CX® Compiler; VisualSpace™ software; and Emulus® software. MultiVendor Architecture™ and MVA™ are trademarks of SAS Institute Inc. SAS Institute also offers SAS Consulting®, SAS Video Productions®, Ambassador Select®, and On-Site Ambassador℠ services. *Authorline*®, Books by Users℠, The Encore Series™, *JMPer Cable*®, *Observations*®, *SAS Communications*®, *SAS Training*®, *SAS Views*®, the SASware Ballot®, and SelecText™ documentation are published by SAS Institute Inc. The SAS Video Productions logo and the Books by Users SAS Institute's Author Service logo are registered service marks and the Helplus logo and The Encore Series logo are trademarks of SAS Institute Inc. All trademarks above are registered trademarks or trademarks of SAS Institute Inc. in the USA and other countries. ® indicates USA registration.

The Institute is a private company devoted to the support and further development of its software and related services.

IBM®, DB2®, and OS/2® are registered trademarks or trademarks of International Business Machines Corporation. ORACLE® is a registered trademark or trademark of Oracle Corporation. ® indicates USA registration.

Other brand and product names are registered trademarks or trademarks of their respective companies.

SAS Institute does not assume responsibility for the accuracy of any material presented in this book.

Contents

Acknowledgments

Books like this don't happen in a vacuum. There are so many people who have helped us along the way that we are amazed when we count them.

We are grateful to all the people at SAS Institute who worked on our book. We would particularly like to thank Jennifer M. Ginn and David D. Baggett, our editors; Patsy J. Poole, our copyeditor; Heather B. Dees, our proofreader; Blanche W. Phillips, our production specialist; and Ginny Matsey and Mike Pezzoni, our designers. Many reviewers provided insightful and nontelegraphic comments that greatly improved the book: M. Michelle Buchecker, Matthew R. Clark, Sanford T. Gayle, Sally Painter, Robina G. Thornton, Susan C. Tideman, Maggie Underberg, Linda Walters, and Michael Williams.

We are also grateful to other people who reviewed parts of our book: John Dickerhoff, Jim Allen, Ted Gould, Myrna Johnston, Chip Northup, Andra Northup, and Shelagh Nugent. Paul Schneeman photographed the authors. Susan Donahue prepared the illustrations for our book proposal. Jay Jaffe suggested that we write a SAS program to do our own index. Michael Delwiche wrote the C program in appendix D. Minghua Zhang provided material for the chapter on debugging programs. Edmond H. Weiss in his book *How to Write a Usable User Manual* (1985, ISI Press) reinforced our original concept for the two-page layout of this book. Susan would like to thank Carolyn Brown, whose red pen struck fear in the hearts of her advanced composition students. Thanks for telling me I should be a writer. Lora would like to thank J. S. Lytle who introduced her to the SAS System, which led to a career in SAS consulting and to writing this book.

Most of all we would like to thank our families, especially Michael and David, for their understanding and support.

Introducing SAS Software

SAS software is used by people all over the world—in over 100 countries, at over 25,000 sites, by an estimated 3 million users. SAS (pronounced sass) is both a company, SAS Institute, and software, the SAS System. When people say SAS, they sometimes mean the software running on their computers and sometimes mean the company. When you lease SAS you are paying for software, and for the services and support provided by the company. In this book, SAS means the software, and the company is referred to as SAS Institute.

People often ask what SAS stands for. Originally the letters S-A-S stood for Statistical Analysis System (not to be confused with Scandinavian Airlines System, San Antonio Shoemakers, or the Society for Applied Spectroscopy). SAS products have become so diverse that a few years back SAS Institute officially dropped the name Statistical Analysis System, now outgrown, and became simply SAS.

The roots of SAS software reach back to the 1970s when it started out as a software package for statistical analysis, but SAS didn't stop there. By the early 1980s SAS had already branched out into graphics, spreadsheets, and online data entry. Today the SAS family tree includes products as diverse as compilers for the C programming language, 3-D animation software, and a terminal emulator for microcomputers. To paraphrase a popular slogan, SAS isn't just statistics anymore. Just as AT&T is now more than telephones and telegraphs, SAS is more than statistics.

While SAS Institute has a diverse family of products, most of these products are integrated; that is, they can be put together like building blocks to construct a seamless system. For example, one day you might read your data using Base SAS, run a statistical analysis using SAS/STAT, and then display the results with SAS/GRAPH, all without leaving interactive SAS. Another time you might use SAS/ACCESS to read data stored in an external data base such as DB2 or ORACLE and analyze it using SAS/OR (operations research and project management), SAS/QC (quality improvement), or SAS/ETS (business planning, forecasting, and decision support), all in a single computer program.

Other software packages often behave differently from one operating system to another, but not SAS. You can take a program written on a personal computer and run it on a mainframe after changing only the operating-system-specific file handling statements. And because SAS programs are as portable as possible, SAS programmers are as portable as possible too. If you know SAS on one operating system, you can switch to another operating system without having to relearn SAS.

SAS Institute is committed to making SAS products available for all major computer operating systems. To facilitate this, SAS software is designed using a Multi-Vendor Architecture, meaning the software is written in as portable a way as possible. Only that small part of the software dealing with host-specific operations such as file handling must be customized for each individual operating system. The remainder of the computer code for SAS software is identical on all systems. As new operating systems emerge, SAS software can be ported quickly and so be available quickly to users.

SAS Institute puts a high percentage of its revenue into research and development, and each year SAS users help determine how that money will be spent by voting on the SASware Ballot. The ballot is a list of suggestions for new features and enhancements. All SAS users are eligible to vote and thereby influence the future development of SAS software. You can make your own suggestions for the SASware Ballot by writing to SAS Institute.

Sooner or later you will come up with a question to which you can't find the answer. With some software companies, very little technical support is available, or the support is available but only for an extra charge—not so with the Institute. SAS technical support is available to all sites. Further, SAS Institute's low employee turnover means better, more knowledgeable service for users. If you have a question about how to use SAS and can't find the answer yourself, first contact your site's official SAS Software Consultant or site representative. If your consultant cannot answer your question, then he or she will contact SAS technical support at (919) 677-8008 or via electronic mail.

Some people (especially microcomputer users) are surprised to learn that SAS software cannot be owned, only licensed. Licensing software is like leasing it; once a year you pay your rent. Licensing has one important advantage when compared with buying: you automatically get each new release without an extra charge. Since SAS software is continually being improved and new versions released, licensing is helpful. For information about licensing SAS products, contact the Institute:

> SAS Institute Inc.
> SAS Campus Drive
> Cary, NC 27513-2414
> (919) 677-8000

This book was written using Release 6.08 of the SAS System on the Windows operating system, but virtually all of the material covered here applies to any release of Version 6 for any operating system and should apply to future releases. If you are ever unsure of which version of SAS you are running, run a SAS program, any SAS program, and look at the beginning of your SAS log to find the release notes.

1

"An honest tale speeds best being plainly told."

WILLIAM SHAKESPEARE, *KING RICHARD III*

CHAPTER 1

Who, What, and How

1.1 ▶ What This Book Covers and Who Needs It

This book is for all new SAS users in business, government, academia, or anyone who will be doing data analysis using the SAS System. Readers need no prior experience with SAS software, but people who have some experience may still find this book useful for learning techniques they missed or as an easy-to-use reference.

This book introduces readers to the SAS language with lots of practical examples, clear and concise explanations, and as little technical jargon as possible. Most of the features covered here come from Base SAS, which contains the core of features used by all SAS programmers. The only exception is a brief chapter introducing SAS/STAT software. Once you learn to use Base SAS, you will be ready to learn other SAS products (such as SAS/AF, SAS/ETS, SAS/FSP, SAS/OR, or SAS/QC software) if you wish.

We included every feature of Base SAS that a beginning user is likely to need. Some people will be surprised because certain topics, such as arrays, are normally considered advanced. But they appear here because sometimes new users need them. However, that doesn't mean that you need to know everything in this book. On the contrary, this book is designed so you can read just those sections you need to solve your problems. Even if you read this book from cover to cover, you may find yourself returning to refresh your memory as new programming challenges arise.

This book starts with general concepts of the SAS language and then addresses common tasks such as

- ▶ running SAS programs
- ▶ reading raw data
- ▶ modifying data
- ▶ sorting, summarizing, and printing data
- ▶ combining data sets
- ▶ applying basic statistical procedures
- ▶ debugging SAS programs.

In the chapter on statistics, we cover four commonly used procedures for univariate statistics, correlation, regression, and analysis of variance. After you master the procedures in this book, the statements, options, and output available in other statistical procedures will look familiar.

Unfortunately, a book of this type cannot provide a thorough introduction to statistical concepts such as degrees of freedom, or crossed and nested effects. We assume that readers who are interested in statistical computing already know something about statistics. People who want to use statistical procedures but are unfamiliar with these concepts should seek out an introductory statistics text or, better yet, take a course in statistics.

The chapter on debugging is particularly unique and important. New users are sometimes intimidated by error messages, but there is no need to be. This chapter includes all the bugs that people commonly encounter, their possible causes, and how to fix them. Here you will also find advice on programming techniques that will help you to avoid getting bugs in the first place.

The appendices include more in-depth information for people with specific interests or experience:

- ▶ where to go for more information
- ▶ overview of SAS products
- ▶ coming to SAS from SPSS
- ▶ coming to SAS from a programming language
- ▶ coming to SAS from SQL.

To use this book you need no prior knowledge of SAS, but you must know something about your computer and local operating system. The SAS System behaves virtually the same from one operating system to another, but some differences are unavoidable. For example, every operating system has a different way of storing and accessing files. Some operating systems have more of a capacity for interactive computing than others. And the exact commands for printing files may be different even for two physically identical computers because of different local customs. This book addresses operating systems as much as possible, but no book can answer every question about your local operating system. You must have either a working knowledge of your operating system or someone you can turn to with questions.

This little book is not a replacement for the many SAS reference manuals. However, after reading this book, you will be able to go to the reference manuals and confidently find any in-depth information you need.

Last, we tried to make this book as readable as possible and, we hope, even enjoyable. Once you master the contents of this small book you will no longer be a beginning SAS programmer.

1.2 How This Book Works

Modular sections   Our goal in writing this book is to make learning SAS as easy and enjoyable as possible. Let's face it, SAS is a big topic. You may have already spent some time scratching your head in front of a shelf full of SAS manuals. We can't condense that entire shelf into this little book, but we can condense topics into short, readable sections. This entire book is composed of two-page sections, each section a complete topic. This way, you can easily skip over topics which do not apply to you. Of course, we think every section is important, or we would not have included it. You probably don't need to know everything in this book, however, to complete your job. By presenting topics in short digestible sections, we believe that learning SAS will be easier and more fun—like eating three meals a day instead of one giant meal a week.

Graphics   Wherever possible, graphics either identify the contents of the section or help explain the topic. A box with rough edges indicates a raw data file, and a box with nice smooth edges indicates a SAS data set. The squiggles inside the box indicate data—any old data—and a period

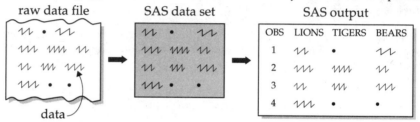

indicates a missing value. The arrow between boxes of these types means that the section explains how to get from data that look like one box to data that look like the other. Some sections have graphics which depict printed output. These graphics look like a stack of papers with variable names printed on the top of the page and observation numbers shown on the left.

Syntax   Some sections show the general form of particular statements (commonly referred to as syntax), and may also give example statements. When showing syntax, what is written in italics is a description of what goes in that spot in the statement, not what you actually type. If it is not in italics, then it is an example of what you could put there. SAS keywords are written in uppercase letters, and must be spelled exactly as shown.

The following shows two VAR statements. The first shows the syntax, or general form of the statement, while the second shows an example of an actual statement as it might appear in a SAS program. Notice that the keyword VAR is the same in both statements and that the descriptive term *variable-list* in the syntax statement has been replaced with actual variable names in the example statement.

	Syntax		Example
	VAR *variable-list*;		VAR lions tigers;

Cross-references   Occasionally, you may need more detail than would be appropriate for this book. To help you at those times, each section ends with cross-references. These cross-references are pointers to the SAS reference manuals where you can find more information on the section's topic. Each cross-reference includes a symbol (call it an icon if you like) for the SAS reference manual and the index item for that manual. By listing the index item rather than the page number or section name, we hope to encourage you to use the index. The index is a valuable tool when you are using SAS as you will always have to look things up. Unless you get very good at flipping to the right page, you will need to use the index. The following symbols are used for the SAS reference manuals:

A typical cross-reference would look like this:

| INPUT statement list input | **L** |

This means to look in the index of *SAS Language: Reference, Version 6, First Edition* for *INPUT statement* and then for *list input*.

---

[1]There is a SAS Companion reference manual for each operating system or environment. SAS tries to make things work the same in every environment, but sometimes this is impossible. The SAS Companion manuals cover topics specific to your environment.

1.3 Layout of Sample Programs

This book contains many sample SAS programs, each complete and executable. Programs are formatted in a way which makes them easy for you to read and understand. You do not have to format your programs this way, as SAS is very flexible, but attention to some of these details will make your programs easier to read. Easy-to-read programs are time savers for you, or the consultant you hire at $100 per hour, when you need to go back and decipher the program months or years later.

Each sample program is formatted in the following way:

Capitalization   All SAS keywords appear in uppercase letters. A keyword is an instruction to SAS and must be spelled correctly. Anything in lowercase letters is something that the programmer has made up: a variable name, a name for a SAS data set, a comment, or a title. For example, the following SAS statement shows the keyword INPUT in upper case and the variable names `lions` and `tigers` in lower case:

```
INPUT lions tigers;
```

SAS doesn't care if statements are in upper or lower case. This is an aid for you so you can easily see which words are SAS keywords and which are not.

Indention   The different parts of the program are shown by indenting all statements after the first in a step. This is a simple way to make your programs more readable, and it's a good habit to form. SAS doesn't really care where statements start or even if they are all on one line. In the following program, the INFILE and INPUT statements are indented, indicating that they belong with the DATA statement:

```
* Read animals' weights from file. Print the results.;
DATA animals;
   INFILE 'zoo.dat';
   INPUT lions tigers;
PROC PRINT;
RUN;
```

Comments   When appropriate, programs in this book have comments to help explain what the program does. The comments used in this book start with an asterisk (*) and end with a semicolon (;). It doesn't matter what's between the asterisk and the semicolon, SAS doesn't look at it. You could put your favorite cookie recipe in there if you want. However, comments are usually used to annotate the program, making it easier for someone to read your program and understand what you have done and why. For example, the preceding program starts with a comment statement describing the purpose of the program.

Another style of comment starts with a slash asterisk (/*) and ends with an asterisk slash (*/). This style of comment, unlike the asterisk-semicolon style, can be used within a SAS statement and can contain embedded semicolons. The following program shows this style of comment statement:

```
   /* Read animals' weights from file */
DATA animals;
   INFILE 'zoo.dat';
   INPUT lions tigers;
PROC PRINT;  /* Print the results */
RUN;
```

Since some operating systems interpret a slash asterisk (/*) in the first column as the end of a job, be careful when using this style of comment not to place it in the first column. For this reason, we chose the asterisk-semicolon style of comment for this book.

comment statement

2

"Nobody is too old to learn—but a lot of people keep putting it off."

WILLIAM O'NEILL

CHAPTER 2

Getting Started Using SAS® Software

2.1 The SAS Language

Many software applications are either menu driven, or command driven (enter a command—see the result). SAS is neither. With SAS, you use statements to write a series of instructions called a SAS program. The program communicates what you want to do and is written using the SAS language. There are some menu-driven front ends to SAS, SAS/ASSIST software for example, which make SAS appear like a point-and-click program. However, these front ends still use the SAS language to write programs for you. You will have much more flexibility using SAS if you learn to write your own programs using the SAS language. Maybe learning a new language is the last thing you want to do, but be assured that although there are parallels between SAS and languages you know (be they English or FORTRAN), SAS is much easier to learn.

SAS programs   A SAS program is a sequence of statements executed in order. A statement gives information or instructions to SAS and must be appropriately placed in the program. An everyday analogy to a SAS program is a trip to the bank. You enter your bank, stand in line, and when you finally reach the teller's window, you say what you want to do. The statements you give can be written down in the form of a program:

```
I would like to make a withdrawal.
   My account number is 0937.
   I would like $200.
   Give me five 20s and two 50s.
```

Note that you first say what you want to do, then give all the information the teller needs to carry out your request. The order of the subsequent statements may not be important, but you must start with the general statement of what you want to do. You would not, for example, go up to a bank teller and say, "Give me five 20s and two 50s." This is not only bad form but would probably make the teller's heart skip a beat or two. You must also make sure that all the subsequent statements belong with the first. You would not say, "I want the largest box you have" when making a withdrawal from your checking account. This statement belongs with "I would like to open a safe deposit box." A SAS program is an ordered set of SAS statements like the ordered set of instructions you use when you go to the bank.

Rules   As with any language, there are a few rules to follow when writing SAS programs. Fortunately for us, the rules for writing SAS programs are much fewer and simpler than those for English.

The most important rule is

Every SAS statement ends with a semicolon.

This sounds simple enough. But while children generally outgrow the habit of forgetting the period at the end of a sentence, SAS programmers never seem to outgrow forgetting the semicolon at the end of a SAS statement. Even the most experienced SAS programmer will at least occasionally forget the semicolon. You will be two steps ahead if you remember this simple rule.

Other rules govern the naming of variables and SAS data sets. You make up names for the variables in your data and for the data sets themselves. It is helpful to make up names that identify what the data represent, especially for variables. While the variable names A, B, and C might seem like perfectly fine, easy-to-type names when you write your program, the names SEX, HEIGHT, and WEIGHT will probably be more helpful when you go back to look at the program six months later. Follow these simple rules when making up names:

- Names must be eight characters or fewer in length.[1]
- Names must start with a letter or an underscore (_).
- Names can contain only letters, numerals, and the underscore (_). No %$!*&#@, please.

(Future releases of SAS may loosen the restrictions on naming, so check your version.)

There really aren't any rules about how to format your SAS program. While it is helpful to have a neat looking program with each statement on a line by itself and indentions to show the various parts of the program, it isn't necessary. SAS program statements can

- be in upper or lower case
- continue on the next line (as long as you don't split words in two)
- be on the same line as other statements
- start in any column.

So you see, SAS is so flexible that it is possible to write programs so disorganized that no one can read them, not even you. (Of course we don't recommend this.)

Errors   People who are just learning SAS often get frustrated because their programs do not work correctly the first time they write them. To make matters worse, SAS errors often come up in bright red letters, and for the poor person whose results turn out more red than black, this can be a very humbling experience. You should expect errors. Most programs simply don't work the first time, if for no other reason than that you are human. You forget a semicolon, misspell a word, have your fingers in the wrong place on the keyboard. It happens. Often one small mistake can generate a whole list of errors. Don't panic if you see red.

names

---

[1] It is possible, using the LABEL statement, to create labels up to 40 characters long for your variables. These labels can be printed in place of the variable names. Sections 3.11 and 5.1 discuss the LABEL statement.

2.2 SAS Data Sets

Before you run an analysis, before you write a report, before you do anything with your data, you must put it into a SAS data set. SAS expects your data to be in this special form. Getting your data into a SAS data set is usually quite simple as SAS is very flexible and can read almost any data. Once your data have been read into a SAS data set, SAS keeps track of what is where and in what form. All you have to do is specify the name and location of the data set you want, and SAS figures out what is in it.

Variables and observations   Data, of course, are the primary constituent of any data set. In SAS terminology the data consist of variables and observations. SAS data sets are sometimes described as rectangular, like a spreadsheet. Below you see a table containing a small data set. The rows are observations, and the columns are variables. The data point Charlie is one of the values of the variable NAME and is also part of the second observation.

Variables

		ID	NAME	HEIGHT	WEIGHT
	1	53	Susie	42	41
	2	54	Charlie	46	55
Observations	3	55	Calvin	40	35
	4	56	Lucy	46	52
	5	57	Dennis	44	.
	6	58		43	50

Data types   Raw data come in many different forms, but SAS simplifies this. In SAS there are just two data types: numeric and character. Numeric fields are, well, numbers. They can be added and subtracted, can have any number of decimal places, and can be positive or negative. In addition to numerals, numeric fields can contain plus signs (+), minus signs (-), decimal points (.), or E for scientific notation. Character data are everything else. They may contain numerals, letters, or special characters (such as $ or !) and can be up to 200 characters long.

If a variable contains letters or special characters, it must be character data. However, if it contains only numbers, then it may be numeric or character. You should base your decision on how you will use the variable.[1] Sometimes data that consist solely of numerals make more sense as character data than as numeric. ZIP codes, for example, are made up of numerals, but it just doesn't make sense to add, subtract, multiply, or divide ZIP codes. Such numbers make more sense as character data. In the previous data set, NAME is obviously a character variable, and HEIGHT and WEIGHT are numeric. ID, however, could be either numeric or character. It's your choice.

Missing data Sometimes despite your best efforts, your data may be incomplete. The value of a particular variable may be missing for some observations. In those cases, missing character data are represented by blanks, and missing numeric data are represented by a single period (.). In the data set above, the value of WEIGHT for observation 5 is missing, and its place is marked by a period. The value of NAME for observation 6 is missing and is just left blank. The use of a period for missing numeric data turns out to be very useful.

Documentation In addition to your actual data, SAS data sets contain information about the data set, such as its name, the date that you created, and the version of SAS with which you created. SAS also stores information about each variable, including its name, type (numeric or character), length (or storage size), and position within the data set. This information is sometimes called the descriptor portion of the data set, and it makes SAS data sets self-documenting.

| missing values in input data |
| numeric data definition of |
| character data definition of |

---

[1] If disk space is a problem, you may also choose to base your decision on storage size. You can use the LENGTH statement, discussed in section 8.14, to control the storage size of variables.

2.3 The Two Parts of a SAS Program

SAS programs are constructed from two basic building blocks: DATA steps and PROC steps. A typical program starts with a DATA step to create a SAS data set and then passes the data to a PROC step for analysis. Here is a simple program that converts miles to kilometers in a DATA step and prints the results with a PROC step:

```
DATA step      DATA distance;
                  miles = 23;
                  kilometr = 1.61 * miles;

PROC step      PROC PRINT DATA = distance;
               RUN;
```

DATA and PROC steps are made up of statements. A step may have as few as one or as many as hundreds of statements. Most statements work in only one type of step—in DATA steps but not PROC steps, or vice versa. A common mistake made by beginners is to try to use a statement in the wrong kind of step. You're not likely to make this mistake if you remember that DATA steps read and modify data while PROC steps perform specific analyses or functions.

Data steps start with the DATA statement, which starts, not surprisingly, with the word DATA. This keyword is followed by a name that you make up for a SAS data set. The DATA step above produces a SAS data set named DISTANCE. In addition to reading data from external, raw data files, DATA steps can include DO loops, IF-THEN/ELSE logic, and a large assortment of numeric and character functions. DATA steps can also combine data sets in just about any way you want, including concatenation and match-merge.

Procedures, on the other hand, start with a PROC statement in which the keyword PROC is followed by the name of the procedure (PRINT, SORT, or PLOT, for example). Most SAS procedures have only a handful of possible statements. Like following a recipe, you use basically the same statements or ingredients each time. SAS procedures do everything from simple sorting and printing to analysis of variance and 3D graphics. Other SAS procedures perform utility functions such as copying data sets and data entry.

A step ends when SAS encounters a new step (marked by a DATA or PROC statement), a RUN statement, or the end of the program.[1] RUN statements tell SAS to run all the preceding lines of the step and are one of those rare statements that are not part of a DATA or PROC step. In the program above, SAS knows that the DATA step has ended when it reaches the PROC statement. The PROC step ends with a RUN statement, which coincides with the end of the program.

While a typical program starts with a DATA step to input or modify data and then passes the data to a PROC step, that is certainly not the only pattern for mixing DATA and PROC steps. Like building blocks that can be stacked in any order. You can arrange DATA and PROC steps in any order. A program could even consist entirely of DATA steps or conceivably (though rarely) consist entirely of PROC steps.

---

[1] If you use SAS long enough, you may run into an exception. Steps can also end with a QUIT, STOP, or ABORT statement.

To review, the table below outlines the basic differences between DATA and PROC steps:

DATA steps	PROC steps
▶ begin with DATA statements	▶ begin with PROC statements
▶ read and modify data	▶ perform specific analysis or function
▶ create a SAS data set	▶ produce results or report

As you read this table, keep in mind that it is a simplification. Because SAS is so flexible, the differences between DATA and PROC steps are, in reality, more blurry. The table above is not meant to imply that PROC steps never create SAS data sets (some do), or that DATA steps never produce reports (they can). Nonetheless, you will find it much easier to write SAS programs if you understand the basic functions of DATA and PROC steps.

2.4 The DATA Step's Built-in Loop

DATA steps read and modify data. They do it in a way that is flexible, giving you lots of control over what happens to your data. DATA steps also have an underlying structure, a built-in loop. This loop is implicit, and SAS does it automatically. Memorize this:

DATA steps execute line by line and observation by observation.

This basic concept is rarely stated explicitly. Consequently, new users often grow into old users before they figure this out on their own.

The idea that DATA steps execute line by line is fairly straightforward and easy to understand. It means that, by default, SAS executes line one of your DATA step before it executes line two, and line two before line three, and so on. That seems common sense, and yet it is common for new users to run into problems because they try to use a variable before they create it. If a variable named Z is the product of X and Y, then you better make sure that the statements creating X and Y come before the statements creating Z.

What is not so obvious is that while DATA steps execute line by line, they also execute observation by observation. That means SAS takes the first observation and runs it all the way through the DATA step (line by line, of course) before looping back to pick up the second observation. In this way, SAS *sees* only one observation at a time.

Imagine a SAS program running in slow motion: SAS reads observation number one from your input data set. Then SAS executes your DATA step using that observation. If SAS reaches the end of the DATA step without encountering any serious errors, then SAS writes the current observation to a new, output data set and returns to the beginning of the DATA step to process the next observation. After the last observation has been written to the output data set, SAS terminates the DATA step and moves on to the next step, if there is one. End of slow motion, please return to normal megahertz.

This diagram illustrates how an observation flows through a DATA step:

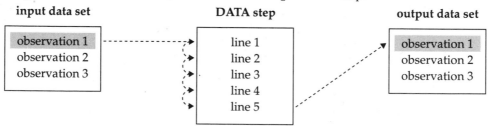

SAS takes observation number one and processes it using line one of the DATA step, then line two, and so on until SAS reaches the end of the DATA step. Then SAS writes the observation in the output data set. This diagram shows the first execution of the line-by-line loop. Once SAS finishes with the first observation, it loops back to the top of the DATA step and picks up observation two. When SAS reaches the last observation, it automatically stops.[1]

Here is an analogy. DATA step processing is a bit like voting. When you arrive at your polling place, you stand in line behind other people who have come to vote. When you reach the front of the line you are asked standard questions: "What is your name? Where do you live?" Then you sign your name, and you cast your vote. In this analogy, the people are observations, and the voting process is the DATA step. People vote one at a time (or observation by observation). Each voter's choices are secret, and peeking at your neighbor's ballot is definitely frowned upon. In addition, each person completes each step of the process in the same order (line by line). You cannot cast your vote before you give your name and address. Everything must be done in the proper order.

DATA step
flow of

---

[1] If this seems a bit too structured, don't worry. You can override the line-by-line and observation-by-observation structure in a number of ways. For example, you can use the RETAIN statement, discussed in section 4.9, to make data from the previous observation available to the current observation. You can also use the OUTPUT statement, discussed in sections 6.11 and 6.12, to control how observations are written to the output data set.

2.5 Executing a SAS Program

So far we have talked about writing SAS programs, but simply writing a program does not give you any results. Just like writing a letter to your representative in Congress does no good unless you mail it, a SAS program does nothing until you submit or execute it. You can execute a SAS program several ways, but not all methods are available for all operating systems. Check in the SAS Companion for your operating system or with your SAS site representative to find out which methods are available to you. The method you choose for executing a SAS program will depend on your preferences and what is most appropriate for your application and your environment. If you are using SAS at a large site with many users, then ask around and find out which is the most accepted method of executing SAS. If you are using SAS on your own personal computer, then choose the method that suits you.

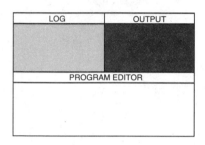

Display manager mode The SAS Display Manager System is a collection of windows where you can edit SAS programs, execute programs, and see the results. Display manager has windows for help, setting parameters, customizing SAS, and much more. All operating systems have display manager in one form or another, and it works basically the same in all environments. The appearance of display manager varies according to the operating system and the type of terminal or monitor you are using. If you use SAS on a personal computer with a nice color graphics monitor, display manager will look slick. If you use SAS on a mainframe computer with a non-graphics, monochrome terminal, display manager will look rather crude. The display manager is usually started by typing SAS at the system prompt and pressing ENTER, or by clicking on the SAS icon.

Non-interactive mode Non-interactive mode is where your SAS program statements are in a file on your system and you start up SAS by specifying that you want to execute that file. SAS immediately starts to process your file and ties up your computer, or window, until it is finished. The results are usually placed in a file or files, and you are returned to your system prompt.

Non-interactive mode is useful in many situations. This mode is good if you want your program to execute immediately, but you do not want to or cannot use display manager. If memory is a problem (common for the PC-DOS version), this mode will save considerable memory compared with using display manager. Some sites use this method while using SAS/GRAPH software.

Non-interactive mode is usually started by typing SAS at your system prompt (shown here as $), followed by the filename containing your program statements:

```
$ SAS myfile.sas
```

Batch or background mode   With batch or background mode, your SAS program is in a file. You submit the file for processing with SAS. Your SAS program may start executing immediately, or it could be put in a queue behind other jobs. Batch processing is used a lot on mainframe computers, which are capable of executing many processes at one time. You can continue to work on your computer while your job is being processed, or better yet, you can go to the baseball game and let the computer work in your absence. Batch processing is usually less expensive than other methods and is especially good for large jobs which can be set up to execute at off hours when the rates are at their lowest. When your job is complete, the results will be placed in a file or files, which you can display or print at any time.

Batch processing is not available for every operating system. Check in the SAS Companion for your operating system to see if it is available, then check with your SAS site representative to find out how to submit SAS programs for batch processing. Even sites with the same operating system may have different ways of submitting jobs in batch mode.

Interactive line mode   This mode is mentioned only because you might see it in the SAS documentation, and you might get into it by accident. In interactive line mode, you are prompted for SAS statements one line at a time. There is no easy way to correct mistakes once you have entered them, so unless you are an excellent typist, and an excellent programmer, interactive line mode is exceedingly frustrating.

If you do find yourself in this mode, (you will know when you get a 1? as a prompt), you can get out by typing ENDSAS; and pressing ENTER. For example:

```
1? ENDSAS;
```

Seek assistance from your SAS site representative to find out why you got into line mode and how to avoid it in the future.

methods of operation	L

batch mode batch processing	C

2.6 Reading the SAS Log and Output

When you execute a SAS program, you expect to get something back; what you get is the log and output. The log contains the program statements you submitted plus messages from SAS about the execution of your program. The output contains printable results, if any exist, from SAS procedures you ran. In the output (sometimes called the listing) you may find reports, tables, statistics, or plots. Every time you run a SAS job, you generate a SAS log. Output, however, is created only when there is something to put in it. So, for example, if your program bombs because of errors, or if you modify your data but don't produce any printable results, then you will not find any output.

Where to find the SAS log The location of the SAS log and output varies depending on the operating system you use, the mode you use (batch, display manager, or non-interactive), and local settings. If you submit a program in display manager, you will, by default, receive the results in display manager. If you submit a program in batch or non-interactive mode, the results will be written to a disk file that you can view or print. The commands to view or print these files depend on how your local system is set up. Likewise, the name given to log and output files depends on your local system, though it is generally some permutation of the name you gave to the original program. For example, if you named your SAS program POPCORN.SAS, then it is a good bet that your log file will be POPCORN.LOG and your output will be POPCORN.OUT (or POPCORN.LIS). At some installations the log and output files are written to a single file, so don't be surprised if you find them together.

Many SAS programmers ignore the SAS log and go straight to the output. That's understandable but dangerous. It is possible—and sooner or later it happens to all of us—to get bogus results that look fine in the output. The only way to know they are bad is to check the SAS log. Just because it runs doesn't mean it's right.

What the log contains People tend to think of the SAS log as either a rehash of their program or as just a lot of gibberish. OK, we admit, there is some technical trivia in the SAS log, but there is also a wealth of important information. Here is a simple program that converts miles to kilometers and prints the result:

```
* Create a SAS data set named distance;
* Convert miles to kilometers;
DATA distance;
   miles = 23;
   kilometr = 1.61 * miles;
* Print the results;
PROC PRINT DATA = distance;
RUN;
```

If you run this program, SAS will produce a log similar to this:

```
❶NOTE: Copyright(c) 1989 by SAS Institute Inc., Cary, NC USA.
  NOTE: SAS (r) Proprietary Software Release 6.08 TS404
        Licensed to XYZ Inc., Site 0028541001
  ❷1           * Create a SAS data set named distance;
   2           * Convert miles to kilometers;
   3           DATA distance;
   4              miles = 23;
   5              kilometr = 1.61 * miles;
   6           * Print the results;
```

```
❸NOTE: The data set WORK.DISTANCE has 1 observations and
       2 variables.
❹NOTE: DATA statement used 6.41 seconds.
❷7          PROC PRINT DATA = distance;
 8          RUN;

❺NOTE: The PROCEDURE PRINT printed page 1.
❹NOTE: PROCEDURE PRINT used 3.79 seconds.
```

The SAS log above is a blow-by-blow account of how SAS executes the program.

❶ It starts with notes about the version of SAS and the SAS site number.

❷ It contains the original program statements with line numbers added on the left.

❸ The DATA step is followed by a note containing the name of the SAS data set created (WORK.DISTANCE), and the number of observations (1) and variables (2). A quick glance is enough to assure you that you did not lose any observations or accidentally create a lot of unwanted variables.

❹ Both DATA and PROC steps produce a note about the computer resources used. At first you probably won't care in the least. But if you run on a multi-user system or have long jobs with large data sets, these statistics may start to pique your interest. If you ever find yourself wondering why your job takes so long to run, a glance at the SAS log will tell you which steps are the culprits.

❺ PROC steps produce a note telling you which page (or pages) of the output contains the results of that procedure. You may not care if your output is short, but if the report you want starts on page 237, it is nice to be able to find it without searching through all those pages.

If there were error messages, they would appear in the log, indicating where SAS got confused and what action it took. You may also find warnings and other types of notes which sometimes indicate errors and other times just provide useful information.

The output   Here is the final product, the SAS output:

```
                        The SAS System                      1

              OBS     MILES     KILOMETR

               1       23       37.03
```

SAS log

2.7 Using Display Manager Commands and Windows

Display manager is a windowing system for editing and executing SAS programs. From display manager you can edit and submit your SAS programs, view and save the results, set options, get help, and a lot more. Display manager is available for all systems but it may not look the same. On systems that are graphical in nature, display manager takes advantage of that and provides scroll bars, pop-up windows, and other features you are accustomed to. On systems which are not graphical, like mainframe computers with simple, non-graphical terminals, display manager looks rather crude, but still functions much the same. The following are examples of what display manager could look like. Since you have control over many aspects of display manager, your display might be different.

Display Manager in:

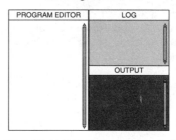

Display manager has three primary windows: the PROGRAM EDITOR window, the LOG window, and the OUTPUT window. You may see all three windows at first, or you may just see the PROGRAM EDITOR and LOG windows depending on your system.

> The PROGRAM EDITOR window is a text editor. You can use it to edit and submit SAS programs or to edit other text files, like data files and output files.
> The LOG window contains the SAS log. After you submit a program, the SAS log will show any notes, errors, or warnings associated with the submitted SAS program as well as the program statements themselves.
> The OUTPUT window contains the results of SAS procedures. Not all SAS procedures produce printed output, but if they do, you will see the results in the OUTPUT window.

There are many other display manager windows besides these three. There are windows for help (HELP), displaying and changing titles which appear on the output (TITLES), defining function keys (KEYS), managing output (OUTPUT MANAGER), and many others.

Each display manager window has a set of valid commands. You can enter commands on the command line or use a menu system. Use the command line by typing the command on the command line (located at the top of the window) and pressing ENTER. For example, the following command clears the window:

```
Command ===> clear
```

You can accomplish the same thing using menus. Select EDIT from the pull-down menu (also called action bar) and select CLEAR TEXT:

All systems can operate in command-line mode, and most have some kind of menu system. You decide which is best for you and your system; you can always switch between the two. The following table shows selected display manager commands (there may be minor differences between operating systems).

Description	Command Line	Menu Path
Save contents of window	file *'filename'*	file → save as → write to file
Clear contents of window	clear	edit → clear text
Change size of window	zoom	*not applicable*
Get help	help	help → SAS System
Display KEYS window	keys	help → keys
Display OPTIONS window	options	globals → global options → SAS options
Display PROGRAM EDITOR, LOG, or OUTPUT window	program log output	globals → program log output
Close window	end	edit → end *or* file → end
End SAS Session	bye	file → exit
Execute operating system commands	x	globals → command → host command
Change to menus	pmenu	*not applicable*
Change to command line	*not applicable*	globals → command → command line
PROGRAM EDITOR only		
Bring external file in the program editor	include *'filename'*	file → open → read file
Submit SAS program for proceessing	submit	locals → submit
Recall submitted program statements to program editor	recall	locals → recall text

output, printing routing output C	display manager commands definitions by category, table L

2.8 Editing Programs in Display Manager

The PROGRAM EDITOR window is one of the primary windows of the SAS Display Manager System. It is a text editor which you can use for creating, editing, and submitting SAS programs. You can also use it to create or edit data files, or just view files without leaving the SAS System. The appearance of the PROGRAM EDITOR window, like display manager, changes according to the operating environment.

Graphical environment   If you are working under a graphical environment with a mouse, then you will be able to select text with the mouse, cut and paste, and do many of the things you expect of a word processor. Most of the editing commands are under the Edit menu. There are standard word processing items like: Undo, Copy, Find, and so on. When entering text, you will either be in insert or overstrike mode. The INSERT key, if you have one, toggles between the two modes and changes the shape of the cursor. If you can't find your INSERT key, or if it doesn't seem to be working, then check with your local SAS site representative.

Non-graphical environment   In a non-graphical environment, editing is not as easy but is still manageable in the PROGRAM EDITOR window. Instead of using a mouse to select text, you use line commands to operate on lines or blocks of lines in your program. To use line commands, you must turn on line numbers. If you do not see line numbers in the PROGRAM EDITOR window, turn them on by entering nums on on the command line (command===> nums on) or selecting the edit-options-numbers (first choose Edit, then under Edit choose Options, then under Options choose Numbers) menu item.

Use line commands by typing the command over the top of the appropriate line number. It doesn't matter which part of the line number you type over. For example, if you want to delete line number 00003, you would type a d anywhere on the number: 0d003, d0003, or 0000d all do the trick.

```
00001  Jack be nimble,
00002  Jack be quick,
00d03  Jack be quick,
00004  Jack jump over the candlestick
```

To delete a block of lines, you would type **dd** on the first line number of the block and **dd** on the last line number. Some operations, like move, require you to specify where to move the line. For these operations, use the line commands **a** or **b** to specify after or before the line. For example, the following will move lines 00008 and 00009 before line 00001.

```
00b01  And everywhere that Mary went
00002  The lamb was sure to go.
00003
00004  It followed her to school one day,
00005  That was against the rule;
00006  It made the children laugh and play
00007  To see the lamb at school.
0mm08  Mary had a little lamb,
0mm09  Its fleece was white as snow;
00010
```

The following table shows the commonly used line commands:

Command	Description
A	indicates after line (move and copy commands)
B	indicates before line (move and copy commands)
C and CC	copies one or more lines
COLS	displays a line ruler that marks horizontal columns
D and DD	deletes one or more lines
I or I#	inserts one or # new lines (where # is any number)
M and MM	moves one or more lines
R and RR or R# and RR#	repeats one or more lines # number of times
TC	connects two lines of text
TS	splits text at cursor

Once you've typed in and edited your program, you may want to save it for later use or to print. Use the FILE command (`command===> FILE 'filename'`) or the menu item file-save as-write to file to save the current contents of the window in a file.

If you decide that you really do not like the program editor, but still want to use display manager, you can create your SAS programs in another text editor and bring them into the program editor to execute. Use the INCLUDE command (`command===> INCLUDE 'filename'`) or the menu item file-open-read file to bring your program into the program editor. If you are using a word processor, be sure to save the file in text or non-document mode before attempting to bring it into the program editor.

| PROGRAM EDITOR window |
| text, editing |
| line commands |

Naturally, after going to the trouble of writing SAS programs, you want to see some results. With display manager, your SAS program must be in the PROGRAM EDITOR window in order to submit it. You may use the program editor to create your program, or you can bring the program into the PROGRAM EDITOR window from a file. The file may have been created with the program editor during a previous session, or it could have been created with another text editor. Use the INCLUDE command (command===> include 'myfile.sas') or the file-open-read file (first choose File, then under File choose Open, then under Open choose Read file) menu item to bring a file into the PROGRAM EDITOR window.

Submitting the program   Once your program appears in the PROGRAM EDITOR window, you can execute it using the SUBMIT command or the locals-submit menu item. Make sure there is a RUN statement at the end of your program; without it SAS will not execute the last step of your program.

PROGRAM EDITOR	LOG
locals	
submit	
DATA distance;	
miles=23;	
kilometr=1.6*miles;	OUTPUT
PROC PRINT;	
RUN;	

Viewing the log and output   After you submit your program, it disappears from the PROGRAM EDITOR window. The SAS log appears in the LOG window, and the output, if any exists, appears in the OUTPUT window. (Don't worry; the program you spent so long writing is not gone forever.) If you submit more programs, the log and output from those will be tacked onto the end of whatever is already in the windows. The CLEAR command or edit-clear text menu item erases the contents of the active window (the window where you typed or selected the command) and allows you to start with a clean slate.

PROGRAM EDITOR	LOG
5 lines submitted	1 DATA distance;
	2 miles=23;
	3 kilometr=1.6*miles;
	NOTE: The data set WORK.DIS
	OUTPUT
	The SAS System
	OBS MILES KILOMETR
	1 23 37.03

To view the SAS log or output, move your cursor to the appropriate window by either clicking on it with your mouse, typing the name of the window on the command line and pressing ENTER, or using the globals-log or globals-output menu items. You may scroll through the contents of the window using the scroll bars, if you have them; the page-up and page-down keys; or the BACKWARD and FORWARD commands. Not all systems have mice for scroll bars or appropriate keys, but the commands always work. Some systems have function keys assigned to the most commonly used commands. To see how your function keys are defined, if at all, get into the KEYS window by entering KEYS on the command line, or selecting help-keys from the menu items.

Getting your program back Many people panic when they see their program vanish before their eyes after submitting it. Rest assured, SAS still remembers your program and has it tucked away in a safe place. SAS also remembers everything else you have done in your current SAS session. Any temporary SAS data sets you have created will be stored along with other settings like titles and system options. These things are stored in memory or disk until you end your SAS session, change the settings or data sets, or the power goes out.

To get your SAS program statements back, use the RECALL command or locals-recall text menu item from the PROGRAM EDITOR window. This will bring back the last block of submitted statements into the PROGRAM EDITOR window. If you use the RECALL command again, it will insert the block of statements submitted before the last one, and so on and so on until it retrieves all the statements you submitted. Using this RECALL command, you can correct any errors in your program and resubmit it. If it ran perfectly, you might want to save the program to a file.

PROGRAM EDITOR	LOG
locals recall text	1 DATA distance; 2 miles=23; 3 kilometr=1.6*miles; NOTE: The data set WORK.DIS
	OUTPUT
	The SAS System OBS MILES KILOMETR 1 23 37.03

PROGRAM EDITOR	LOG

5 lines recalled
 	
DATA distance;
  miles=23;
  kilometr=1.6*miles;
PROC PRINT;
RUN;
	1 DATA distance;
	2 miles=23;
	3 kilometr=1.6*miles;
	
	NOTE: The data set WORK.DIS

	OUTPUT
	The SAS System OBS MILES KILOMETR 1 23 37.03

RECALL display manager command
SUBMIT display manager command

2.10   Using SAS System Options

System options are parameters you can change that affect the SAS System—how it works, what the output looks like, how much memory is used, error handling, and a host of other things. The SAS System makes many assumptions about how you want it to work. This is good. You do not want to specify every little detail each time you use SAS. However, you may not always like the assumptions SAS makes. System options give you a way to change some of these assumptions.

A long list of system options can be found in the *SAS Language, Reference* manual. The options are grouped by the following general areas:

> initialization
> reading and writing data
> log and procedure output
> SAS data set control
> error handling
> macro facility
> product interface.

Not all options are available for all operating systems. A list of options specific to your operating system appears in the SAS Companion manual for your environment. If you don't have the companion manual at your fingertips, you can get a list of system options and their current values using the OPTIONS procedure. Submit the following SAS program, and view the results in the SAS output:

```
PROC OPTIONS;
RUN;
```

There are four ways to specify system options. Some options can only be specified using some of these methods. The SAS Companion manual tells you which methods are valid for each system option:

1. Your system administrator (this could be you if you are using a PC) can create a SAS configuration file which contains settings for the system options. This file is accessed by the SAS System every time SAS is started.
2. Specify system options at the time you start up SAS from your system's prompt (called the invocation).
3. Change selected options in the OPTIONS window if you are using the SAS display manager.
4. Use the OPTIONS statement as a part of your SAS program.

The methods are listed here in order of increasing precedence; method 2 will override method 1, method 3 will override method 2, and so forth. If you are using display manager, methods 3 and 4, the OPTIONS window and OPTIONS statement, will override each other—so whichever was used last will be in effect. Only the last two methods are covered here. The first two are very system dependent; to find out more about these methods see the SAS Companion manual for your system.

OPTIONS window   The OPTIONS window is one of the SAS display manager windows. To access the OPTIONS window, either enter OPTIONS on the display manager command line or use the pull-down menu item <u>globals</u>-<u>global options</u>-<u>SAS options</u>. The OPTIONS window will display a partial list of SAS system options and their current settings. To change the value for an option, move the cursor to the current value and replace it with the desired value. Close the window, or type SAVE on the command line of the OPTIONS window to make the new value take effect. This new value will stay in effect for the rest of your SAS session unless you change it again through the OPTIONS window or the OPTIONS statement.

OPTIONS statement   The OPTIONS statement is part of a SAS program and affects all steps that follow it. It starts with the keyword OPTIONS and follows with a list of options and their values. For example

```
OPTIONS LINESIZE = 80 NODATE;
```

The OPTIONS statement is one of the special SAS statements which do not belong to either a PROC or a DATA step. The statement can appear anywhere in your SAS program, but it usually makes the most sense to let it be the first line in your program. This way you can easily see which options are in effect. If the OPTIONS statement is in a DATA or PROC step, then it affects that step and the following steps. Any subsequent OPTIONS statements in a program override previous ones.

Common options   The following are some common system options which affect the appearance of your SAS output:

CENTER | NOCENTER   This option works as a switch. CENTER centers your output on the page. NOCENTER left justifies your output.

DATE | NODATE   This is also a switch. With DATE, today's date will appear at the top of each page of output, with NODATE it will not.

NUMBER | NONUMBER   This switch controls whether or not page numbers appear on each page of SAS output.

LINESIZE = n With LINESIZE you can control the maximum length of output lines. Possible values for n are 64–256.

PAGESIZE = n PAGESIZE controls the maximum number of lines per page of output. Possible values for n are 15–32767.

LINESIZE and PAGESIZE are both helpful to customize the output for your printer or screen. Sometimes the effect of using PAGESIZE is not seen because SAS automatically starts a new page for each new part of the output. Each table, for example, starts on a new page.

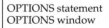

OPTIONS statement
OPTIONS window   L

SAS system options   C

3

> " **Practice is the best of all instructors.** "

PUBLILIUS SYRUS, *CIRCA* 42 B.C.

> " **We all learned by doing, by experimenting (and often failing), and by asking questions.** "

JAY JACOB WIND, SAS® USER SINCE 1980

From *Bartlett's Familiar Quotations* 13th edition, by John Bartlett, copyright 1955 by Little, Brown and Company. Public doman.
From the SAS L listserv, March 15, 1994. Reprinted by permission of the author.

CHAPTER 3

Getting Your Data into the SAS® System

3.1 Telling SAS Where to Find Your Raw Data

Before you can analyze your data with SAS software, you must get your data into a SAS data set. Often data are in raw data files, also referred to as text, ASCII, sequential, or flat files. A raw data file can be viewed (or printed) using operating system commands like *type* in DOS or *cat* in UNIX. If, for example, you try using the DOS type command to look at a spreadsheet file (which is not a raw data file), you will probably see lots of funny special characters you can't find on your keyboard. It may cause your computer to beep and chirp, making you wish you had that private office down the hall. It looks nothing like the nice neat rows and columns you see when you use your spreadsheet software to view the same file.

Raw data can be internal or external to the SAS program. Internal data are lines embedded in the SAS program, whereas external data are contained in a separate file. Sometimes it is useful to have internal data. When there are small amounts of data or you are testing a program with a small test data set, it may be easier to maintain only one file with both the data and the SAS program statements. However, usually you will want to use external data files. External data make the SAS program easier to read, eliminate the chance that data may be accidentally altered when editing the SAS program, and allow more than one SAS program access to the data. Most of the programs in this book use external data.

Internal data The CARDS statement is used to indicate internal data and is the same for all operating systems. All lines in the SAS program following the CARDS statement are considered data until SAS encounters a semicolon. The semicolon can be on a line by itself or at the end of a SAS statement which follows the data lines. The CARDS statement must be the last statement in the DATA step. The term CARDS is a holdover from when computing was done on computer cards instead of terminals. The following SAS program illustrates the use of the CARDS statement. (The INPUT statement in the program tells SAS how to read the data. The INPUT statement is discussed in sections 3.2 through 3.9.)

```
* Read internal data into SAS data set uspres;
DATA uspres;
   INPUT pres $ party $ number;
   CARDS;
Adams      F  2
Lincoln    R 16
Grant      R 18
Kennedy    D 35
   ;
RUN;
```

External files The INFILE statement is used for external files and tells SAS the filename and path, if appropriate, of the external file containing the data. After the INFILE keyword, the file path and name are enclosed in single quotes. Examples from several operating systems follow:

DOS, Windows, OS/2:	INFILE 'c:\mydir\presiden.dat';
Macintosh:	INFILE 'my disk:my folder:presiden.dat';
UNIX:	INFILE '/home/mydir/presiden.dat';

```
Open VMS, VMS:    INFILE '[username.mydir]presiden.dat';

         MVS:    INFILE 'MYID.PRESIDEN.DAT';

         CMS:    INFILE 'presiden data a';
```

Suppose the following data are in a file called PRESIDEN.DAT in the directory MYDIR on the C: drive (DOS, Windows, OS/2):

```
Adams      F  2
Lincoln    R 16
Grant      R 18
Kennedy    D 35
```

The following program shows the use of the INFILE statement to read the external data file:

```
* Read data from external file into SAS data set;
DATA uspres;
   INFILE 'c:\mydir\presiden.dat';
   INPUT pres $ party $ number;
RUN;
```

The SAS log Whenever you read data from an external file, SAS gives some very valuable information about the file in the SAS log. The following is an excerpt from the SAS log after running the previous program. Always check this information after you read a file as it could indicate problems. A simple comparison of the number of records read from the infile with the number of observations in the SAS data set can tell you a lot about whether or not SAS is reading your data correctly.

```
NOTE: The infile 'c:\mydir\presiden.dat' is:
      FILENAME=c:\mydir\presiden.dat,RECFM=V,LRECL=132
NOTE: 4 records were read from the infile 'c:\mydir\presiden.dat'.
      The minimum record length was 14.
      The maximum record length was 14.
NOTE: The data set WORK.USPRES has 4 observations and 3 variables.
```

Long records On some operating systems, SAS assumes external files have a record length of 132 or less. (The record length is the number of characters, including spaces, on a data line.) If your data lines are long, and it looks like SAS is not reading all your data, then use the LRECL= option in the INFILE statement to specify a record length at least as long as the longest record in your data file.

```
INFILE 'c:\mydir\presiden.dat' LRECL=2000;
```

Check the SAS log to see that the maximum record length listed is as long as you think it should be.

INFILE statement
CARDS statement

3.2 Reading Raw Data Separated by Spaces

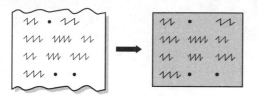

If the values in your data file are all separated by at least one space,[1] then using list input (also called free formatted input) to read the data may be appropriate. List input is the easiest way to read data into SAS, but with ease comes a few limitations. Periods indicate missing data. Character data, if present, must be simple: no embedded spaces, and no values greater than eight characters in length.[2] If the data file contains dates or other values which need special treatment, then list input may not be appropriate. This may sound like a lot of restrictions, but a surprising number of data files can be read using list input.

List input is great for small files when the creator does not want to be bothered with keeping data in neat columns. (Beware that files of this type may be difficult to proofread.) Data files which originate from other programs, like spreadsheets or database programs, are also possible candidates for list input. Data files do not have to look messy to be read with list input as long as they meet all the stated requirements.

To write an INPUT statement using list input, simply list the variable names after the INPUT keyword in the order they appear in the data file. Variable names must be eight characters or fewer, start with a letter or an underscore, and contain only letters, underscores, or numerals. If the values are character (not numbers) then place a $ after the variable name. Leave at least one space between names, and remember to place a semicolon after the last name to complete the statement.

Example   Your hometown has been overrun with toads this year. A local resident, having heard of frog jumping in California, had the idea of a toad jump to cap off the annual town fair. For each contestant you have the toad's name, weight, and the jump distance from three separate attempts. If the toad is disqualified for any jump, then a period is used to indicate missing data. Here is what the data file TOADJUMP.DAT looks like:

```
Lucky 2.3 1.9 . 3.0
Spot 4.6 2.5 3.1 .5
Tubs 7.1 . . 3.8
Hop 4.5 3.2 1.9 2.6
Noisy 3.8 1.3 1.8
1.5
Winner 5.7 . . .
```

This data file does not look very neat, but it does meet all the requirements for list input: the character data are eight characters or fewer and have no embedded spaces, all values are separated by at least one space, and missing data are indicated by a period. Notice that the data for Noisy has spilled over to the next data line. This is no problem since, by default, SAS will go to the next data line to read more data if there are more variables in the INPUT statement than there are values in the data line.

---

[1] SAS can read files with other delimiters such as commas or tabs using list input. This is discussed in sections 3.10 and 3.14.
[2] It is possible to override this constraint using the LENGTH statement, discussed in section 8.12, which can change the length of character variables from the default of 8 to anything between 1 and 200.

Here is the SAS program that will read the data:

```
* Create a SAS data set named toads;
* Read the data file toadjump.dat using list input;
DATA toads;
   INFILE 'toadjump.dat';
   INPUT toadname $ weight jump1 jump2 jump3;
* Print the data to make sure the file was read correctly;
PROC PRINT;
 TITLE 'SAS Data Set Toads';
RUN;
```

The variables TOADNAME, WEIGHT, JUMP1, JUMP2, and JUMP3 are listed after the keyword INPUT in the same order as they appear in the file. A dollar sign ($) after TOADNAME indicates that it is a character variable; all the other variables are numeric. A PROC PRINT statement is used to print the data values after reading them to make sure they are correct. The PRINT procedure, in its simplest form, prints the values for all variables and all observations in a SAS data set. The TITLE statement after the PROC PRINT, tells SAS to put the text enclosed in quotes on the top of each page of output. If you had no TITLE statement in your program, SAS would put the words "The SAS System" at the top of each page.

The output will look like this:

```
                        SAS Data Set Toads                    1

      OBS    TOADNAME    WEIGHT    JUMP1    JUMP2    JUMP3

       1      Lucky        2.3      1.9       .       3.0
       2      Spot         4.6      2.5      3.1      0.5
       3      Tubs         7.1       .        .       3.8
       4      Hop          4.5      3.2      1.9      2.6
       5      Noisy        3.8      1.3      1.8      1.5
       6      Winner       5.7       .        .        .
```

Because SAS had to go to a second data line to get the data for Noisy's final jump, the following note appears in the SAS log:

NOTE: SAS went to a new line when INPUT statement reached past the end of a line.

If you find this note in your SAS log when you didn't expect it, then you may have a problem. If so, look in section 8.4 which discusses this note in more detail.

INPUT statement
list input

3.3 Reading Raw Data Arranged in Columns

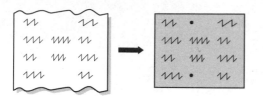

Some data files do not have spaces (or other delimiters) between all the values, or periods for missing data—so the files can't be read using list input. But if each of the variable's values are always found in the same place in the data line, then you can use column input as long as all the values are character or standard numeric. Standard numeric data contain only numbers, decimal points, minus signs, and E for scientific notation. Dates or numbers with embedded commas, for example, are not standard.

Column input has the following advantages over list input:

- ▶ spaces are not required between values
- ▶ missing values can be left blank
- ▶ character data can have embedded spaces
- ▶ you can skip unwanted variables.

Survey data are good candidates for column input. Most answers to survey questionnaires are single digits (0–9). If a space is entered between each value, then the file will be twice the size and require twice the typing of a file without spaces. Data files with street addresses, which often have embedded blanks, are also good candidates for column input. The street Martin Luther King Jr. Boulevard should be read as one variable not five, as it would be with list input. Data which can be read with column input can often also be read with formatted input or a combination of input styles (discussed in the following three sections).

With column input, the INPUT statement takes on the following form. After the INPUT keyword, list the first variable's name. If the variable is character, leave a space; then place a $. After the $, or variable name if it is numeric, leave a space; then list the column or range of columns for that variable. The columns are positions of the characters or numbers in the data line and are not to be confused with columns like you see in a spreadsheet. Repeat this for all the variables you want to read.

Example   The local minor league baseball team, the Walla Walla Sweets, is keeping records about concession sales. A ballpark favorite are the sweet onion rings which are sold at the concession stands and also by vendors in the bleachers. The ballpark owners have a feeling that in games with lots of hits and runs more onion rings are sold in the bleachers than at the concession stands. They think they should send more vendors out into the bleachers when the game heats up but need more evidence to back up their feelings.

For each home game they have the following information: name of opposing team, onion ring sales at the concession stands and in the bleachers, the number of hits for each team and the final score for each team. The following is a sample of the data file named ONIONS.DAT. For your reference, a rule showing the column numbers has been placed above the data:

```
----+----1----+----2----+----3----+----4
Columbia Peaches     35 67  1 10  2  1
Plains Peanuts      210     2  5  0  2
Gilroy Garlics      151035 12 11  7  6
Sacramento Tomatoes 124 85 15  4  9  1
```

Notice that the data file has the following characteristics, all making it a prime candidate for column input. All the values line up in columns, the team names have imbedded blanks, missing values are blank, and in one case there is not a space between data values. (Those Gilroy Garlic fans must really love onion rings.)

The following program shows how to read these data using column input:

```
* Create a SAS data set named sales;
* Read the data file onions.dat using column input;
DATA sales;
   INFILE 'onions.dat';
   INPUT vteam $ 1-20 csales 21-24 bsales 25-28 ourhits 29-31
         vhits 32-34 ourruns 35-37 vruns 38-40;
* Print the data to make sure the file was read correctly;
PROC PRINT;
   TITLE 'SAS Data Set Sales';
RUN;
```

The variable VTEAM is character (indicated by a $) and reads the visiting team's name in columns 1 through 20. The variables CSALES and BSALES read the concession and bleacher sales in columns 21 through 24 and 25 through 28, respectively. The number of hits for the home team, OURHITS, and the visiting team, VHITS, are read in columns 29 through 31 and 32 through 34, respectively. The number of runs for the home team, OURRUNS, is read in columns 35 through 37, while the number of runs for the visiting team, VRUNS, is in columns 38 through 40.

The output will look like this:

```
                          SAS Data Set Sales                      1

OBS          VTEAM        CSALES BSALES OURHITS VHITS OURRUNS VRUNS

 1    Columbia Peaches       35     67      1     10      2      1
 2    Plains Peanuts        210      .      2      5      0      2
 3    Gilroy Garlics         15   1035     12     11      7      6
 4    Sacramento Tomatoes   124     85     15      4      9      1
```

INPUT statement
column input

3.4 Reading Raw Data Not in Standard Format

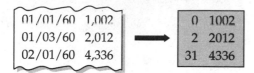

Sometimes raw data are not straightforward numeric or character. For example, we humans easily read the number 1,000,001 as one million and one, but your trusty computer sees it as a character string. While the embedded commas make the number easier for us to interpret, they make the number impossible for the computer to recognize without some instructions. In SAS, informats are used to tell the computer how to interpret these types of data.

Informats are useful anytime you have non-standard data. (Standard numeric data contain only numbers, decimal points, minus signs, and E for scientific notation.) Numbers with embedded commas or dollar signs are examples of non-standard data. Other examples include data in hexadecimal or packed decimal formats. SAS has informats for reading these types of data as well.

Dates[1] are perhaps the most common non-standard data. Using date informats, SAS will convert conventional forms of dates like 10-31-87 or 31OCT87 into a number, the number of days since January 1st, 1960. (Why January 1st, 1960? Who knows? Maybe 1960 was a good year for the SAS founders.) This turns out to be extremely useful when you want to do calculations with dates. For example, you can easily find people's current ages by subtracting their birth dates from today's date and dividing by the number of days per year [(today's date – birth date)/365.25].

There are three general types of informats: character, numeric, and date. A table of selected SAS informats appears in section 3.5. The three types of informats have the following general forms:

Character	**Numeric**	**Date**
$informatw.	informatw.d	informatw.

The $ indicates character informats, INFORMAT is the name of the informat, w is the total width, and d is the number of decimal places (numeric informats only). Two informats do not have names: $w., which reads character data, and w.d, which reads standard numeric data. The period in the informat is very important because it distinguishes an informat from a variable name, which cannot contain any special characters except the underscore.

Use informats by placing the informat after the variable name in the INPUT statement; this is called formatted input. The columns read for each variable are determined by the starting point and the width of the informat. SAS always starts with the first column; so if the first variable has an informat of 5. (like the number 24000, for example), it would be read in columns 1–5. If it had an informat of 5.2 (like the number 19.95, for example), it would still be read in columns 1–5 because the width includes any decimal places and the decimal point itself. The starting point for the second variable is now column 6 because SAS reads through column 5 and starts reading the next variable in column 6. So if the second variable had an informat of 7.1, it would be read in columns 6–12.

---

[1] Using dates in SAS is discussed in more detail in section 4.7.

Example   This example illustrates the use of informats for reading data. The following data file, PUMPKIN.DAT, represents the results from a local pumpkin carving contest. Each line includes the contestant's name, age, type (carved or decorated), the date they entered their pumpkin, and their scores from each of five judges.

```
Alicia Grossman   13 c 10-28-93 7.8 6.5 7.2 8.0 7.9
Matthew Lee        9 D 10-30-93 6.5 5.9 6.8 6.0 8.1
Elizabeth Garcia  10 C 10-29-93 8.9 7.9 8.5 9.0 8.8
Lori Newcombe      6 D 10-30-93 6.7 5.6 4.9 5.2 6.1
Jose Martinez      7 d 10-31-93 8.9 9.510.0 9.7 9.0
Brian Williams    11 C 10-29-93 7.8 8.4 8.5 7.9 8.0
```

The following program reads these data. Please note there are many ways to input these data, so if you imagined something else, that's OK.

```
* Create a SAS data set named contest;
* Read the file pumpkin.dat using formatted input;
DATA contest;
   INFILE 'pumpkin.dat';
   INPUT name $16. age 3. +1 type $1. +1 date MMDDYY8.
       (score1 score2 score3 score4 score5) (4.1);
* Print the data set to make sure the file was read correctly;
PROC PRINT;
   TITLE 'Pumpkin Carving Contest';
RUN;
```

The variable NAME has an informat of $16., meaning that it is a character variable 16 columns wide. Variable AGE has an informat of 3., is numeric, 3 columns wide, and has no decimal places. The +1 skips over one column. Variable TYPE is character, and it is one column wide. Variable DATE, informat MMDDYY8., reads dates in the form 10-31-93 or 10/31/93, each 8 columns wide. The remaining variables, SCORE1 through SCORE5, all require the same informat, 4.1. By putting the variables and the informat in separate sets of parentheses, you only have to list the informat once. Here are the results:

```
                    Pumpkin Carving Contest                      1

OBS       NAME         AGE TYPE  DATE² SCORE1 SCORE2 SCORE3 SCORE4 SCORE5

  1  Alicia Grossman    13  c   12354   7.8    6.5    7.2    8.0    7.9
  2  Matthew Lee         9  D   12356   6.5    5.9    6.8    6.0    8.1
  3  Elizabeth Garcia   10  C   12355   8.9    7.9    8.5    9.0    8.8
  4  Lori Newcombe       6  D   12356   6.7    5.6    4.9    5.2    6.1
  5  Jose Martinez       7  d   12357   8.9    9.5   10.0    9.7    9.0
  6  Brian Williams     11  C   12355   7.8    8.4    8.5    7.9    8.0
```

> INPUT statement
>   formatted input
> informats
>   definition

---

[2] Notice that these dates are printed as the number of days since January 1, 1960. Section 5.5 discusses how to format these values into readable dates.

3.5 Selected Informats

The table in this section spans both pages. The left page gives definitions of the informats along with the default width and width range, while the right page shows examples using the informats. These are the most commonly used informats, but there are many others. So if you don't find what you need here, check *SAS Language, Reference* for a complete list.

		width range	default width
Character			
$CHAR*w*.	Reads character data—does not trim leading or trailing blanks	1-200	1 or length of variable
$HEX*w*.	Converts hexadecimal data to character data	1-200	2
$*w*.	Reads character data—trims leading blanks	1-200	none
Date Time, and Datetime[1]			
DATE*w*.	Reads dates in form: *ddmmmyy* or *ddmmmyyyy*	7-32	7
DATETIME*w*.	Reads datetime values in the form: *ddmmmyy hh:mm:ss.ss*	13-40	18
JULIAN*w*.	Reads Julian dates in form: *yyddd* or *yyyyddd*	5-32	5
MMDDYY*w*.	Reads dates in form: *mmddyy* or *mmddyyyy*	6-32	6
TIME*w*.	Reads time in form: *hh:mm:ss.ss* (hours:minutes:seconds—24-hour clock)	5-32	8
Numeric			
COMMA*w.d*	Removes embedded commas and $, converts left parentheses to minus sign	1-32	1
HEX*w*.	Converts hexadecimal to floating-point values if *w* is 16. Otherwise, converts to fixed-point.	1-16	8
IB*w.d*	Reads integer binary data	1-8	4
PD*w.d*	Reads packed decimal data	1-16	1
PERCENT*w*.	Converts percentages to numbers	1-32	6
w.d	Reads standard numeric data	1-32	none
ZD*w.d*	Reads zoned decimal data	1-32	1

---

[1] SAS date values are the number of days since January 1, 1960. Time values are the number of seconds past midnight, and datetime values are the number of seconds past midnight January 1, 1960.

	Input data	INPUT statement	Results
Character			

$CHAR*w*.	my cat
	  my cat
		INPUT animal $CHAR10.;	my cat
			  my cat

$HEX*w*.	6C6C	INPUT name $HEX4.;	11 (ASCII)or %% (EBCDIC)[2]
$*w*.	my cat my cat	INPUT animal $10.;	my cat my cat
Date, Time, and Datetime			
DATE*w*.	1jan1961 1 jan 61	INPUT day DATE10.;	366 366
DATETIME*w*.	1jan1960 10:30:15 1jan1961,10:30:15	INPUT dt DATETIME18.;	37815 31660215
JULIAN*w*.	61001 1961001	INPUT day JULIAN7.;	366 366
MMDDYY*w*.	01-01-61 01/01/61	INPUT day MMDDYY8.;	366 366
TIME*w*.	10:30 10:30:15	INPUT time TIME8.;	37800 37815
Numeric			
COMMA*w.d*	$1,000,001 (1,234)	INPUT income COMMA10.;	1000001 -1234
HEX*w*.	F0F3	INPUT value HEX4.;	61683
IB*w.d*	[3]	INPUT value IB4.;	255
PD*w.d*	[3]	INPUT value PD4.;	255
PERCENT*w*.	5% (20%)	INPUT value PERCENT5.;	0.05 -0.2
w.d	1234 -12.3	INPUT value 5.1;	123.4 -12.3
ZD*w.d*	[3]	INPUT value ZD4.;	255

informats
definition by category, table

---

[2] The EBCDIC character set is used on most IBM mainframe computers while the ASCII character set is used on most other computers. So, depending on the computer you are using, you will get one or the other.
[3] These values cannot be printed.

3.6 Mixing Input Styles

Each of the three major input styles has its own advantages. List style is the easiest; column style is a bit more work; and formatted style is the hardest of the three. However, column and formatted styles do not require spaces (or other delimiters) between variables and can read embedded blanks. Formatted style can read special data such as dates. Sometimes you use one style, sometimes another, and sometimes the easiest way is to use a combination of styles. SAS is so flexible, that you can mix and match any of the input styles for your own convenience.

Example   The following raw data contain information about U.S. national parks: name, state (or states as the case may be), year established, and size in acres.

```
Yellowstone             ID/MT/WY 1872    4,065,493
Everglades              FL 1934          1,398,800
Yosemite                CA 1864            760,917
Great Smoky Mountains   NC/TN 1926         520,269
Wolf Trap Farm          VA 1966                130
```

You could write the INPUT statement for these data in many ways—that is the point of this section. The following program shows one way to do it:

```
* Create a SAS data set named natparks;
* Read a data file park.dat mixing input styles;
DATA natparks;
   INFILE 'park.dat';
   INPUT parkname $ 1-22 state $ year @43 acreage COMMA9.;
PROC PRINT;
   TITLE 'Selected National Parks';
RUN;
```

Notice that the variable PARKNAME is read with column style input, STATE and YEAR are read with list style input, and ACREAGE is read with formatted style input. The output looks like this:

```
                     Selected National Parks                    1

       OBS    PARKNAME                 STATE      YEAR    ACREAGE

        1     Yellowstone              ID/MT/WY   1872    4065493
        2     Everglades               FL         1934    1398800
        3     Yosemite                 CA         1864     760917
        4     Great Smoky Mountains    NC/TN      1926     520269
        5     Wolf Trap Farm           VA         1966        130
```

Sometimes programmers run into problems when they mix input styles. When SAS reads a line of raw data it uses a pointer to mark its place, but each style of input uses the pointer a little differently. When you read a variable with list style input, SAS automatically scans to the next non-blank field and starts reading. When you read a variable with column style input, SAS starts reading that variable in the exact column you specify. But with formatted input, SAS just starts reading—wherever the pointer is, that is where SAS reads. Sometimes you need to move the pointer explicitly, and you can do that by using the column pointer, @n, where n is the number of the column SAS should move to.

In the preceding program, the column pointer @43 tells SAS to move to column 43 before reading ACREAGE. If you removed the column pointer from the INPUT statement, as shown in the following statement, then SAS would start reading ACREAGE right after YEAR:

```
INPUT parkname $ 1-22 state $ year acreage COMMA9.;
```

The resulting output would look like this:

```
                  Selected National Parks                        1

      OBS    PARKNAME                 STATE     YEAR    ACREAGE

       1     Yellowstone              ID/MT/WY  1872    4065
       2     Everglades               FL        1934       .
       3     Yosemite                 CA        1864       .
       4     Great Smoky Mountains    NC/TN     1926       5
       5     Wolf Trap Farm           VA        1966       .
```

Because ACREAGE was read with formatted input, SAS started reading right where the pointer was. Here is the data file with a ruler for counting columns at the top and asterisks marking the place where SAS started reading the variable ACREAGE:

```
----+----1----+----2----+----3----+----4----+----5-
Yellowstone              ID/MT/WY 1872 *  4,065,493
Everglades               FL 1934 *        1,398,800
Yosemite                 CA 1864 *          760,917
Great Smoky Mountains    NC/TN 1926 *       520,269
Wolf Trap Farm           VA 1966 *              130
```

The COMMA9. informat told SAS to read 9 columns, and SAS did that even when those columns were completely blank.

The column pointer, @*n*, has other uses too and can be used anytime you want SAS to skip backwards or forwards within a data line. You could use it, for example, to skip over unneeded data, reading some variables and not others.

INPUT statement
column pointer controls

3.7 Reading Multiple Lines of Raw Data per Observation

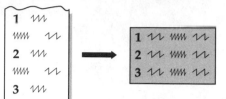

In a typical raw data file each line of data represents one observation, but sometimes the data for each observation are spread out over more than one line. Since SAS will automatically go to the next line if it runs out of data before it has read all the variables in an INPUT statement, you could just let SAS take care of figuring out when to go to a new line. But if you know that your data file has multiple lines of raw data per observation, it is better for you to explicitly tell SAS when to go to the next line than to make SAS figure it out. That way you won't get that suspicious SAS-went-to-a-new-line message in your log. To tell SAS when to skip to a new line, you simply add line pointers to your INPUT statement.

The line pointers, slash (/) and pound-*n* (#*n*), are like road signs telling SAS, "Go this way." To read more than one line of raw data for a single observation, you simply insert a slash into your INPUT statement when you want to skip to the next line of raw data. The #*n* line pointer performs the same action except that you specify the line number. The *n* in #*n* stands for the number of the line of raw data for that observation; so #2 means to go to the second line for that observation, and #4 means go to the fourth line. You can even go backwards using the #*n* line pointer, reading from line 4 and then from line 3, for example. The slash is simpler, but #*n* is more flexible.

Example   A colleague is trying to plan his next summer vacation, but he wants to go someplace where the weather is just right. He obtains data from a meteorology database. Unfortunately, he has not quite figured out how to export from this database and makes a rather odd file.

The file contains information about temperatures for the month of July for Alaska, Florida, and North Carolina. (If your colleague chooses the last state, maybe he can visit SAS Institute headquarters.) The first line contains the city and state; the second line lists the normal high temperature and normal low; and the third line contains the record high and low:

```
Nome AK
55 44
88 29
Miami FL
90 75
97 65
Raleigh NC
88 68
105 50
```

The following program reads the weather data from a file named TEMPERAT.DAT:

```
* Create a SAS data set named highlow;
* Read the data file using line pointers;
DATA highlow;
   INFILE 'temperat.dat';
   INPUT city $ state $
         / normhigh normlow
         #3 rechigh reclow;
PROC PRINT;
   TITLE 'High and Low Temperatures for July';
RUN;
```

The INPUT statement reads the variables CITY and STATE from the first line of data. Then the slash tells SAS to move to column 1 of the next line of data before reading NORMHIGH and NORMLOW. Likewise, the #3 tells SAS to move to column 1 of the third line of data for that observation before reading RECHIGH and RECLOW. As usual, there is more than one way to write this INPUT statement. You could replace the slash with #2 or replace #3 with a slash.

This note appears in the log:

```
NOTE: 9 records were read from the infile 'temperat.dat'.
      The minimum record length was 5.
      The maximum record length was 10.
NOTE: The data set WORK.HIGHLOW has 3 observations and 6 variables.
```

Notice that while nine records were read from the infile, the SAS data set contains just three observations. Usually this would set off alarms in your mind, but here it confirms that indeed three data lines were read for every observation just as planned. You should always check your log, particularly when using line pointers. The output looks like this:

```
              High and Low Temperatures for July            1

   OBS   CITY     STATE   NORMHIGH   NORMLOW   RECHIGH   RECLOW
    1    Nome      AK        55         44        88        29
    2    Miami     FL        90         75        97        65
    3    Raleigh   NC        88         68       105        50
```

INPUT statement
line pointer controls

3.8 Reading Multiple Observations per Line of Raw Data

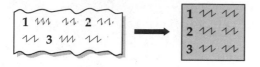

There ought to be a Murphy's law of data: whatever form data can take, it will. Normally SAS assumes that each line of raw data represents exactly one observation, no more and no less. When you have multiple observations per line of raw data, you can use double trailing at signs (@@) at the end of your INPUT statement. This line-hold specifier is like a stop sign telling SAS, "Stop, hold that line of raw data." SAS will hold that line of data, continuing to read observations until it either runs out of data or reaches an INPUT statement that does not end with a double trailing @.

Example Suppose you have a colleague, who is planning a vacation and has obtained a file containing data about rainfall for the three cities he is considering. The variables are city, state, normal rainfall for the month of July, and normal number of days with measurable precipitation in July. The raw data look like this:

```
Nome AK 2.5 15 Miami FL 6.75
18 Raleigh NC . 12
```

Notice that in this data file the first line stops in the middle of an observation. The following program reads these data from a file named PRECIP.DAT and uses an @@ so SAS does not automatically go to a new line of raw data for each observation:

```
* Create a SAS data set using the @@ line pointer;
* Read the data file precip.dat;
DATA rainfall;
   INFILE 'precip.dat';
   INPUT city $ state $ normrain daysrain @@;
PROC PRINT;
   TITLE 'Normal Total Precipitation and';
   TITLE2 'Mean Days with Precipitation for July';
RUN;
```

This note will appear in the log:

```
NOTE: 2 records were read from the infile 'precip.dat'
      The minimum record length was 18.
      The maximum record length was 28.
NOTE: SAS went to a new line when INPUT statement reached past the
      end of a line.
NOTE: The data set WORK.RAINFALL has 3 observations and
      4 variables.
```

While only two records were read from the raw data file, the RAINFALL data set contains three observations. The log also includes the note SAS went to a new line when INPUT statement reached past the end of a line. This means that SAS came to the end of a line in the middle of an observation and continued reading with the next line of raw data. Normally these messages would indicate a problem, but in this case they are exactly what you want.

The output will look like this:

```
                     Normal Total Precipitation and            1
                  Mean Days with Precipitation for July

        OBS    CITY       STATE    NORMRAIN    DAYSRAIN

         1     Nome        AK        2.50         15
         2     Miami       FL        6.75         18
         3     Raleigh     NC         .           12
```

INPUT statement
line-hold specifiers

3.9 Reading Part of a Raw Data File

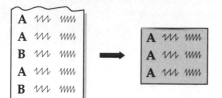

At some time you may find that you need to read a small fraction of the observations in a large data file. For example, you might be reading U.S. census data and only want female heads-of-household with incomes above $75,000 living in Walla Walla, Washington. You could read all the observations in the data file and then throw out the unneeded ones, but that would waste time.

Luckily, you don't have to read all the data before you tell SAS whether to keep an observation. Instead, you can read just enough variables to decide whether to keep the current observation, then end the INPUT statement with an at-sign (@), called a trailing at, telling SAS to hold that line of raw data. While the trailing @ holds that line, you can test the observation with an IF statement to see if it's one you want to keep. If it is, then you can read the remaining variables with a second INPUT statement. Without the trailing @, SAS would automatically start reading the next line of raw data with each INPUT statement.

The trailing @ is really a special case of the column pointer, @*n*, introduced earlier. By specifying a number after the @ sign, you tell SAS to move to a particular column. By using an @ without specifying a column, it is as if you are telling SAS, "Stay tuned for more information. Don't touch that dial!" SAS will hold that line of data until it reaches either the end of the DATA step, or an INPUT statement that does not end with a trailing @.

Example You want to read part of a raw data file containing local traffic data for freeways and surface streets. The data include four variables: type of street, name of street, the average number of vehicles per hour traveling that street during the morning, and the average number of vehicles per hour for the evening. Here are the data:

```
freeway 408                         3684 3459
surface Martin Luther King Jr. Blvd. 1590 1234
surface Broadway                    1259 1290
surface Rodeo Dr.                   1890 2067
freeway 608                         4583 3860
freeway 808                         2386 2518
surface Lake Shore Dr.              1590 1234
surface Pennsylvania Ave.           1259 1290
```

Suppose you only want to see the freeway data at this point so you read the raw data file TRAFFIC.DAT with this program:

```
* Use a trailing @ to delete surface streets;
DATA freeways;
   INFILE 'traffic.dat';
   INPUT type $ @;
   IF type = 'surface' THEN DELETE;
   INPUT name $ 9-38 amtraff pmtraff;

PROC PRINT;
   TITLE 'Traffic for Freeways';
RUN;
```

Notice that there are two INPUT statements. The first reads the character variable TYPE and then ends with an @. The trailing @ holds each line of data while the IF statement tests it. The second INPUT statement reads three variables: NAME (in columns 9-38), AMTRAFF, and PMTRAFF. If an observation has a value of surface for the variable TYPE, then the second INPUT statement never executes. Instead SAS returns to the beginning of the DATA step to process the next observation and does not add the unwanted observation to the FREEWAYS data set. (Do not pass go, do not collect $200.)

When you run this program, the log will contain these two notes, one saying that eight records were read from the input file and another saying that the new data set has just three observations:

```
NOTE: 8 records were read from the infile 'traffic.dat'.
NOTE: The data set WORK.FREEWAYS has 3 observations and 4 variables.
```

The other five observations were dropped because they did not satisfy the IF statement. The output looks like this:

```
                    Traffic for Freeways                     1

          OBS    TYPE      NAME    AMTRAFF    PMTRAFF

           1     freeway    408     3684       3459
           2     freeway    608     4583       3860
           3     freeway    808     2386       2518
```

The double trailing @, discussed in the previous section, is similar to the trailing @. Both are line-hold specifiers; the difference is how long they hold a line of data for input. The trailing @ holds a line of data for subsequent INPUT statements and releases that line of data at the end of the DATA step. The double trailing @ holds a line of data for subsequent INPUT statements even when SAS starts reading a new observation. In both cases, the line of data is released if SAS reaches a subsequent INPUT statement that does not contain a line-hold specifier.

INPUT statement line-hold specifiers	

3.10 Using Options on the INFILE Statement

So far in this chapter, we have seen ways to use the INPUT statement to read many different types of raw data. When reading raw data files, SAS makes certain assumptions about how to read them. For example, SAS starts reading with the first data line and, if you are using list input, SAS assumes that there are spaces between data values. Most of the time this is OK, but some data files can't be read using the default assumptions. The options in the INFILE statement change the way SAS reads raw data files. The following options are useful for reading particular types of data files. Place these options after the filename on the INFILE statement.

FIRSTOBS= The FIRSTOBS= option tells SAS at what line to begin reading data. This is useful if you have a data file that contains descriptive text or header information at the beginning, and you want to skip over these lines to begin reading the data. The following data file, for example, has a description of the data in the first two lines:

```
Ice-cream sales data for the summer of 1993
Flavor     Location   Boxes sold
Chocolate  213        123
Vanilla    213        512
Chocolate  415        242
```

The following program uses the FIRSTOBS= option to tell SAS to start reading data on the third line of the file:

```
DATA icecrm;
   INFILE 'sales.dat' FIRSTOBS = 3;
   INPUT flavor $ 1-9 loc boxes;
RUN;
```

MISSOVER By default, SAS will go to the next data line to read more data if SAS has reached the end of the data line and it still has more variables to read. The MISSOVER option tells SAS that if it runs out of data, don't go to the next data line. Instead, assign missing values to any remaining variables. The following data file illustrates where this option may be useful. This file contains test scores for a self-paced course. Since not all students complete all the tests, some have more scores than others.

```
Nguyen 89 76 91 82
Ramos 67 72 80 76 86
Robbins 76 65 79
```

The following program reads the data for the five test scores, assigning missing values to tests not completed:

```
DATA class102;
   INFILE 'scores.dat' MISSOVER;
   INPUT name $ test1 test2 test3 test4 test5;
RUN;
```

PAD   The PAD option is needed when you are reading data using column or formatted input and some data lines are shorter than others. This option will pad the end of data lines with blanks up to the length defined by the LRECL= option on the INFILE statement, if there is one, or the default record length. The default record length is system dependent; see the SAS Companion documentation for your operating system to find the default record length. This INFILE statement, for example, will pad data lines to a length of 200:

```
INFILE 'address.dat' PAD LRECL = 200;
```

The following INFILE statement, under SAS for Windows, will pad data lines to a length of 132, the system default:

```
INFILE 'address.dat' PAD;
```

The next file contains people's addresses and must be read using column or formatted input because the street names have embedded blanks. Note that the data lines are all different lengths:

```
John Garcia      114  Maple Ave.
Slyvia Chung    1302  Washington Drive
Martha Newton     45  S.E. 14th St.
```

This program uses column input to read the addresses file but needs the PAD option to fill in the short lines. Without the PAD option, SAS would try to go to the next line to read the remaining data for the first and third lines.

```
DATA homeadd;
   INFILE 'address.dat' PAD;
   INPUT name $ 1-15 number 16-19 street $ 22-37;
RUN;
```

DLM=   List input, by default, requires a space between data values. The DLM=, or DELIMITER=, option allows you to read data files with other delimiters. The following file is comma delimited where students' names are followed by the number of books they read for each week in a summer reading program:

```
Grace,3,1,5,2,6
Martin,1,2,4,1,3
Scott,9,10,4,8,6
```

This program uses list input to read the student data file specifying the comma as the delimiter:

```
DATA reading;
   INFILE 'books.dat' DLM = ',';
   INPUT name $ week1 week2 week3 week4 week5;
RUN;
```

More discussion of reading delimited raw data files can be found in section 3.14.

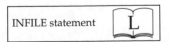

INFILE statement   L

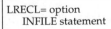

LRECL= option
INFILE statement   C

3.11 Listing the Contents of a SAS Data Set

To use a SAS data set, all you need to do is tell SAS the name and location of the data set you want, and SAS figures out what is in it. SAS can do this because SAS data sets are self documenting, which is another way of saying that SAS automatically stores information about the data set (sometimes called the descriptor portion) along with the data. You can't display a SAS data set on your computer screen like an ordinary text file. However, there is an easy way to find out what is in a SAS data set; you simply run PROC CONTENTS.

PROC CONTENTS is a simple procedure. In most cases you just type the keywords PROC CONTENTS and specify the data set you want with the DATA= option:

```
PROC CONTENTS DATA = dataset-name;
```

If you leave out the DATA= option, then by default SAS will use the most recently created SAS data set.

Example   The following DATA step creates a SAS data set named FUNNIES so that we can run PROC CONTENTS:

```
DATA funnies;
   INPUT id name $ height weight dob MMDDYY8.;
   LABEL id   = 'Identification no.'
      height = 'Height in inches'
      weight = 'Weight in pounds'
      dob    = 'Date of birth';
   INFORMAT dob MMDDYY8.;
   FORMAT dob WORDDATE18.;
   CARDS;
53 Susie    42  41  07-11-81
54 Charlie  46  55  10-26-54
55 Calvin   40  35  01-10-81
56 Lucy     46  52  01-13-55
   ;
* Use PROC CONTENTS to describe data set funnies;
PROC CONTENTS DATA = funnies;
RUN;
```

Note that the DATA step above includes a LABEL statement. For each variable, you can specify a label up to 40 characters long. These optional labels allow you to document your variables in more detail than is possible with just variable names. If you specify a LABEL statement in a DATA step, then the descriptions will be stored in the data set and will be printed by PROC CONTENTS. You can also use LABEL statements in PROC steps to customize your reports, but then the labels apply only for the duration of the PROC step and are not stored in the data set.

INFORMAT and FORMAT statements also appear in this program. You can use these optional statements to associate informats or formats with variables. Just as informats give SAS special instructions for reading a variable, formats give SAS special instructions for writing a variable. If you specify an INFORMAT or FORMAT statement in a DATA step, then the name of that informat or format will be saved in the data set and printed by PROC CONTENTS. FORMAT statements, like LABEL statements, can be used in PROC steps to customize your reports, but then the name of the format is not stored in the data set.[1]

The output looks like this:

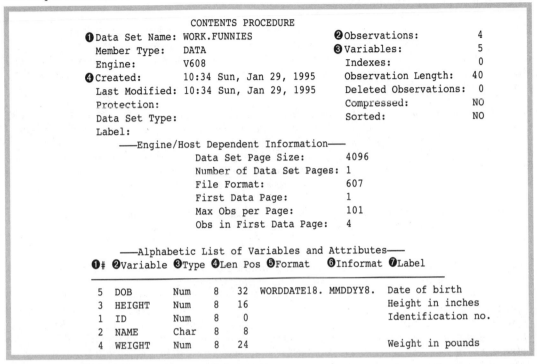

The output from PROC CONTENTS is like a table of contents for your data set. It starts with general information about your data set and then describes each variable in alphabetical order. The major points of interest are

For the data set

❶ Data set name
❷ Number of observations
❸ Number of variables
❹ Date created

For each variable

❶ Internal order
❷ Variable name
❸ Type (numeric or character)
❹ Length (storage size in bytes)
❺ Format for printing (if any)
❻ Informat for input (if any)
❼ Label (if any)

| CONTENTS procedure | P |

---

[1] Sections 5.5 and 5.6 discuss standard SAS formats more thoroughly.

3.12 Temporary versus Permanent SAS Data Sets

SAS data sets come in two varieties: temporary and permanent. A temporary SAS data set is one that exists only during the current job or session and is automatically erased by SAS when you finish. If a SAS data set is permanent, that doesn't mean that it lasts for eternity, just that it remains when the job or session is finished.

Each type of data set has its own advantages. Sometimes you want to keep a data set for later use and sometimes you don't. In this book, most of our examples use temporary data sets because we don't want to clutter up your disks. But, in general, if you use a data set more than once, it is more efficient to save it as a permanent SAS data set than to create a new temporary SAS data set every time you want to use the data.

SAS data set names   All SAS data sets have a two-level name such as WORK.BANANA, with the two levels separated by a period. The first level of a SAS data set name, WORK in this case, is called its libref (short for SAS data library reference). A libref is like an arrow pointing to a particular location. On some operating systems a libref refers to a physical location, such as a disk. On other systems it refers to a logical location, such as a directory or file. The second level, BANANA, is the member name that uniquely identifies the data set within that library.

Both the libref and member name follow the standard rules for valid SAS names. Specifically, they must be eight characters or shorter; start with a letter or underscore; and contain only letters, numerals, or underscores.

You never explicitly tell SAS to make a data set temporary or permanent, it is just implied by the name you give the data set when you create it. Most data sets are created in DATA steps, but PROC steps can also create data sets. If you specify a two-level name (and the libref is something other than WORK) then your data set will be permanent. If you specify just one level of the data set name (as we have in all examples so far in this book), then your data set will be temporary. SAS will use your one-level name as the member name and automatically append the libref WORK. By definition, any SAS data set with a libref of WORK is a temporary data set and will be erased by SAS at the end of your job or session. Here are some sample DATA statements and the characteristics of the data sets they create:

DATA statement	Libref	Member name	Type
`DATA apple;`	WORK	apple	temporary
`DATA WORK.orange;`	WORK	orange	temporary
`DATA mylib.grape;`	mylib	grape	permanent

Temporary SAS data sets   The following program creates a temporary SAS data set named WORK.DISTANCE:

```
DATA distance;
   miles = 23;
   kilometr = 1.61 * miles;
RUN;
```

Notice that the libref WORK does not appear in the DATA statement. Because the data set has just a one-level name, SAS assigns the default library, WORK, and uses DISTANCE as the member name within that library. The log contains this note with the complete, two-level name:

```
NOTE: The data set WORK.DISTANCE has 1 observations and 2 variables.
```

Permanent SAS data sets   Before you can use a libref, you need to define it. The most universal (and therefore most portable) method is with a LIBNAME statement. On some computers librefs can also be defined using operating system control language. The examples in this book use LIBNAME statements to define librefs, but it may be customary at your installation to define a libref without a LIBNAME statement.[1]

The following program is the same as the preceding one except that it creates a permanent SAS data set. The LIBNAME statement defines a libref called SASBOOK which points to a directory named MYSASLIB on the C drive. This is the syntax for LIBNAME statements on the DOS, OS/2, and Windows operating systems. LIBNAME statements may be different on your operating system and are discussed in more detail in the next section. Notice that a two-level name appears in the DATA statement.

```
LIBNAME sasbook 'c:\mysaslib';
DATA sasbook.distance;
   miles = 23;
   kilometr = 1.61 * miles;
RUN;
```

This time the log contains this note:

```
NOTE: The data set SASBOOK.DISTANCE has 1 observations and 2 variables.
```

This is a permanent SAS data set because its LIBREF is not WORK.

SAS data sets, permanent
WORK library

---

[1] With MVS you may use Job Control Language (JCL). With CMS you can create, read, and write permanent SAS data sets on your A disk without either a LIBNAME statement or CMS commands. You just use the two-level name in your DATA or PROC statements. The libref will be the CMS filetype, and the member name will be the CMS filename. To use a SAS data set on some disk other than your A disk, use a LIBNAME statement. To find out more, see the SAS Companion documentation for your operating system or contact your local SAS software consultant.

3.13 Using LIBNAME Statements with Permanent SAS Data Sets

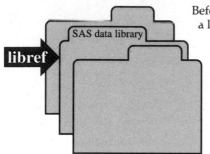

Before you can write or read a permanent SAS data set, you must define a libref for that data set. A libref is a word that corresponds to the location of a SAS data library. When you use a libref as the first level in the name of a SAS data set, SAS knows to look for that data set in that location.

You can define a libref using either a LIBNAME statement or, with some computers, operating system control language. This book focuses on the use of the LIBNAME statement because it is the most universal (and therefore most portable) method. The basic form of the LIBNAME statement is

```
LIBNAME libref 'your-SAS-data-library';
```

After the keyword LIBNAME, you specify the libref and then the location of your permanent SAS data set in quotes. Librefs must be eight characters or shorter; start with a letter or underscore; and contain only letters, numerals, or underscores. Here is the syntax of LIBNAME statements for individual operating systems:

DOS, OS/2, Windows: `LIBNAME libref 'drive:\directory';`

Macintosh: `LIBNAME libref 'disk:folder';`

UNIX: `LIBNAME libref '/home/path';`

Open VMS, VMS: `LIBNAME libref '[userid.directory]';`

CMS: `LIBNAME libref 'filemode';`

MVS: `LIBNAME libref 'OS.data.set.name';`

Creating a permanent SAS data set The following example creates a permanent SAS data set containing information about magnolia trees. The raw data file includes six variables: scientific name, common name, maximum height, age at first blooming when planted from seed, whether evergreen or deciduous, and color of flowers.

```
M. grandiflora Southern Magnolia 80 15 E white
M. campbellii                    80 20 D rose
M. liliiflora  Lily Magnolia     12  4 D purple
M. soulangiana Saucer Magnolia   25  3 D pink
M. stellata    Star Magnolia     10  3 D white
```

This program sets up a libref named PLANTS pointing to the MYSASLIB directory on the C drive (DOS, OS/2, Windows systems). Then it reads the raw data from a file called MAG.DAT, creating a permanent SAS data set named PLANTS.MAGNOLIA.

```
LIBNAME plants 'c:\mysaslib';
DATA plants.magnolia;
   INFILE 'mag.dat';
   INPUT sciname $ 1-14 comname $ 16-32 maxhigh
      agebloom type $ color $;
RUN;
```

The log contains this note showing the two-level data set name:

```
NOTE: The data set PLANTS.MAGNOLIA has 5 observations and 6 variables.
```

If you print a directory of files on your computer, you will not see a file named PLANTS.MAGNOLIA. That is because operating systems have their own system for naming files. When run under Windows with Version 6 of the SAS System, this data set will be called MAGNOLIA.SD2. Under MVS, the file name would be *OS.data.set.name*. Under CMS, it would be MAGNOLIA PLANTS. On other operating systems, the name will usually be a two-level name that starts with the SAS member name and then has a standard extension.

Reading a permanent SAS data set   To use a permanent SAS data set, you only need to include a LIBNAME statement in your program and refer to the data set by its two-level name. For instance, if you wanted to go back later and print the permanent data set created in the last example, all you would need are the following statements:

```
LIBNAME example 'c:\mysaslib';
PROC PRINT DATA = example.magnolia;
   TITLE 'Magnolias';
RUN;
```

This time the libref in the LIBNAME statement is EXAMPLE instead of PLANTS, but it points to the same location as before, the MYSASLIB directory on the C drive. The libref can change, but the member name, MAGNOLIA, stays the same.

The output looks like this:

```
                      Magnolias                          1

    OBS     SCINAME          COMNAME      MAXHIGH AGEBLOOM TYPE COLOR

     1   M. grandiflora  Southern Magnolia    80      15     E    white
     2   M. campbellii                        80      20     D    rose
     3   M. liliiflora   Lily Magnolia        12       4     D    purple
     4   M. soulangiana  Saucer Magnolia      25       3     D    pink
     5   M. stellata     Star Magnolia        10       3     D    white
```

LIBNAME statement   L

LIBNAME statement   C

3.14 Importing Data from Other Sources

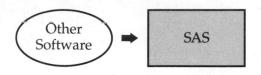

Because SAS is not the only program out there, and because people could never decide on just one format for data files even if it were possible, you will probably find someday that the data you want to analyze isn't in a SAS data set or raw data file. Data can come from a number of sources: Data Base Management Systems (DBMS) like ORACLE or DB2, spreadsheets like Excel or Lotus 123, or other statistical analysis programs like SPSS or BMDP. Because each software application keeps data in its own special format, SAS cannot directly read these data.

You can import data from other applications in the following ways:

▶ You can create a raw (also called ASCII, text, flat, or sequential) data file from the application and read the file using the INPUT statement just as you would any raw data file.

▶ You can read the data in its native format using SAS data engines if an engine exists for your application.

▶ You can share data with the application using SAS/ACCESS software, or through Dynamic Data Exchange (DDE) or Open Data Base Connectivity (ODBC).

The first method is almost always an option as most applications can create raw data files. The last two methods are available for a limited number of applications and operating systems, and in the case of SAS/ACCESS, may require the purchase of additional software since it is licensed separately from the Base SAS software.

Delimited raw data files Most applications can convert their data into raw data files. Some applications give a lot of control over the format of the file whereas others only output files in one format. An easy format for import into SAS is a space delimited file where missing values are indicated with a period. Space delimited means that there is at least one space between each value in the file. If character data have embedded spaces, then a comma delimited file may be better. The following data file, TOADS2.DAT, is an example of a comma delimited file:

```
Lucky,2.3,1.9,,3.0
Spot,4.6,2.5,3.1,.5
Tubs,7.1,,,3.8
Hop,4.5,3.2,1.9,2.6
Noisy,3.8,1.3,1.8,1.5
Winner,5.7,,,,
```

This file can be read using a list style INPUT statement by specifying the comma as the delimiter in the DLM= option of the INFILE statement. Because this file has two consecutive delimiters rather than periods for missing values you need the DSD (Delimiter Separated Data) option (available in Release 6.07 and higher) of the INFILE statement to make SAS read the two delimiters as a missing value. The DSD option also allows you to read embedded delimiters in quoted strings. (For example, you might have "Peter, Paul, and Mary" as a field in a comma-delimited file. With the DSD option, SAS will read the field as Peter, Paul, and Mary. The quotations are dropped.)

The following program will read the comma-delimited file shown earlier:

```
* Read raw data using the DLM= and DSD options;
DATA toads;
    INFILE 'toads2.dat' DLM = ',' DSD;
    INPUT toadname $ weight jump1 jump2 jump3;
RUN;
```

Tab-delimited files Some applications create tab-delimited files. These types of files are best avoided if possible but can be read using the EXPANDTABS option in the INFILE statement (available in Release 6.06 and higher). This option replaces the tab character with spaces, allowing you to read the file using list input:

```
INFILE 'toads3.dat' EXPANDTABS;
```

Alternatively, you can use the option DLM = '09'x in the INFILE statement if your computer uses the ASCII character set (most computers except IBM mainframes). In ASCII, 09 is the hexadecimal equivalent of a tab character, and the notation '09'x means a hexadecimal 09:

```
INFILE 'toads3.dat' DLM = '09'x;
```

Data Engines A data engine is an internal set of instructions which tell SAS how to read the data file. The default engine reads and writes SAS data sets, but there are other engines available. Check the SAS Companion documentation for your system for a complete list of engines available for you. The following engines are available for most systems and read files in their native formats: **SPSS, BMDP** and **OSIRIS**.

SAS/ACCESS, DDE, and ODBC[1] The SAS/ACCESS products, which are licensed separately, allow access to data in popular DBMS systems like ORACLE. You can access files directly without conversion or even copying. This means that data can be stored and updated in one location, ensuring that you are using the most current data for your analysis.

Dynamic Data Exchange (DDE) and open database connectivity (ODBC) are industry standards available for personal computers running Windows (OS/2 also supports DDE). As with SAS/ACCESS, you can share data with other applications running on your computer without converting or copying the data. Many applications running on these platforms support DDE and ODBC. See your SAS Companion documentation for more information about DDE and ODBC.

engines
    LIBNAME statement, assigning with
INFILE statement
    EXPANDTABS option
    DELIMITER= option

---

[1] Support for ODBC is available in Release 6.10 and higher and may require the purchase of additional software.

3.15 Transporting SAS Data Sets between Computers

Generally, SAS data sets created on one computer are not directly useable on another unless both computers are the same type and use the same operating system.[1] This is because each computer has its own way of representing data, and they don't understand each other's language (they are binary incompatible—or, in human terms, they have irreconcilable differences). Fortunately, you can convert your SAS data sets to the SAS transport format, move the transport file to the new computer, and then convert it back to a SAS data set.

This section covers transporting SAS data sets only, via files on disk, for Release 6.06 and higher. If you are dealing with an older version of SAS, want to transport other types of SAS files, or want to read or write files directly to tape, you will need to use other methods. These topics are discussed in detail in the SAS Technical Report P-195, *Transporting SAS Files between Host Systems*.

For maximum portability, SAS transport files should have the following attributes:

- ▶ record length of 80
- ▶ fixed block records with 8000 characters per block.

If you are transferring your transport files over a network, be sure to use binary transfer methods. This minimizes the chance of one of the previous attributes being altered during the transfer.

You can use the COPY procedure[2] to read or write SAS transport files. The program has three parts, the LIBNAME statement for the SAS data set, the LIBNAME statement for the transport file, and the COPY procedure. To write a transport file you specify the libref (library reference) for the transport file in the OUT= option and the libref for the SAS data set in the IN= option. To read a transport file, reverse the librefs—transport file in the IN= option and SAS data set in the OUT= option. The following shows the general form of the program:

```
LIBNAME libref 'drive:path';
LIBNAME libref XPORT 'drive:path\filename';
PROC COPY IN = libref OUT = libref;
```

Transport files can contain more than one SAS data set, and by default PROC COPY copies all the SAS data sets in the library or transport file. If you don't want them all, you can add the SELECT or EXCLUDE statements after the PROC COPY statement to list the SAS data sets you want (SELECT *data-set-names;* or EXCLUDE *data-set-names;*).

The LIBNAME statement for the SAS data set (whether you are creating it from a transport file, or converting it to a transport file) is the same one you normally use to read or write a SAS data set on your system.

The LIBNAME statement for the transport file is a little different. Instead of specifying just the location of the file as you would in most LIBNAME statements, you give the actual file name, and

---

[1] You may not need to transport data sets between MVS and CMS or between UNIX systems if they share a file system.
[2] It is possible to read and write SAS transport files in a DATA step and to create them in other procedures. However, if all you want to do is copy a SAS data set to a transport file or vice versa, then PROC COPY is generally more efficient.

path if appropriate. In addition, between the libref and the file specification, you put the engine name XPORT. This tells SAS that this is a transport file and not a SAS data set. The following gives the syntax for this LIBNAME statement for several operating systems:

Windows, OS/2: `LIBNAME libref XPORT 'drive:\directory\filename';`

Macintosh: `LIBNAME libref XPORT 'disk:folder:filename';`

UNIX: `LIBNAME libref XPORT '/home/path/filename';`

VMS, Open VMS: `LIBNAME libref XPORT '[userid.dir]filename.ext' CC=NONE;`[3]

CMS: `LIBNAME libref XPORT 'filename filetype filemode';`

MVS: `LIBNAME libref XPORT;`[4]

Example The following program reads data about the toad jumping contest using a CARDS statement and creates a permanent SAS data set (example is for Windows or OS/2 operating systems):

```
LIBNAME mylib 'c:\mysaslib';
DATA mylib.toads;
   INPUT toadname $ weight jump1 jump2 jump3;
   CARDS;
Lucky 2.3 1.9 . 3.0
Spot 4.6 2.5 3.1 .5
Tubs 7.1 . . 3.8
;
RUN;
```

The next program creates a SAS transport file from the permanent SAS data set just created above and puts it on the diskette labeled PCDISK in the A drive. The SELECT statement ensures that just the TOADS data set is copied to the transport file:

```
LIBNAME mylib 'c:\mysaslib';
LIBNAME trans XPORT 'a:\toads.tra';
PROC COPY IN = mylib OUT = trans;
   SELECT toads;
RUN;
```

Finally, this program reads the transport file on a Macintosh computer and recreates the SAS data set on the disk named Hard Disk in a folder named SAS data:

```
LIBNAME sdata 'Hard Disk:SAS data';
LIBNAME trans XPORT 'pcdisk:toads.tra';
PROC COPY IN = trans OUT = sdata;
RUN;
```

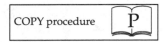

COPY procedure

---

[3] The CC=NONE option is available for SAS Release 6.08 TS405 or later. If you are using an earlier version and you want to transfer the file over a network, you will need to change the carriage control attributes of the transport file to NONE before transferring. Contact your site's SAS software consultant for information on how to do this.
[4] Under MVS you need to define the libref in either a DD statement in the JCL or in a TSO allocate command. If you are creating the transport file, be sure to specify the correct DCB information (RECFM=FB, LRECL=80, BLKSIZE=8000).

3.16 Writing Raw Data Files

Generally people use SAS to produce a report or analysis, but sometimes your goal might be to create a raw data file. A common reason for writing raw data files is to transfer data from SAS to a spreadsheet or word processor. If those software packages don't read SAS data sets, you can put the data into a raw data file and treat it like a text file.

You can write raw data the same way that you read raw data, with just a few changes. Instead of naming your external file in an INFILE statement, you name it in a FILE statement. Instead of reading variables with an INPUT statement, you write them with a PUT statement. To say it another way, you use INFILE and INPUT statements to get raw data into SAS, and FILE and PUT statements to get raw data out.

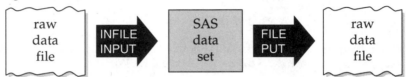

Example   A market research company has conducted a random telephone survey of toothcare preferences. Respondents were asked, "What do you think is the best color for toothpaste? On a scale of 1 to 5, with 1 being 'like a lot' and 5 being 'dislike a lot', how would you rate these flavors of toothpaste: cool mint, luscious banana, and crazy cola?" Respondents were also asked, "Do you squeeze the tube in the middle or at the end?" Here is a sample of the raw data:

```
white     1 5 4 end
blue      2 4 3 mid
white     1 5 2 end
green     2 4 1 mid
magenta   3 2 2 mid
```

The following program uses INFILE and INPUT statements to read the data from a file called TOOTH.DAT and puts it in a permanent SAS data set named SURVEY.TEETH in the MYSASLIB directory on the C drive (DOS, OS/2, Windows). The LIBNAME statement may differ on your operating system.

```
LIBNAME survey 'c:\mysaslib';
DATA survey.teeth;
   INFILE 'tooth.dat';
   INPUT favcolor $ mint banana cola squeeze $;
PROC PRINT;
RUN;
```

Suppose you have a colleague who wants to put the data in a spreadsheet on his PC. You can write it in the form he wants using FILE and PUT statements:

```
LIBNAME survey 'c:\mysaslib';
DATA _NULL_;
   SET survey.teeth;
   FILE 'newfile.dat';
   PUT mint banana cola favcolor squeeze;
RUN;
```

The word _NULL_ appears in the DATA statement instead of a SAS data set name. You could put a data set name there, but _NULL_ is a special keyword that tells SAS not to bother making a new SAS data set. By not writing a new SAS data set, you save computer time.

The SET statement simply tells SAS to read the SAS data set SURVEY.TEETH.[1] The FILE statement tells SAS the name of the output file you want to create. Then, the PUT statement tells SAS what to write and where.

PUT statements can be in list, column, or formatted style, just like INPUT statements. But since SAS already knows whether a variable is numeric or character, you don't have to put a $ after character variables. Both the INPUT and PUT statements in the preceding program are in list format, but only the INPUT statement requires a $ to identify character variables.

If you run this program, your log will contain the following note telling how many records were written to the output file:

```
NOTE: 5 records were written to the file 'newfile.dat'.
```

The output file looks like this:

```
1 5 4 white end
2 4 3 blue mid
1 5 2 white end
2 4 1 green mid
3 2 2 magenta mid
```

Because the PUT statement was in list format, SAS automatically put one space between each variable. If you use column or formatted styles of PUT statements, SAS will put the variables wherever you specify.

For a spreadsheet you may want commas between each variable and everything in neat columns. Luckily, you can add any string of characters simply by enclosing it in quotes, and you can control the spacing with the @n pointer. PUT statements use the same pointers as INPUT statements (@n to move to column n, / to skip to the next line, #n to skip to line n, and the trailing @ to hold the current line). Here is the revised PUT statement:

```
PUT mint ', ' banana ', ' cola ', ' favcolor @21 ', ' squeeze;
```

The new output with commas and orderly columns looks like this:

```
1 , 5 , 4 , white   , end
2 , 4 , 3 , blue    , mid
1 , 5 , 2 , white   , end
2 , 4 , 1 , green   , mid
3 , 2 , 2 , magenta , mid
```

FILE statement
PUT statement

---

[1] For more information about this kind of SET statement, see section 6.1.

4

"Contrariwise," continued Tweedledee, "if it was so, it might be; and if it were so, it would be; but as it isn't, it ain't. That's logic."

From *Alice Through the Looking Glass* by Lewis Carroll. Public domain.

CHAPTER 4

Working with Your Data

4.1 Creating and Redefining Variables

If someone compiled a list of the ten most popular things to do with SAS software, creating and redefining variables would be near the top. Fortunately, SAS is flexible and uses a common sense approach to these tasks. You create and redefine variables with assignment statements using this basic form:

```
variable = expression;
```

On the left side of the equation is a variable name, either new or old. The right side of the equation may be a constant, another variable, or a mathematical expression. Here are examples of these basic types of assignment statements:

Assignment statement	Type of expression
qwerty = 10;	numeric constant
qwerty = 'ten';	character constant
qwerty = oldvar;	a variable
qwerty = oldvar + 10;	addition
qwerty = oldvar - 10;	subtraction
qwerty = oldvar * 10;	multiplication
qwerty = oldvar / 10;	division
qwerty = oldvar ** 10;	exponentiation

Whether the variable QWERTY is numeric or character depends on the expression that defines it. When the expression is numeric, QWERTY will be numeric; when it is character, QWERTY will be character.

When deciding how to execute your equation, SAS follows the standard mathematical rules of precedence: SAS performs exponentiation first, then multiplication and division, followed by addition and subtraction. You can use parentheses to override that order. Here are two similar SAS statements showing that a couple of parentheses can make a big difference:

Assignment statement	Result
x = 10 * 4 + 3 ** 2;	x = 49
x = 10 * (4 + 3 ** 2);	x = 130

While SAS can read equations with or without parentheses, people often can't. If you use parentheses, your programs will be a lot easier to read.

Example   The following raw data are from a survey of home gardeners. Gardeners were asked to estimate the number of pounds they harvested for four crops: tomatoes, zucchini, peas, and grapes.

```
Gregor  10  2  40     0
Molly   15  5  10  1000
Luther  50 10  15    50
Susan   20  0   .    20
```

This program reads the data from a file called GARDEN.DAT and then modifies the data:

```
* Modify home data set with assignment statements;
DATA home;
   INFILE 'garden.dat';
   INPUT name $ 1-7 tomato zucchini peas grapes;
   year = 1995;
   type = 'home';
   zucchini = zucchini * 10;
   total = tomato + zucchini + peas + grapes;
   pertom = (tomato / total) * 100;
PROC PRINT;
   TITLE 'Home Gardening Survey';
RUN;
```

This program contains five assignment statements. The first creates a new variable, YEAR, equal to a numeric constant, 1995. The variable TYPE is set equal to a character constant, home. The variable ZUCCHINI is multiplied by 10 because that just seems natural for zucchini. TOTAL is the sum for all the types of plants. PERTOM is not a genetically engineered tomato but the percent of harvest which were tomatoes. The report from PROC PRINT contains all the variables, old and new:

```
                        Home Gardening Survey                       1

    OBS NAME   TOMATO ZUCCHINI PEAS GRAPES YEAR TYPE  TOTAL  PERTOM

     1  Gregor   10      20     40      0   1995 home    70  14.2857
     2  Molly    15      50     10   1000   1995 home  1075   1.3953
     3  Luther   50     100     15     50   1995 home   215  23.2558
     4  Susan    20       0      .     20   1995 home     .       .
```

Notice that the variable ZUCCHINI appears only once because the new value replaced the old value. The other four assignment statements each created a new variable. When a variable is new, SAS adds it to the data set you are creating. When a variable already exists, SAS replaces the original value with the new one. Using an existing name has the advantage of not cluttering your data set with a lot of similar variables. However, you don't want to overwrite a variable unless you are really sure you won't need the original value later.

The variable PEAS had a missing value for the last observation. Because of this, the variables TOTAL and PERTOM, which are calculated from PEAS, were also set to missing and this message appeared in the log:

```
NOTE: Missing values were generated as a result of performing an operation
      on missing values.
```

This message is a flag that often indicates an error. However, in this case it is not an error but simply the result of incomplete data collection.[1]

| arithmetic operators assignment statements | 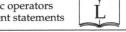 |

---

[1] If you want to add only non-missing values, you can use the SUM function discussed in section 8.7.

4.2 Using SAS Functions

Sometimes a simple equation, using only arithmetic operators, does not give you the new value you are looking for. This is where functions are very handy. Functions simplify your programming task because SAS has already done the programming for you. All you need to do is plug in the right values to the function and out comes the result—like putting a dollar in a change machine and getting back four quarters.

SAS has close to 150 functions in the following general areas:

Arithmetic	Quantile
Array	Random Number
Character	Sample Statistics
Date and Time	Special Functions
Financial	State and ZIP Code
Mathematical	Trigonometric and Hyperbolic
Probability	Truncation

Section 4.3, "Selected SAS Functions," gives a sample of the most common SAS functions.

Functions perform a calculation on or a transformation of the arguments given in parentheses following the function name. SAS functions have the following general form:

```
function-name(argument, argument, ...)
```

All functions must have parentheses even if they don't require any arguments. Arguments are separated by commas and can be variable names, constant values such as numbers or characters enclosed in quotes, or expressions. The following statement computes BIRTHDAY as a SAS date value using the function MDY and the variables MONBORN, DAYBORN, and YEARBORN. The MDY function takes three arguments, one each for the month, day, and year:

```
birthday = MDY(monborn, dayborn, yearborn);
```

Functions can be nested, where one function is the argument of another function. For example, the following statement calculates NEWVALUE using two nested functions, INT and LOG:

```
newvalue = INT(LOG(10));
```

The result for this example is 2, the integer portion of the natural log of the numeric constant 10 (2.3026). Just be careful when nesting functions that each parenthesis has a mate.

Example Data from a pumpkin carving contest illustrates the use of several functions. The contestants' names are followed by their age, type of pumpkin (carved or decorated), date of entry, and the scores from five judges:

```
Alicia Grossman   13 c 10-28-93 7.8 6.5 7.2 8.0 7.9
Matthew Lee        9 D 10-30-93 6.5 5.9 6.8 6.0 8.1
Elizabeth Garcia  10 C 10-29-93 8.9 7.9 8.5 9.0 8.8
Lori Newcombe      6 D 10-30-93 6.7 5.6 4.9 5.2 6.1
Jose Martinez      7 d 10-31-93 8.9 9.510.0 9.7 9.0
Brian Williams    11 C 10-29-93 7.8 8.4 8.5 7.9 8.0
```

The following program reads the data, creates two new variables (AVGSC and DAYENTER) and transforms another (TYPE):

```
DATA contest;
   INFILE 'pumpkin.dat';
   INPUT name $16. age 3. +1 type $1. +1 date MMDDYY8.
         (sc1 sc2 sc3 sc4 sc5) (4.1);
   avgsc = MEAN(sc1, sc2, sc3, sc4, sc5);
   dayenter = DAY(date);
   type = UPCASE(type);
PROC PRINT;
   TITLE 'Pumpkin Carving Contest';
RUN;
```

The variable AVGSC is created using the MEAN function, which returns the mean of the non-missing arguments. This differs from simply adding the arguments together and dividing by their number, which would return a missing value if any of the arguments were missing.

The variable DAYENTER is created using the DAY function, which returns the day of the month. SAS has all sorts of functions for manipulating dates, and what's great about them is that you don't have to worry about things like leap year—SAS takes care of that for you.

The variable TYPE is transformed using the UPCASE function. SAS is case sensitive when it comes to variable values; a 'd' is not the same as 'D'. The data file has both lowercase and uppercase letters for the variable TYPE, so the function UPCASE is used to make all the values upper case.

Here are the results:

```
                    Pumpkin Carving Contest                      1

 OBS       NAME       AGE TYPE  DATE SC1 SC2  SC3 SC4 SC5 AVGSC DAYENTER

   1  Alicia Grossman  13  C   12354 7.8 6.5  7.2 8.0 7.9  7.48   28
   2  Matthew Lee       9  D   12356 6.5 5.9  6.8 6.0 8.1  6.66   30
   3  Elizabeth Garcia 10  C   12355 8.9 7.9  8.5 9.0 8.8  8.62   29
   4  Lori Newcombe     6  D   12356 6.7 5.6  4.9 5.2 6.1  5.70   30
   5  Jose Martinez     7  D   12357 8.9 9.5 10.0 9.7 9.0  9.42   31
   6  Brian Williams   11  C   12355 7.8 8.4  8.5 7.9 8.0  8.12   29
```

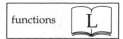

functions L

4.3 Selected SAS Functions

The table in this section spans both pages. The left page gives the syntax and definition of functions while the right page shows examples. These are the most commonly used functions, but there are many others. So if you don't find what you need here, check *SAS Language, Reference* for a complete list.

Function name	Syntax[1]	Definition
Numeric		
INT	INT(*arg*)	Returns the integer portion of argument
LOG	LOG(*arg*)	Natural logarithm
LOG10	LOG10(*arg*)	Logarithm to the base 10
MAX	MAX(*arg,arg,...*)	Largest non-missing value
MIN	MIN(*arg,arg,...*)	Smallest non-missing value
MEAN	MEAN(*arg,arg,...*)	Arithmetic mean of non-missing values
ROUND	ROUND(*arg, round-off-unit*)	Rounds to nearest round-off unit
SUM	SUM(*arg,arg,...*)	Sum of non-missing values
Character		
LEFT	LEFT(*arg*)	Left aligns a SAS character expression
LENGTH	LENGTH(*arg*)	Returns the length of an argument not counting trailing blanks (missing values have a length of 1)
SUBSTR	SUBSTR(*arg,position,n*)	Extracts a substring from an argument starting at 'position' for 'n' characters or until end if no 'n'[2]
TRANSLATE	TRANSLATE(*source,to-1, from -1,...to-n,from-n*)	Replaces 'from' characters in 'source' with 'to' characters (one to one replacement only—you can't replace one character with two, for example)
TRIM	TRIM(*arg*)	Removes trailing blanks from character expression
UPCASE	UPCASE(*arg*)	Converts all letters in argument to uppercase
Date		
DATEJUL	DATEJUL(*julian-date*)	Converts a Julian date to a SAS date value[3]
DAY	DAY(*date*)	Returns the day of the month from a SAS date value
MDY	MDY(*month,day,year*)	Returns a SAS date value from month, day, and year values
MONTH	MONTH(*date*)	Returns the month (1-12) from a SAS date value
QTR	QTR(*date*)	Returns the yearly quarter (1-4) from a SAS date value
TODAY	TODAY()	Returns the current date as a SAS date value

---

[1] arg is short for argument, which means a literal value, variable name, or expression.
[2] SUBSTR has a different function when on the left side of an equals sign.
[3] A SAS date value is the number of days since January 1, 1960.

Function name	Example	Result	Example	Result
Numeric				
INT	x=INT(4.32);	x=4	y=INT(5.789);	y=5
LOG	x=LOG(1);	x=0.0	y=LOG(10);	y=2.30259
LOG10	x=LOG10(1);	x=0.0	y=LOG10(10);	y=1.0
MAX	x=MAX(9.3,8,7.5);	x=9.3	y=MAX(-3,.,5);	y=5
MEAN	x=MEAN(1,4,7,2);	x=3.5	y=MEAN(2,.,3);	y=2.5
MIN	x=MIN(9.3,8,7.5);	x=7.5	y=MIN(-3,.,5);	y=-3
ROUND	x=ROUND(12.65);	x=13	y=ROUND(12.65,.1);	y=12.7
SUM	x=SUM(3,5,1);	x=9.0	y=SUM(4,7,.);	y=11
Character				
LEFT	a=' cat'; x=LEFT(a);	x='cat '	a=' my cat'; y=LEFT(a);	y='my cat '
LENGTH	a='my cat'; x=LENGTH(a);	x=6	a=' my cat '; y=LENGTH(a);	y=7
SUBSTR	a='(916)734-6281'; x=SUBSTR(a,2,3);	x='916'	y=SUBSTR('1cat',2);	y='cat'
TRANSLATE	a='6/16/93'; x=TRANSLATE(a, '-', '/';	x='6-16-93'	a='my cat can'; y=TRANSLATE(a, 'r', 'c');	y='my rat ran'
TRIM	a='my '; b='cat'; x=TRIM(a)||b;[4]	x='mycat '	a='my cat '; b='s'; y=TRIM(a)||b;	y='my cats '
UPCASE	a='MyCat'; x=UPCASE(a);	x='MYCAT'	y=UPCASE('Tiger');	y='TIGER'
Date				
DATEJUL	a=60001; x=DATEJUL(a);	x=0	a=60365; y=DATEJUL(a);	y=364
DAY	a=MDY(4,18,89); x=DAY(a);	x=18	a=MDY(9,3,60); y=DAY(a);	y=3
MDY	x=MDY(1,1,60);	x=0	m=2; d=1; y=60; date=MDY(m,d,y);	date=31
MONTH	a=MDY(4,18,89); x=MONTH(a);	x=4	a=MDY(9,3,60); y=MONTH(a);	y=9
QTR	a=MDY(4,18,89); x=QTR(a);	x=2	a=MDY(9,3,60); y=QTR(a);	y=3
TODAY	x=TODAY();	x=today's date	x=TODAY()-1;	x=yesterday's date

functions

---

[4] The concatenation operator | | concatenates character strings.

4.4 Using IF-THEN Statements

Frequently, you want an assignment statement to apply to some observations but not all—under some conditions, but not others. This is called conditional logic, and you do it with IF-THEN statements:

```
IF condition THEN action;
```

The condition is an expression comparing one thing to another, and the action is what SAS should do when the expression is true, usually an assignment statement. For example

```
IF model = 'Mustang' THEN make = 'Ford';
```

This statement tells SAS to set the variable MAKE equal to Ford whenever the variable MODEL equals Mustang. The terms on either side of the comparison may be constants, variables, or expressions. Those terms are separated by a comparison operator, which may be either symbolic or mnemonic. The decision of whether to use symbolic or mnemonic operators depends on your personal preference and the symbols available on your keyboard. Here are the basic comparison operators:

Symbolic	Mnemonic	Meaning
=	EQ	equals
¬ =, ^ =, or ~ =	NE	not equal
>	GT	greater than
<	LT	less than
> =	GE	greater than or equal
< =	LE	less than or equal

The IN operator also makes comparisons, but it works a bit differently. IN compares the value of a variable to a list of values. Here is an example:

```
IF model IN ('Corvette', 'Camaro') THEN make = 'Chevrolet';
```

This statement tells SAS to set the variable MAKE equal to Chevrolet whenever the value of MODEL is Corvette or Camaro.

A single IF-THEN statement can only have one action. If you add the keywords DO and END, then you can execute more than one action. For example

```
IF condition THEN DO;        IF model = 'Mustang' THEN DO;
   action;                      make = 'Ford';
   action;                      size = 'compact';
END;                         END;
```

The DO statement causes all SAS statements coming after it to be treated as a unit until a matching END statement appears. Together, the DO statement, the END statement, and all the statements in between are called a DO group.

You can also specify multiple conditions with the keywords AND and OR:

```
IF condition AND condition THEN action;
```

For example

```
IF model = 'Mustang' AND year < 1970 THEN status = 'classic';
```

Like the comparison operators, AND and OR may be symbolic or mnemonic:

Symbolic	Mnemonic	Meaning
&	AND	all comparisons must be true
|, ¦, or !	OR	only one comparison must be true

Be careful with long strings of comparisons; they can be a logical maze.

Example   Here are data about used cars. The variables are model, year, make, number of seats, and color:

```
Corvette 1955 .      2 black
XJ6      1985 Jaguar 2 teal
Mustang  1966 Ford   4 red
Miata    1992 .      . silver
CRX      1991 Honda  2 black
Camaro   1990 .      4 red
```

The following program reads the data from a file called CARS.DAT, uses a series of IF-THEN statements to fill in missing data, and creates a new variable, STATUS:

```
DATA sporty;
   INFILE 'cars.dat';
   INPUT model $ year make $ seats color $;
   IF year < 1970 THEN status = 'classic';
   IF model = 'Corvette' OR model = 'Camaro' THEN make = 'Chevy';
   IF model = 'Miata' THEN DO;
      make = 'Mazda';
      seats = 2;
   END;
PROC PRINT;
   TITLE "Eddy's Excellent Emporium of Used Sports Cars";
RUN;
```

This program contains three IF-THEN statements. The first is a simple IF-THEN that creates the new variable STATUS based on the value of YEAR. That is followed by a compound IF-THEN using an OR. The last IF-THEN uses DO and END. The output looks like this:

```
        Eddy's Excellent Emporium of Used Sports Cars          1

    OBS    MODEL      YEAR    MAKE     SEATS    COLOR     STATUS

     1     Corvette   1955    Chevy      2      black     classic
     2     XJ6        1985    Jaguar     2      teal
     3     Mustang    1966    Ford       4      red       classic
     4     Miata      1992    Mazda      2      silver
     5     CRX        1991    Honda      2      black
     6     Camaro     1990    Chevy      4      red
```

IF statement operators   L

4.5 Grouping Observations with IF-THEN/ELSE Statements

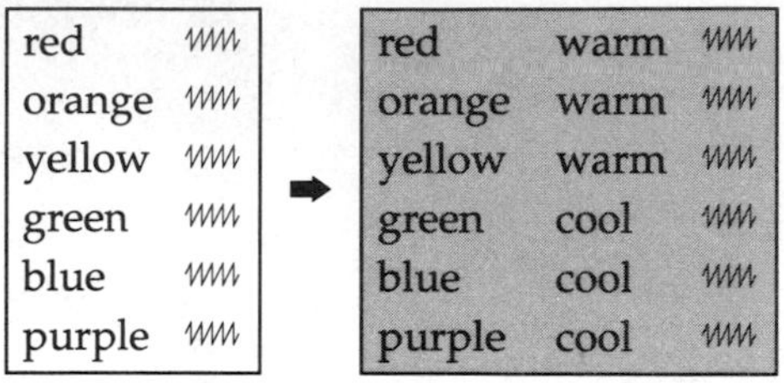
red
orange
yellow
green
blue
purple
red warm
orange warm
yellow warm
green cool
blue cool
purple cool

One of the most common uses of IF-THEN statements is for grouping observations. Perhaps a variable has too many different values and you want to print a more compact report, or perhaps you are going to run an analysis based on specific groups of interest. There are many possible reasons for grouping data, so sooner or later you'll probably need to do it.

The simplest and most common way to create a grouping variable is with a series of IF-THEN statements.[1] By adding the keyword ELSE to your IF statements, you can tell SAS that these statements are related. IF-THEN/ELSE logic takes this basic form:

```
IF condition THEN action;
   ELSE IF condition THEN action;
   ELSE IF condition THEN action;
```

Notice that the ELSE statement is simply an IF-THEN statement with an ELSE tacked onto the front. You can have any number of these statements.

IF-THEN/ELSE logic has two advantages when compared to a simple series of IF-THEN statements without any ELSE statements. First, it is more efficient, using less computer time; once an observation satisfies a condition, SAS skips the rest of the series. Second, ELSE logic ensures that your groups are mutually exclusive so you don't accidentally have an observation fitting into more than one group.

Sometimes the last ELSE statement in a series is a little different, containing just an action, with no IF or THEN. Note the final ELSE statement in this series:

```
IF condition THEN action;
   ELSE IF condition THEN action;
   ELSE action;
```

An ELSE of this kind becomes a default which is automatically executed for all observations failing to satisfy any of the previous IF statements. You can only have one of these statements, and it must be the last in the IF-THEN/ELSE series.

Example Here are data from a survey of home improvements. Each observation contains three variables: owner's name, description of the work done, and cost of the improvements in dollars:

```
Bob     kitchen cabinet face-lift   1253.00
Shirley bathroom addition          11350.70
Silvia  paint exterior                  .
Al      backyard gazebo             3098.63
Norm    paint interior               647.77
Kathy   second floor addition      75362.93
```

[1] Other ways to create grouping variables include using a SELECT statement, or using a PUT function with a user-defined format from PROC FORMAT.

This program reads the raw data from a file called HOME.DAT and then assigns a grouping variable called COSTGRP. This variable has a value of high, medium, low, or missing, depending on the value of COST:

```
* Group observations by cost;
DATA homefix;
   INFILE 'home.dat';
   INPUT owner $ 1-7 descrip $ 9-33  cost;
   IF cost = . THEN costgrp = 'missing';
      ELSE IF cost < 2000 THEN costgrp = 'low';
      ELSE IF cost < 10000 THEN costgrp = 'medium';
      ELSE costgrp = 'high';
PROC PRINT;
   TITLE 'Home Improvement Cost Groups';
RUN;
```

Notice that there are four statements in this IF-THEN/ELSE series, one for each possible value of the variable COSTGRP. The first statement deals with observations that have missing data for the variable COST. Without this first statement, observations with a missing value for COST would be incorrectly assigned a COSTGRP of low. SAS considers missing values to be smaller than non-missing values, smaller than any printable character for character variables, and smaller than negative numbers for numeric variables. Unless you are sure that your data contain no missing values, you should allow for missing values when you write IF-THEN/ELSE statements.

The results look like this:

```
                        Home Improvement Cost Groups                 1

       OBS   OWNER    DESCRIP                   COST       COSTGRP

        1    Bob      kitchen cabinet face-lift   1253.00   low
        2    Shirley  bathroom addition          11350.70   high
        3    Silvia   paint exterior                  .     missing
        4    Al       backyard gazebo             3098.63   medium
        5    Norm     paint interior               647.77   low
        6    Kathy    second floor addition      75362.93   high
```

IF-THEN/ELSE statement
missing values
   order after sorting data

4.6 Subsetting Your Data

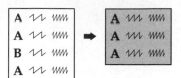

Often programmers find that they want to use some of the observations in a data set and exclude the rest. The most common way to do this is with a subsetting IF statement in a DATA step.[1] The basic form of a subsetting IF is

```
IF expression;
```

Consider this example:

```
IF sex = 'f';
```

At first subsetting IF statements may seem odd. People naturally ask, "IF sex = 'f', then what?" The subsetting IF looks incomplete, as if a careless typist pressed the delete key too long. But it is really a special case of the standard IF-THEN statement. In this case the action is merely implied. If the expression is true, then SAS continues with the DATA step. If the expression is false, then no further statements are processed for that observation; that observation is not added to the data set being created; and SAS moves on to the next observation. You can think of the subsetting IF as a kind of on-off switch. If the condition is true, then the switch is on and the observation is processed. If the condition is false, then that observation is turned off.

If you don't like subsetting IFs, there is another alternative, the DELETE statement. DELETE statements do the opposite of subsetting IFs. While the subsetting IF statement tells SAS which observations to include, the DELETE statement tells SAS which observations to exclude:

```
IF expression THEN DELETE;
```

The following two statements are equivalent (assuming there are only two values for the variable sex, and no missing data):

```
IF sex = 'f';        IF sex = 'm' THEN DELETE;
```

Example The members of a local amateur playhouse want to choose a Shakespearean comedy for this spring's play. You volunteer to compile a list of titles using data from an online encyclopedia. The variables are title, approximate year of first performance, and type of play:

```
A Midsummer Night's Dream 1595 comedy
Comedy of Errors          1590 comedy
Hamlet                    1600 tragedy
Macbeth                   1606 tragedy
Richard III               1594 history
Romeo and Juliet          1596 tragedy
Taming of the Shrew       1593 comedy
Tempest                   1611 romance
```

---

[1] Other ways to subset data include using multiple INPUT statements (discussed in section 3.9), and the WHERE statement (discussed in section 5.2 and appendix E).

This program reads the data from a raw data file called SHAKESP.DAT and then uses a subsetting IF statement to select only comedies:

```
* Choose only comedies;
DATA comedy;
    INFILE 'shakesp.dat';
    INPUT title $ 1-26 year type $;
    IF type = 'comedy';
PROC PRINT;
    TITLE 'Shakespearean Comedies';
RUN;
```

The output looks like this:

```
                       Shakespearean Comedies                    1

            OBS    TITLE                     YEAR    TYPE

             1     A Midsummer Night's Dream  1595    comedy
             2     Comedy of Errors           1590    comedy
             3     Taming of the Shrew        1593    comedy
```

These notes appear in the log stating that although eight records were read from the input file, the data set WORK.COMEDY contains only 3 observations:

```
NOTE: 8 records were read from the infile 'shakesp.dat'
NOTE: The data set WORK.COMEDY has 3 observations and 3 variables.
```

It is always a good idea to check the SAS log when you subset observations to make sure that you ended up with what you expected.

In the program above, you could substitute the statement

```
IF type = 'tragedy' OR type = 'romance' OR type = 'history' THEN DELETE;
```

for the statement

```
IF type = 'comedy';
```

But you would have to do a lot more typing. Generally, you use the subsetting IF when it is easier to specify a condition for including observations, and use the DELETE statement when is easier to specify a condition for excluding observations.

IF statement, subsetting

4.7 Working with SAS Dates

Dates can be tricky to work with. Some months have 30 days, some 31, some 28, and don't forget leap year. SAS dates simplify all this. A SAS date is the number of days since January 1, 1960.[1] The table below lists four dates and their values as SAS dates:

Date	SAS date value
January 1, 1959	–365
January 1, 1960	0
January 1, 1961	366
January 1, 2001	14976

SAS has special tools for working with dates: informats for reading dates, functions for manipulating dates, and formats for printing dates.[2] A table of selected date informats, formats, and functions is in the next section.

Informats   To read variables that are dates, you use formatted style input with a date informat. The INPUT statement below tells SAS to read a variable named BDATE using the MMDDYY8. informat:

```
INPUT bdate MMDDYY8.;
```

SAS has a variety of date informats for reading dates in many different forms. All of these informats convert your data to a number equal to the number of days since January 1, 1960.[3]

When SAS sees a date like 07/04/95, SAS assumes, by default, that the year is 1995 rather than 1895 or 2095. You can change that with the YEARCUTOFF= system option which specifies the first year of a hundred year span for SAS to use when reading dates. The default value for this option is 1900, but this statement tells SAS to interpret two-digit dates as occurring between 1950 and 2049:

```
OPTIONS YEARCUTOFF = 1950;
```

Dates in SAS expressions   Once a variable has been read with a SAS date informat, it can be used in arithmetic expressions like other numeric variables. For example, if a library book is due in three weeks, you could find the due date by adding 21 days to the date it was checked out:

```
datedue = datechek + 21;
```

You can use a date as a constant in a SAS expression by adding quotes and a letter D. The assignment statement below creates a variable named HALWN95, which is equal to the SAS date value for October 31,1995:

```
halwn95 = '31OCT95'D;
```

Functions   SAS date functions perform a number of handy operations. For example, the TODAY function returns a SAS date value equal to today's date. The statement below uses the TODAY function to compute a person's current age:

```
age = (TODAY() - dob) / 365.25;
```

---

[1] We don't know why this date was chosen, but since SAS dates are relative, January 1, 1960, is as good as any other date.
[2] SAS also has informats, functions, and formats for working with time values (the number of seconds since midnight), and datetime values (the number of seconds since midnight, you guessed it, January 1, 1960).
[3] For more information about informats see section 3.4, for functions section 4.2, and for formats section 5.5.

The variable AGE is equal to today's date minus the variable DOB (date of birth) divided by the number of days in a year. Given a SAS date value, other functions return the day, month, or quarter. Some functions convert other forms of dates, such as Julian dates, into SAS date values.

Formats If you print a SAS date value, SAS will by default print the actual value—the number of days since January 1, 1960. Since this is not very meaningful to most people, SAS has a variety of formats for printing dates in different forms. The FORMAT statement below tells SAS to print the variable BDATE using the WEEKDATE17. format:

```
FORMAT bdate WEEKDATE17.;
```

Example A local library has a data file containing details about library cards. The file has three variables—the card holder's name, birthdate, and the date that card became effective:

```
A. Jones     01jan60 09-15-90
M. Rincon    05oct49 01-24-92
Z. Grandage  18mar88 10-10-93
K. Kaminaka  29feb80 05-29-94
```

The program below reads the raw data from a file named DATES.DAT using the DATE8. and MMDDYY8. informats. Then the variable EXPDATE (for expiration date) is computed by adding three years (365.25 multiplied by 3) to the variable EFFDATE. The variable EXPQTR (the quarter the card expires) is computed using the QTR function and the variable EXPDATE. An IF statement uses a date constant to identify cards issued after January 1, 1994:

```
DATA libcards;
   INFILE 'dates.dat';
   INPUT name $12. bdate DATE8. effdate MMDDYY8.;
   expdate = effdate + (365.25 * 3);
   expqtr = QTR(expdate);
   IF effdate > '01jan94'D THEN newcard = 'yes';
PROC PRINT;
   FORMAT effdate MMDDYY8. expdate WEEKDATE17.;
   TITLE 'SAS Dates without and with Formats';
RUN;
```

Here is the output from PROC PRINT. Notice that the variable BDATE is printed without a date format, while EFFDATE and EXPDATE use formats:

```
                SAS Dates without and with Formats                    1

   OBS    NAME        BDATE    EFFDATE       EXPDATE      EXPQTR  NEWCARD

    1   A. Jones          0   09/15/90  Tue, Sep 14, 1993   3
    2   M. Rincon     -3740   01/24/92  Mon, Jan 23, 1995   1
    3   Z. Grandage   10304   10/10/93   Wed, Oct 9, 1996   4
    4   K. Kaminaka    7364   05/29/94  Wed, May 28, 1997   2       yes
```

| SAS date and time values | L |

4.8 Selected Date Informats, Functions, and Formats

The table in this section spans both pages. The left page gives the syntax and definitions while the right page shows examples. These are the most commonly used date informats, functions, and formats, but there are others. Check *SAS Language, Reference* for a complete list.

Informats		width range	default width
DATE*w*.	Reads dates in form: ddmmmyy or ddmmmyyyy	7-32	7
JULIAN*w*.	Reads Julian dates in form: yyddd or yyyyddd	5-32	5
MMDDYY*w*.	Reads dates in form: mmddyy or mmddyyyy	6-32	6

Functions	Syntax	Definition
DATEJUL	DATEJUL(*julian-date*)	Converts a Julian date to a SAS date value[1]
DAY	DAY(*date*)	Returns the day of the month from a SAS date value
MDY	MDY(*month,day,year*)	Returns a SAS date value from month, day, and year values
MONTH	MONTH(*date*)	Returns the month (1-12) from a SAS date value
QTR	QTR(*date*)	Returns the yearly quarter (1-4) from a SAS date value
TODAY	TODAY()	Returns the current date as a SAS date value

Formats		width range	default width
DATE*w*.	Writes SAS date values in form: *ddmmmyy*	5-9	7
DAY*w*.	Writes the day of the month from a SAS date value	2-32	2
JULIAN*w*.	Writes a Julian date from a SAS date value	5-7	5
MMDDYY*w*.	Writes SAS date values in form: *mmddyy*	2-8	8
WEEKDATE*w*.	Writes SAS date values in form: *day-of-week, month-name dd, yy or yyyy*	3-37	29
WORDDATE*w*.	Writes SAS date values in form: *month-name dd, yyyy*	3-32	18
YYQ*w*.	Writes the year and quarter of a SAS date value	4-6	6

---

[1] A SAS date value is the number of days since January 1, 1960.

Informats	Input data	INPUT statement	Results
DATE*w*.	1jan1961	`INPUT day DATE10.;`	366
JULIAN*w*.	61001	`INPUT day JULIAN7.;`	366
MMDDYY*w*.	01-01-61	`INPUT day MMDDYY8.;`	366

Functions	Example	Result	Example	Result
DATEJUL	`a=60001;` `x=DATEJUL(a);`	x=0	`a=60365;` `y=DATEJUL(a);`	y=364
DAY	`a=MDY(4,18,89);` `x=DAY(a);`	x=18	`a=MDY(9,3,60);` `y=DAY(a);`	y=3
MDY	`x=MDY(1,1,60);`	x=0	`m=2; d=1; y=60;` `date=MDY(m,d,y);`	date=31
MONTH	`a=MDY(4,18,89);` `x=MONTH(a);`	x=4	`a=MDY(9,3,60);` `y=MONTH(a);`	y=9
QTR	`a=MDY(4,18,89);` `x=QTR(a);`	x=2	`a=MDY(9,3,60);` `y=QTR(a);`	y=3
TODAY	`x=TODAY();`	x=today's date	`x=TODAY()-1;`	x=yesterday's date

Formats	Input data	PUT statement[2]	Results
DATE*w*.	8966	`PUT birth DATE7.;` `PUT birth DATE9.;`	19JUL84 19JUL1984
DAY*w*.	8966	`PUT birth DAY2.;` `PUT birth DAY7.;`	19 19
JULIAN*w*.	8966	`PUT birth JULIAN5.;` `PUT birth JULIAN7.;`	84201 1984201
MMDDYY*w*.	8966	`PUT birth MMDDYY8.;` `PUT birth MMDDYY6.;`	07/19/84 071984
WEEKDATE*w*.	8966	`PUT birth WEEKDATE15.;` `PUT birth WEEKDATE29.;`	Thu, Jul 19, 84 Thursday, July 19, 1984
WORDDATE*w*.	8966	`PUT birth WORDDATE12.;` `PUT birth WORDDATE18.;`	Jul 19, 1984 July 19, 1984
YYQ*w*.	8966	`PUT birth YYQ6.;`	1984Q3

L

---

[2] Formats can be used in PUT statements and PUT functions in DATA steps, and in FORMAT statements in either DATA or PROC steps.

4.9 Using the RETAIN and Sum Statements

When reading raw data, SAS sets the values of all variables equal to missing at the start of each iteration of the DATA step. If a variable is not assigned a new value in either an INPUT statement or an assignment statement, then it will have a missing value in the output data set. The RETAIN and sum statements change this. If a variable appears in a RETAIN statement, then its value will be retained from one iteration of the DATA step to the next. So a variable normally has missing values if it is not assigned a value in the DATA step. With the RETAIN statement, though, a variable is assigned its value from the previous iteration of the DATA step. A sum statement is a special SAS statement which also retains values from the previous iteration of the DATA step.

RETAIN statement   The RETAIN statement can appear anywhere in the DATA step and has the following form, where all variables to be retained are listed after the RETAIN keyword:

    RETAIN variables;

You can also specify an initial value, other than missing, to the variables. All variables listed before an initial value will start the first iteration of the DATA step with that value:

    RETAIN variables initial-value;

Sum statement   A sum statement also retains values from the previous iteration of the DATA step, but use it for the special cases where you simply want to cumulatively add the value of an expression to a variable. A sum statement, like an assignment statement, contains no keywords. It has the following form:

    variable + expression;

No, there is no typo here and no equals sign either. This statement adds the value of the expression to the variable while retaining the variable's value from one iteration of the DATA step to the next. The variable must be numeric and has the initial value of zero. This statement can be re-written using the RETAIN statement and SUM function as follows:

    RETAIN variable 0;
    variable = SUM(variable, expression);

As you can see, a sum statement is really a special case of using RETAIN.

Example This example illustrates the use of both the RETAIN and sum statements. The minor league baseball team, the Walla Walla Sweets, has the following data about their games. The date the game was played and the team played are followed by the number of hits and runs for the game:

```
6-19 Columbia Peaches      8  3
6-20 Columbia Peaches     10  5
6-23 Plains Peanuts        3  4
6-24 Plains Peanuts        7  2
6-25 Plains Peanuts       12  8
6-30 Gilroy Garlics        4  4
7-1  Gilroy Garlics        9  4
7-4  Sacramento Tomatoes  15  9
7-4  Sacramento Tomatoes  10 10
7-5  Sacramento Tomatoes   2  3
```

The team wants two additional variables in their data set. One shows the cumulative number of runs for the season, and one shows the maximum number of runs in a game to date. The following program uses a sum statement to compute the cumulative number of runs, and the RETAIN statement and MAX function to determine the maximum number of runs in a game to date:

```
DATA runs;
   INFILE 'games.dat';
   INPUT  month 1 day 3-4 team $ 6-25 hits 27-28 runs 30-31;
   RETAIN maxruns;
   maxruns = MAX(maxruns, runs);
   runstodt + runs;
PROC PRINT;
   TITLE "Season's Record to Date";
RUN;
```

The variable MAXRUNS is set equal to the maximum of its value from the previous iteration of the DATA step, since it appears in the RETAIN statement, and the variable RUNS. The variable RUNSTODT adds the number of runs per game, RUNS, to itself while retaining its value from one iteration of the DATA step to the next. This produces a cumulative record of the number of runs.

Here are the results:

```
                        Season's Record to Date                      1

    OBS  MONTH  DAY       TEAM          HITS  RUNS  MAXRUNS  RUNSTODT

     1     6     19   Columbia Peaches    8     3      3         3
     2     6     20   Columbia Peaches   10     5      5         8
     3     6     23   Plains Peanuts      3     4      5        12
     4     6     24   Plains Peanuts      7     2      5        14
     5     6     25   Plains Peanuts     12     8      8        22
     6     6     30   Gilroy Garlics      4     4      8        26
     7     7      1   Gilroy Garlics      9     4      8        30
     8     7      4   Sacramento Tomatoes 15     9      9        39
     9     7      4   Sacramento Tomatoes 10    10     10        49
    10     7      5   Sacramento Tomatoes  2     3     10        52
```

sum statement
RETAIN statement

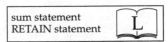

4.10   Simplifying Programs with Arrays

Sometimes you want to do the same thing to many variables. You may want to take the log of every numeric variable or change every occurrence of zero to a missing value. You could write a series of assignment statements or IF statements, but if you have a lot of variables to transform, using arrays will simplify and shorten your program.

An array is an ordered group of similar items. You might think your local mall has a nice array of stores to choose from. In SAS, an array is a group of variables. You can define an array to be any group of variables you like, as long as they are either all numeric or all character. The variables can be ones that already exist in your data set, or they can be new variables that you want to create.

Arrays are defined using the ARRAY statement in the DATA step. The ARRAY statement has the following general form:

```
ARRAY name (#) $ variable-list;
```

In this statement, *name* is a name you give to the array, and # is the number of variables in the array. Following the (#) is a list of variable names. The number of variables in the list must equal the number given in parentheses. (You may use {} or [] instead of parentheses if you like.) This is called an explicit array, where you explicitly state the number of variables in the array. The $ is needed if the variables are character and is only necessary if the variables have not previously been defined.

The array itself is not stored with the data set; it is only defined for the duration of the DATA step. You can give the array any name, as long as it does not match any of the variable names in your data set or any SAS keywords. The rules for naming arrays are the same as those for naming variables (must be eight characters or fewer and start with a letter or underscore followed by letters, numerals, or underscores).

To reference a variable using the array name, give the array name and the subscript for that variable. The first variable in the variable list has subscript 1, the second has subscript 2, and so forth. So if you have an array defined as

```
ARRAY store (4) macys penneys sears target;
```

STORE(1) is the variable MACYS, STORE(2) is the variable PENNEYS, STORE(3) is the variable SEARS, and STORE(4) is the variable TARGET. This is all just fine, but simply defining an array doesn't do anything for you. You want to be able to use the array to make things easier for you.

Example   The radio station WBRK is conducting a survey asking people to rate ten different songs. Songs are rated on a scale of 1 to 5, where 1 = change the station when it comes on, and 5 = turn up the volume when it comes on. If listeners had not heard the song or didn't care to comment on it, a 9 was entered for that song. The following are the data collected:

```
Albany      54 4 3 5 9 9 2 1 4 4 9
Richmond    33 5 2 4 3 9 2 9 3 3 3
Oakland     27 1 3 2 9 9 9 3 4 2 3
Richmond    41 4 3 5 5 5 2 9 4 5 5
Berkeley    18 3 4 9 1 4 9 3 9 3 2
```

The listener's city of residence, age, and their responses to all ten songs are listed. The following program changes all the 9's to missing values. (The variables are named using the first letters of the words in the song's title.)

```
DATA songs;
   INFILE 'wbrk.dat';
   INPUT city $ 1-15 age domk wj hwow simbh kt aomm libm tr filp ttr;
   ARRAY song (10) domk wj hwow simbh kt aomm libm tr filp ttr;
   DO i = 1 TO 10;
      IF song(i) = 9 THEN song(i) = .;
   END;
PROC PRINT;
   TITLE 'WBRK Song Survey';
RUN;
```

An array, SONG, is defined as having ten variables, the same ten variables that appear in the INPUT statement representing the ten songs. Next comes an iterative DO statement. All statements between the DO statement and the END statement are executed, in this case, ten times, once for each variable in the array.

The variable I is used as an index variable and is incremented by 1 each time through the DO loop. The first time through the DO loop, the variable I has a value of 1 and the IF statement would read `IF song(1)=9 then song(1)=.;`, which is the same as: `IF domk=9 then domk=.;`. The second time through, I has a value of 2 and the IF statement would read `IF song(2)=9 then song(2)=.;`, which is the same as: `IF wj=9 then wj=.;`. This continues through all 10 variables in the array.

Here are the results:

```
                           WBRK Song Survey                              1

  OBS    CITY      AGE DOMK WJ HWOW SIMBH KT AOMM LIBM TR FILP TTR   I
   1    Albany     54   4   3   5     .   .   2    1   4   4    .   11
   2    Richmond   33   5   2   4     3   .   2    .   3   3    3   11
   3    Oakland    27   1   3   2     .   .   .    3   4   2    3   11
   4    Richmond   41   4   3   5     5   5   2    .   4   5    5   11
   5    Berkeley   18   3   4   .     1   4   .    3   .   3    2   11
```

Notice that the array members SONG(1) to SONG(10) did not become part of the data set, but the variable I did. You could have written ten IF statements instead of using arrays and accomplished the same result. In this program it would not have made a big difference, but if you had 100 songs in your survey instead of ten, then using arrays would clearly be a better solution.

array processing
ARRAY statement, explicit
DO statement, iterative

4.11 Using Shortcuts for Lists of Variable Names

As the title states, this section is about shortcuts, shorthand ways of writing lists of variable names. While writing SAS programs, you will often need to write a list of variable names. When defining ARRAYS, using functions like MEAN or SUM, or using SAS procedures, you must specify which variables to use. Now, if you only have a handful of variables, you might not feel a need for a shortcut. But if, for example, you need to define an array with 100 elements, you might be a little grumpy after typing in the 49th variable name knowing you still have 51 more to go. You might even think, "There must be an easier way." Well, there is.

You can use an abbreviated list of variable names anywhere you can use a regular variable list. In functions, abbreviated lists must be preceded by the keyword OF (for example, `SUM(OF cat8 - cat12)`). Otherwise, you simply replace the regular list of variables with the abbreviated one.

Numbered range lists   Variables which start with the same characters and end with consecutive numbers can be part of a numbered range list. The numbers can start and end anywhere as long as the number sequence between is complete. For example, the following shows a variable list and its abbreviated form:

Variable list	Abbreviated list
`INPUT cat8 cat9 cat10 cat11 cat12;`	`INPUT cat8 - cat12;`

Name range lists   Name range lists depend on the internal order, or position, of the variables in the SAS data set. This is determined by the order of appearance of the variable in the DATA step. For example, if you had the following DATA step, then the internal variable order would be Y A C H R B:

```
DATA example;
   INPUT y a c h r;
   b = c + r;
RUN;
```

To specify a name range list, put the first variable, then two hyphens, then the last variable. The following PUT statements show the variable list and its abbreviated form using a named range:

Variable list	Abbreviated list
`PUT y a c h r b;`	`PUT y -- b;`

If you are not sure of the internal order, you can find out using PROC CONTENTS with the POSITION option. The following program will list the variables in the permanent SAS data set DISTANCE sorted by position.

```
LIBNAME mydir 'c:\mysaslib';
PROC CONTENTS DATA = mydir.distance POSITION;
RUN;
```

Use caution when including name range lists in your programs. Although they can save on typing, they may also make your programs more difficult to understand and debug.

Special SAS name lists The special name lists, _ALL_, _CHARACTER_, and _NUMERIC_ can also be used any place you want either all the variables, all the character variables, or all the numeric variables in a SAS data set. These name lists are useful when you want to do something like compute the mean of all the numeric variables for an observation (MEAN(OF _NUMERIC_)), or list the values of all variables in an observation (PUT _ALL_;).

Example The radio station WBRK wants to modify the program from the previous section, which changes all 9's to missing values. Now, instead of changing the original variables, they use the following program to create new variables (SONG1 through SONG10) which will have the new missing values:

```
DATA songs;
   INFILE 'wbrk.dat';
   INPUT city $ 1-15 age domk wj hwow simbh kt aomm libm tr filp ttr;
   ARRAY new (10) song1 - song10;
   ARRAY old (10) domk -- ttr;
   DO i = 1 TO 10;
      IF old(i) = 9 THEN new(i) = .;
         ELSE new(i) = old(i);
   END;
   avgsc = MEAN(OF song1 - song10);
PROC PRINT;
   TITLE 'WBRK Song Survey';
RUN;
```

Note that both ARRAY statements use abbreviated variable lists, array NEW uses a numbered range list and array OLD uses a name range list. Inside the iterative DO loop, the SONG variables (array NEW) are set equal to missing if the original variable (array OLD) had a value of 9. Otherwise, they are set equal to the original values. After the DO loop, a new variable, AVGSC, is created using an abbreviated variable list in the function MEAN. The output includes variables from both the OLD array (DOMK, WJ, ... TTR) and NEW array (SONG1 – SONG10):

```
                    WBRK Song Survey                              1

                                              S
              S                  S S S S S S S S O        A
        C     D  H I  A L   F    O O O O O O O O O N       V
  O  I  A O   W M  O I   I T  N N N N N N N N N G         G
  B  T  G M W O B K M B T L T  G G G G G G G G G 1        S
  S  Y  E K J W H T M M R P R  1 2 3 4 5 6 7 8 9 0   I    C

  1 Albany   54 4 3 5 9 9 2 1 4 4 9 4 3 5 . . 2 1 4 4 .  11 3.28571
  2 Richmond 33 5 2 4 3 9 2 9 3 3 3 5 2 4 3 . 2 . 3 3 3  11 3.12500
  3 Oakland  27 1 3 2 9 9 9 3 4 2 3 1 3 2 . . . 3 4 2 3  11 2.57143
  4 Richmond 41 4 3 5 5 5 2 9 4 5 5 4 3 5 5 5 2 . 4 5 5  11 4.22222
  5 Berkeley 18 3 4 9 1 4 9 3 9 3 2 3 4 . 1 4 . 3 . 3 2  11 2.85714
```

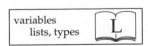

variables
lists, types

5

" **Once in a while the simple things work right off.** "

PHIL GALLAGHER, SAS® USER SINCE 1975

From the SAS L listserv, 1994. Reprinted by permission of the author.

CHAPTER 5

Sorting, Printing, and Summarizing Your Data

5.1 Using SAS Procedures

```
PROC whatever
DATA=        _____
BY           _____
TITLE        _____
FOOTNOTE _____
LABEL        _____
```

Using a procedure, or PROC, is like filling out a form. Someone else designed the form, and all you have to do is fill in the blanks and choose from a list of options. Each PROC has its own unique form with its own list of options. But while each procedure is unique, there are similarities too. This section discusses some of those similarities.

All procedures have required statements, and most have optional statements.[1] PROC PRINT, for example, requires only two words:

```
PROC PRINT;
```

At other times you might use the PRINT procedure and, with optional statements, make it a dozen lines long.

Most procedures write results to your output window or file (sometimes called the listing). You can customize the appearance of that output (centering, dates, linesize, and pagesize) using the system options discussed in section 2.10. Many procedures can also write results to an output SAS data set to be printed or used in a later program.

PROC statement   All procedures start with the keyword PROC followed by the name of the procedure, such as PRINT or CONTENTS. Options, if there are any, follow the procedure name. The DATA= option tells SAS which data set to use as input for that procedure. In this case, SAS will use a temporary SAS data set named banana:

```
PROC CONTENTS DATA = banana;
```

The DATA= option is, of course, optional. If you skip it, then SAS will use the most recently created data set, which is not necessarily the same as the most recently used. Sometimes it is easier to specify the data set you want than to figure out which data set SAS will use by default. To use a permanent SAS data set, just issue a LIBNAME statement to set up a libref pointing to the location of your data set, and put the data set's two-level name in the DATA= option, as discussed in section 3.13.

BY statement   The BY statement is required for only one procedure, PROC SORT. In PROC SORT the BY statement tells SAS how to arrange the observations. In all other procedures, the BY statement is optional, and tells SAS to perform a separate analysis for each combination of values of the BY variables rather than treating all observations as one group. For example, this statement tells SAS to run a separate analysis for each state:

```
BY state;
```

All procedures, except PROC SORT, assume that your data are already sorted by the variables in your BY statement. If your observations are not already sorted, then use PROC SORT to do the job.

---

[1] This book covers required statements and the most frequently used options. To find a complete listing of required and optional statements for each procedure, check the relevant guide such as the *SAS Procedures Guide, Version 6, Third Edition* or *SAS/STAT User's Guide, Version 6, Fourth Edition, Volume 1* and *Volume 2*. In those guides each procedure has its own chapter, and near the beginning of that chapter you will find a complete list of possible statements.

TITLE and FOOTNOTE statements   You have seen TITLE statements many times in this book. FOOTNOTE works the same way, but prints at the bottom of the page. These statements are not technically part of any step. You can put them anywhere in your program, but since they apply to the procedure output it generally makes sense to put them with the procedure. The most basic TITLE statement consists of the keyword TITLE followed by your title enclosed in quotes. SAS doesn't care if the two quotation marks are single or double as long as they are the same:

```
TITLE 'This is a title';
```

If you find that your title contains an apostrophe, use double quotes around the title, or replace the single apostrophe with two:

```
TITLE "Here's another title";
TITLE 'Here''s another title';
```

You can specify up to ten titles or footnotes by adding numbers to the keywords TITLE and FOOTNOTE:

```
FOOTNOTE3 'This is the third footnote';
```

Titles and footnotes stay in effect until you replace them with new ones or cancel them with a null statement. This statement cancels all current titles:

```
TITLE;
```

When you specify a new title or footnote, it replaces the old title or footnote with the same number and cancels ones with a higher number. For example, a new TITLE2 cancels an existing TITLE3, if there is one.

LABEL statement   By default, SAS uses variable names to label your output. Since variable names are limited to eight characters, sometimes they are a bit more terse than you would like. In those cases you can use the LABEL statement to create more informative labels for your reports. This statement creates labels for the variables RECDATE and POSTDATE. Labels can be up to 40 characters long including blanks and must be enclosed in quotes:

```
LABEL recdate  = 'Date order received'
      postdate = 'Date merchandise mailed';
```

When a LABEL statement is used in a DATA step, the labels become part of the data set; but when used in a PROC, the labels stay in effect only for the duration of that step.

BY statement	P

FOOTNOTE statement	
LABEL statement	L
TITLE statement	

5.2 Subsetting in Procedures with the WHERE Statement

One optional statement for any PROC that reads a SAS data set is the WHERE statement. The WHERE statement tells a procedure to use a subset of the data. There are other ways to subset data, as you probably remember, so you could get by without ever using the WHERE statement.[1] However, the WHERE statement is a shortcut. While the other methods of subsetting work only in DATA steps, the WHERE statement works in PROC steps too.

Unlike subsetting in a DATA step, using a WHERE statement in a procedure does not create a new data set. When you use a WHERE statement, the procedure reads directly from the original data set. That is one of the reasons why WHERE statements are sometimes more efficient than other ways of subsetting.

The basic form of a WHERE statement is

```
WHERE condition;
```

Only observations satisfying the condition will be used by the PROC. This may look familiar since it is similar to a subsetting IF. The left side of that condition is a variable name, and the right side is a variable name, a constant, or a mathematical equation. Mathematical equations can contain the standard arithmetic symbols for addition (+), subtraction (−), multiplication (*), division (/), and exponentiation (**). Between the two sides of the expression, you can use comparison and logical operators; those operators may be symbolic or mnemonic. Here are the most frequently used operators:

Symbolic	Mnemonic	Example
=	EQ	WHERE region = 'Spain';
~=, ^=, ¬=	NE	WHERE region ~= 'Spain';
>	GT	WHERE rainfall > 20;
<	LT	WHERE rainfall < avgrain;
>=	GE	WHERE rainfall >= avgrain + 5;
<=	LE	WHERE rainfall <= avgrain / 1.25;
&	AND	WHERE rainfall > 20 AND temp < 90;
|,¦,!	OR	WHERE rainfall > 20 OR temp < 90;
	IS NOT MISSING	WHERE region IS NOT MISSING;
	BETWEEN AND	WHERE region BETWEEN 'Plain' AND 'Spain';
	CONTAINS	WHERE region CONTAINS 'ain';
	IN (list)	WHERE region IN ('Rain', 'Spain', 'Plain');

---

[1] Subsetting while reading a raw data file is discussed in section 3.9, and the subsetting IF statement is discussed in section 4.6.

Example You have a database containing information about well-known painters. A subset of the data appears below. Each observation includes three variables: the painter's name, primary style, and nation of origin:

```
Mary Cassatt           impressionism      U
Paul Cezanne           post-impressionism F
Edgar Degas            impressionism      F
Paul Gauguin           post-impressionism F
Claude Monet           impressionism      F
Pierre Auguste Renoir  impressionism      F
Vincent van Gogh       post-impressionism N
```

To make this example more realistic, it has two steps. The first creates a permanent SAS data set, then the second uses the data. The first program sets up a libref named ART, which points to the MYSASLIB directory on the C drive (DOS, OS/2, Windows). The LIBNAME statement may be different on your operating system. Then the DATA step reads the data from a file named ARTISTS.DAT into a permanent SAS data set named ART.STYLE:

```
LIBNAME art 'c:\mysaslib';
DATA art.style;
   INFILE 'artists.dat';
   INPUT name $ 1-21 genre $ 23-40 home $ 42;
RUN;
```

Suppose a day later you wanted to print a list of just the impressionist painters. The quick-and-easy way to do this is with a WHERE statement and PROC PRINT. Since the data are in a permanent SAS data set, you must use a LIBNAME statement again. Specify the two-level data set name in the DATA= option of the PROC statement:

```
LIBNAME art 'c:\mysaslib';
PROC PRINT DATA = art.style;
   WHERE genre = 'impressionism';
   TITLE 'Major Impressionist Painters';
   FOOTNOTE 'F = France N = Netherlands U = US';
RUN;
```

The output looks like this:

```
                 Major Impressionist Painters           1

        OBS   NAME                    GENRE          HOME

         1    Mary Cassatt            impressionism    U
         3    Edgar Degas             impressionism    F
         5    Claude Monet            impressionism    F
         6    Pierre Auguste Renoir   impressionism    F

              F = France N = Netherlands U = US
```

WHERE statement

5.3 Sorting Your Data with PROC SORT

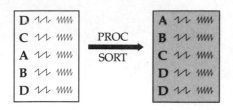

There are many reasons for sorting your data: to organize data for a report, before combining data sets, or before using a BY statement in another PROC or DATA step. Fortunately, PROC SORT is quite simple. The basic form of this procedure is

```
PROC SORT;
    BY variable-1 ... variable-n;
```

The variables named in the BY statement are called BY variables. You can specify as many BY variables as you wish. With one BY variable, SAS sorts the data based on the values of that variable. With more than one variable, SAS sorts observations by the first variable, then by the second variable within categories of the first, and so on. A BY group is all the observations that have the same values of BY variables. If, for example, your BY variable is STATE then all the observations for North Dakota form one BY group.

The DATA= and OUT= options specify the input and output data sets. If you don't specify the DATA= option, then SAS will use the most recently created data set. If you don't specify the OUT= option, then SAS will replace the original data set with the newly sorted version. This sample statement tells SAS to sort the data set named MESSY, and then put the sorted data into a data set named NEAT:

```
PROC SORT DATA = messy OUT = neat;
```

The NODUPKEY option tells SAS to eliminate any duplicate observations that have the same values for the BY variables. To use this option, just add NODUPKEY to the PROC SORT statement:

```
PROC SORT NODUPKEY;
```

By default SAS sorts data in ascending order, from lowest to highest or from A to Z. To have your data sorted from highest to lowest, add the keyword DESCENDING to the BY statement before each variable that should be sorted from highest to lowest. This statement tells SAS to sort first by STATE (from A to Z) and then by CITY (from Z to A) within STATE:

```
BY state DESCENDING city;
```

Example   The following data about whales and sharks includes three variables: name, type, and average length in feet:

```
beluga    whale 15
whale     shark 40
basking   shark 30
gray      whale 50
mako      shark 12
sperm     whale 60
dwarf     shark .5
whale     shark 40
humpback   .   50
blue      whale 100
killer    whale 30
```

This program reads and sorts the data:

```
DATA marine;
   INFILE 'sealife.dat';
   INPUT name $ family $ length;
* Sort the data;
PROC SORT OUT = seasort NODUPKEY;
   BY family DESCENDING length;
PROC PRINT DATA = seasort;
   TITLE 'Whales and Sharks';
RUN;
```

The DATA step reads the raw data from a file called SEALIFE.DAT. Then PROC SORT rearranges the observations by family in ascending order, and by length in descending order. The NODUPKEY option of PROC SORT eliminates any duplicates, while the DATA= option writes the sorted data into a new data set named SEASORT. The output from PROC PRINT looks like this:

```
            Whales and Sharks            1

       OBS    NAME       FAMILY    LENGTH

        1     humpback              50.0
        2     whale      shark      40.0
        3     basking    shark      30.0
        4     mako       shark      12.0
        5     dwarf      shark       0.5
        6     blue       whale     100.0
        7     sperm      whale      60.0
        8     gray       whale      50.0
        9     killer     whale      30.0
       10     beluga     whale      15.0
```

Notice that the humpback with a missing value for family became observation one. That is because missing values are always low for both numeric and character variables. Also, the NODUPKEY option eliminated a duplicate observation for the whale shark. The log contains these notes showing that the sorted data set has one less observation than the original data set.

```
NOTE: The data set WORK.MARINE has 11 observations and 3 variables.

NOTE: 1 observations with duplicate key values were deleted.
NOTE: The data set WORK.SEASORT has 10 observations and 3 variables.
```

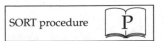
SORT procedure

5.4 ▶ Printing Your Data with PROC PRINT

The PRINT procedure is perhaps the most widely used SAS procedure. You have seen this procedure used many times in this book to print the contents of a SAS data set. In its simplest form, PROC PRINT prints all observations for all variables in the SAS data set. SAS decides the best way to format the output, so you don't have to worry about things like how many variables will fit on a page. But there are a few more features of PROC PRINT that you might want to use.

The general form of the PRINT procedure requires just one statement:

```
PROC PRINT;
```

By default, SAS prints the observation numbers along with the variables' values. If you don't want observation numbers, use the NOOBS option on the PROC PRINT statement. If you define variable labels with a LABEL statement, and you want to print the labels instead of the variable names, then add the LABEL option as well. The following statement shows both of these options together:

```
PROC PRINT NOOBS LABEL;
```

The following are some optional statements that sometimes come in handy:

BY *variable-list*; The BY statement starts a new section in the output for each new value of the BY variables and prints the values of the BY variables at the top of each section. The data must be presorted by the BY variables.

ID *variable-list*; Using the ID statement, the observation numbers are not printed. Instead, the variables in the ID variable list appear on the left-hand side of the page.

SUM *variable-list*; The SUM statement prints sums for the variables in the list.[1]

VAR *variable-list*; The VAR statement specifies which variables to print and the order. Without a VAR statement, all variables in the SAS data set are printed in the order that they occur in the data set.

Example   Students from two fourth-grade classes are selling candy to earn money for a special field trip. The class earning the most money gets a free box of candy. The following are the data for the results of the candy sale. The students' names are followed by their classroom number, the date they turned in their money, the type of candy: mint patties or chocolate dinosaurs, and the number of boxes sold:

```
Adriana   21   3/21/95 MP   7
Nathan    14   3/21/95 CD  19
Matthew   14   3/21/95 CD  14
Claire    14   3/22/95 CD  11
Caitlin   21   3/24/95 CD   9
Ian       21   3/24/95 MP  18
Chris     14   3/25/95 CD   6
Anthony   21   3/25/95 MP  13
Stephen   14   3/25/95 CD  10
Erika     21   3/25/95 MP  17
```

---

[1] You can also use the MEANS procedure to calculate sums along with other summary statistics. The MEANS procedure, however, will not print the individual observations as PROC PRINT does. PROC MEANS is covered in section 5.9.

The class earns $1.25 for each box of candy sold. The teachers want a report giving the money earned for each classroom, the money earned by each student, the type of candy sold, and the date the students returned their money. The following program reads the data, computes money earned (PROFIT), and sorts the data by classroom using PROC SORT. Then, the PROC PRINT step uses a BY statement to print the data by CLASS and a SUM statement to give the totals for PROFIT. The VAR statement lists the variables to be printed:

```
DATA sales;
   INFILE 'candy.dat';
   INPUT name $ 1-11 class @15 returned MMDDYY8. candy $ quantity;
   profit = quantity * 1.25;
PROC SORT;
   BY class;
PROC PRINT;
   BY class;
   SUM profit;
   VAR name returned candy profit;
   TITLE 'Candy Sales for Field Trip by Class';
RUN;
```

Here are the results:

```
                  Candy Sales for Field Trip by Class                 1

        ------------------------------ CLASS=14 ------------------------------

               OBS     NAME     RETURNED    CANDY    PROFIT

                1     Nathan     12863       CD       23.75
                2     Matthew    12863       CD       17.50
                3     Claire     12864       CD       13.75
                4     Chris      12867       CD        7.50
                5     Stephen    12867       CD       12.50
                                                     ------
              CLASS                                   75.00


        ------------------------------ CLASS=21 ------------------------------

               OBS     NAME     RETURNED    CANDY    PROFIT

                6     Adriana    12863       MP        8.75
                7     Caitlin    12866       CD       11.25
                8     Ian        12866       MP       22.50
                9     Anthony    12867       MP       16.25
               10     Erika      12867       MP       21.25
                                                     ------
              CLASS                                   80.00
                                                     ======
                                                     155.00
```

Notice that the values for the variable RETURNED are printed as their SAS date values. You can use formats, covered in the next section, to print dates in readable forms.

PRINT procedure   P

5.5 ▸ Changing the Appearance of Printed Values with Formats

0	1002
2	2012
31	4336

➡

OBS	DATE	POP
1	01/01/60	1,002
2	01/03/60	2,012
3	02/01/60	4,336

When SAS prints your data, it decides which format is best—how many decimal places to print, how much space to allow for each value, and so on. This is very convenient and makes your job much easier, but SAS doesn't always do what you want. Fortunately you're not stuck with the format SAS thinks is best. You can change the appearance of printed values using SAS formats.

SAS has many formats for numeric, character, and date values. For example, you can use the COMMA*w.d* format to print numbers with embedded commas, the $*w*. format to control the number of characters printed, and the MMDDYY*w*. format to print SAS date values (the number of days since January 1, 1960) in a readable form like 12/03/88. You can even print your data in more obscure formats like hexadecimal, zoned decimal, and packed decimal, if you like[1].

The general forms of a SAS format are

Character	**Numeric**	**Date**
$formatw.	formatw.d	formatw.

where the $ indicates character formats, *format* is the name of the format, *w* is the total width including any decimal point, and *d* is the number of decimal places. The period in the format is very important because it distinguishes a format from a variable name, which cannot contain any special characters except the underscore.

FORMAT statement   You can associate formats with variables in a FORMAT statement. The FORMAT statement starts with the keyword FORMAT, followed by the variable name (or names if more than one variable is to be associated with the same format), followed by the format. For example the following FORMAT statement associates the DOLLAR8.2 format with the variables PROFIT and LOSS and associates the MMDDYY8. format with the variable SALEDATE:

```
FORMAT profit loss DOLLAR8.2 saledate MMDDYY8.;
```

FORMAT statements can go in either DATA steps or in PROC steps. If the FORMAT statement is in a DATA step, then the format association is permanent and is stored with the SAS data set. If the FORMAT statement is in a PROC step, then it is temporary—affecting only the results from that procedure.

PUT statement   You can also use formats in PUT statements when writing raw data files or reports. Place a format after each variable name, as in the following example:

```
PUT profit DOLLAR8.2 loss DOLLAR8.2 saledate MMDDYY8.;
```

Example   In the last section, results from the fourth-grade candy sale were printed using the PRINT procedure. The names of the students were printed along with the date they turned in their money, the type of candy sold, and the profit. You may have noticed that the dates printed were

---

[1] You can also create your own formats using the FORMAT procedure covered in section 5.7.

numbers like 12863 and 12867. Using the FORMAT statement in the PRINT procedure, we can print the dates in a readable form. At the same time, we can print the variable PROFIT using the DOLLAR6.2 format so dollar signs appear before the numbers.

Here are the data, where the students' names are followed by their classroom, the date they turned in their money, the type of candy sold: mint patties or chocolate dinosaurs, and the number of boxes sold:

```
Adriana    21  3/21/95 MP  7
Nathan     14  3/21/95 CD 19
Matthew    14  3/21/95 CD 14
Claire     14  3/22/95 CD 11
Caitlin    21  3/24/95 CD  9
Ian        21  3/24/95 MP 18
Chris      14  3/25/95 CD  6
Anthony    21  3/25/95 MP 13
Stephen    14  3/25/95 CD 10
Erika      21  3/25/95 MP 17
```

The following program reads the raw data and computes PROFIT. The FORMAT statement in the PRINT procedure associates the DATE7. format with the variable RETURNED and the DOLLAR6.2 format with the variable PROFIT:

```
DATA sales;
   INFILE 'candy.dat';
   INPUT name $ 1-11 class @15 returned MMDDYY8. candy $ quantity;
   profit = quantity * 1.25;
PROC PRINT;
   VAR name returned candy profit;
   FORMAT returned DATE7. profit DOLLAR6.2;
   TITLE 'Candy Sale Data Using Formats';
RUN;
```

Here are the results:

```
                  Candy Sale Data Using Formats                    1

           OBS    NAME      RETURNED    CANDY    PROFIT

             1    Adriana   21MAR95      MP      $8.75
             2    Nathan    21MAR95      CD     $23.75
             3    Matthew   21MAR95      CD     $17.50
             4    Claire    22MAR95      CD     $13.75
             5    Caitlin   24MAR95      CD     $11.25
             6    Ian       24MAR95      MP     $22.50
             7    Chris     25MAR95      CD      $7.50
             8    Anthony   25MAR95      MP     $16.25
             9    Stephen   25MAR95      CD     $12.50
            10    Erika     25MAR95      MP     $21.25
```

FORMAT statement
formats
definition

5.6 Selected Standard Formats

The table in this section spans both pages. The left page gives the definitions while the right page gives examples. These are the most commonly used formats. For a complete list, see *SAS Language, Reference*.

		width range	default width
Character			
$HEX*w*.	Converts character data to hexidecimal (specify *w* twice the length of the variable)	1-200	4
$*w*.	Writes standard character data—does not trim leading blanks (same as $CHAR*w*.)	1-200	Length of variable or 1
Date Time, and Datetime[1]			
DATE*w*.	Writes SAS data values in form *ddmmmyy* or *ddmmmyyyy*	5-9	7
DATETIME*w.d*	Writes SAS datetime values in form *ddmmmyy:hh:mm:ss.ss*	7-40	16
DAY*w*.	Writes day of month from a SAS date value	2-32	2
JULIAN*w*.	Writes a Julian date from a SAS date value in form *yyddd* or *yyyyddd*	5-7	5
MMDDYY*w*.	Writes SAS date values in form *mmddyy*	2-8	8
TIME*w*.	Writes SAS time values in form *hh:mm:ss.ss*	2-20	8
WEEKDATE*w*.	Writes SAS date values in form *day-of-week, month-name dd, yy* or *yyyy*	3-37	29
WORDDATE*w*.	Writes SAS date values in form *month-name dd, yyyy*	3-32	18
YYQ*w*.	Writes the year and quarter of a SAS date value	4-6	6
Numeric			
BEST*w*.	SAS System chooses best format—this is the default format for writing numeric data	1-32	12
COMMA*w.d*	Writes numbers with commas separating every three digits	2-32	6
DOLLAR*w.d*	Writes numbers with a leading $ and commas separating every three digits	2-32	6
E*w*.	Writes numbers in scientific notation	7-32	12
PD*w.d*	Writes numbers in packed decimal—*w* specifies the number of bytes	1-16	1
w.d	Writes standard numeric data	1-32	none

---

[1]SAS date values are the number of days since January 1, 1960. SAS time values are the number of seconds past midnight, and datetime values are the number of seconds since midnight January 1, 1960.

	Input data	PUT statement	Results
Character			
$HEX*w*	AB	PUT name $HEX4.;	C1C2 (EBCDIC)[2] 4142 (ASCII)
$*w*.	my cat my snake	PUT animal $8. '*';	my cat * my snak*
Date, Time, and Datetime			
DATE*w*.	8966	PUT birth DATE7.; PUT birth DATE9.;	19JUL84 19JUL1984
DATETIME*w*.	12182	PUT start DATETIME13.; PUT start DATETIME18.1;	01JAN60:03:23 01JAN60:03:23:02.0
DAY*w*.	8966	PUT birth DAY2.; PUT birth DAY7.;	19 19
JULIAN*w*.	8966	PUT birth JULIAN5.; PUT birth JULIAN7.;	84201 1984201
MMDDYY*w*.	8966	PUT birth MMDDYY8.; PUT birth MMDDYY6.;	07/19/84 071984
TIME*w.d*	12182	PUT start TIME8.; PUT start TIME11.2;	3:23:02 3:23:02.00
WEEKDATE*w*.	8966	PUT birth WEEKDATE15.; PUT birth WEEKDATE29.;	Thu, Jul 19, 84 Thursday, July 19, 1984
WORDDATE*w*.	8966	PUT birth WORDDATE12.; PUT birth WORDDATE18.;	Jul 19, 1984 July 19, 1984
YYQ*w*.	8966	PUT birth YYQ6.;	1984Q3
Numeric			
BEST*w*.	1200001	PUT value BEST6.; PUT value BEST8.;	1.20E6 1200001
COMMA*w.d*	1200001	PUT value COMMA9.; PUT value COMMA12.2;	1,200,001 1,200,001.00
DOLLAR*w.d*	1200001	PUT value DOLLAR10.; PUT value DOLLAR13.2;	$1,200,001 $1,200,001.00
E*w*	1200001	PUT value E7.;	1.2E+06
PD*w.d*	128	PUT value PD4.;	[3]
w.d	23.635	PUT value 6.3; PUT value 5.2;	23.635 23.64

[2] The EBCDIC character set is used on most IBM mainframe computers while the ASCII character set is used on most other computers. So, depending on the computer you are using, you will get one or the other.
[3] These values cannot be printed.

formats
table by categories

5.7 Creating Your Own Formats Using PROC FORMAT

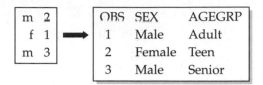

OBS	SEX	AGEGRP
1	Male	Adult
2	Female	Teen
3	Male	Senior

At some time you will probably want to create your own custom formats—especially if you use a lot of coded data. Imagine that you have just completed a survey for your company and to save disk space and time, all the responses to the survey questions are coded. For example, the age categories teen, adult, and senior are coded as numbers 1, 2, and 3. This is convenient for data entry and analysis but bothersome when it comes time to interpret the results. You could present your results along with a code book, and your company directors could look up the codes as they read the results. But this will probably not get you that promotion you've been looking for. A better solution is to create user-defined formats using PROC FORMAT and print the formatted values instead of the coded values.

The FORMAT procedure creates formats that will later be associated with variables in a FORMAT statement. The procedure starts with the statement PROC FORMAT; and follows with one or more VALUE statements (other optional statements are available):

```
PROC FORMAT;
     VALUE name range-1 = 'formatted-text-1'
                 range-2 = 'formatted-text-2'
                      .
                      .
                      .
                 range-n = 'formatted-text-n';
```

NAME is the name of the format you are creating, which can't be longer than eight characters, must not end with a number, and cannot contain any special characters except the underscore. The NAME can't be the name of an existing format, and if the format is for character data, it must start with a $. The RANGEs are the values of a variable that are assigned to the text given in quotes on the right side of the equal sign. The text can be as long as 40 characters, but some procedures will only print the first 8 or 16 characters. The following are examples of valid range specifications:

```
          'R' = 'Republican'
1, 3, 5, 7, 9 = 'Odd'
500000 - HIGH = 'Not Affordable'
      13 -< 20 = 'Teenager'
         OTHER = 'Bad Data'
```

Character values must be enclosed in quotes ('R' for example). If there is more than one value in the range, then separate the values with a comma or use the dash (–) for a continuous range. The keywords LOW and HIGH can be used in ranges to indicate the lowest and the highest non-missing value for the variable. You can also use the symbols < and > in ranges to indicate less than and greater than, and the symbols <= and >= to indicate less than or equal and greater than or equal. The OTHER keyword can be used to assign a format to any values not listed in the VALUE statement.

Example Universe Cars is surveying its customers as to their preferences for car colors. They have information about the customer's age, sex (coded as 1 for male and 2 for female), annual income, and preferred car color (yellow, gray, blue, or white). Here are the data:

```
19 1 14000 Y
45 1 65000 G
72 2 35000 B
31 1 44000 Y
58 2 83000 W
```

The following program reads the data; creates formats for age, sex, and car color using the FORMAT procedure; then prints the data using the new formats:

```
DATA carsurv;
   INFILE 'cars.dat';
   INPUT age sex income color $;
PROC FORMAT;
   VALUE gender 1 = 'Male'
                2 = 'Female';
   VALUE agegroup 13 -< 20 = 'Teen'
                  20 -< 65 = 'Adult'
                  65 - HIGH = 'Senior';
   VALUE $col  'W' = 'Moon White'
               'B' = 'Sky Blue'
               'Y' = 'Sunburst Yellow'
               'G' = 'Rain Cloud Gray';
* Print data using user-defined and standard (DOLLAR8.) formats;
PROC PRINT;
   FORMAT sex gender. age agegroup. color $col. income DOLLAR8.;
   TITLE 'Survey Results Printed with User-Defined Formats';
RUN;
```

This program creates two numeric formats: GENDER for the variable SEX and AGEGROUP for the variable AGE. The program creates a character format, $COL, for the variable COLOR. Notice that the format names do not end with periods in the VALUE statement, but they do in the FORMAT statement.

Here is the output:

```
         Survey Results Printed with User-Defined Formats        1

         OBS    AGE      SEX      INCOME    COLOR

          1     Teen     Male     $14,000   Sunburst Yellow
          2     Adult    Male     $65,000   Rain Cloud Gray
          3     Senior   Female   $35,000   Sky Blue
          4     Adult    Male     $44,000   Sunburst Yellow
          5     Adult    Female   $83,000   Moon White
```

This example creates a temporary format that exists only for the current job or session. Creating and using permanent formats is discussed in the *SAS Procedures Guide*.

FORMAT procedure

5.8 Writing Simple Custom Reports

PROC PRINT is flexible and easy to use. Still, there are times when PROC PRINT just won't do. One of the great features of PROC PRINT is that you don't have to worry about trivia such as spacing and page breaks; SAS takes care of that. But there may be times when you are forced to worry about these details: when your report to a state agency has to be spaced just like their fill-in-the-blank form, or when your client insists that the report contain complete sentences, or when you want one page per observation. Whenever you have to be picky about the format of a report, chances are that PROC PRINT won't do.

At those times you can use the flexibility of the DATA step to produce your report.[1] This is really an extension of section 3.16 on using FILE and PUT statements to write a raw data file. The difference is that this time you will write to a file for the purpose of printing. To do that, add the PRINT option after the file name in your FILE statement. This way, SAS knows to include those special printing instructions such as carriage returns and page breaks.

Example To show how this differs from PROC PRINT, we'll use the candy sales data again. Two fourth-grade classes have sold candy to raise money for a field trip. Here are the data with each student's name, classroom number, the date they turned in their money, the type of candy: mint patties or chocolate dinosaurs, and the number of boxes sold:

```
Adriana    21 3/21/95 MP  7
Nathan     14 3/21/95 CD 19
Matthew    14 3/21/95 CD 14
Claire     14 3/22/95 CD 11
Caitlin    21 3/24/95 CD  9
Ian        21 3/24/95 MP 18
Chris      14 3/25/95 CD  6
Anthony    21 3/25/95 MP 13
Stephen    14 3/25/95 CD 10
Erika      21 3/25/95 MP 17
```

The teachers want a report for each student showing how much money that student earned. They want each student's report on a separate page so it is easy to hand out. Lastly, they want it to be easy for fourth graders to understand, with complete sentences. Here is the program:

```
* Write a report with FILE and PUT statements;
DATA _NULL_;
   INFILE 'candy.dat';
   INPUT name $ 1-11 class @15 returned MMDDYY8. candy $ quantity;
   profit = quantity * 1.25;
   FILE 'student.rep' PRINT;
   TITLE;
   PUT @5 'Candy sales report for ' name 'from classroom ' class
       // @5 'Congratulations!  You sold ' quantity 'boxes of candy'
       / @5 'and earned ' profit DOLLAR6.2 ' for our field trip.';
   PUT _PAGE_;
RUN;
```

---

[1] Other ways to create reports include PROC TABULATE for reports in rows and columns, PROC REPORT for interactive or batch reports, and PROC FORMS for reports with a regular pattern such as mailing labels.

Notice that the keyword _NULL_ appears in the DATA statement instead of a data set name. Since our goal is to create a report not a SAS data set, the keyword _NULL_ tells SAS not to bother. The FILE statement creates the output file for the report, and the PRINT option tells SAS to include carriage returns and page breaks. The null TITLE statement tells SAS to eliminate all automatic titles.

A PUT statement tells SAS exactly what to write and where, like an INPUT statement in reverse. Like INPUT statements, PUT statements can use column and line pointers, as well as list, column, and formatted styles of output. In addition to printing your data, you can print any literal by enclosing it in quotes. The first PUT statement in this program starts with a pointer, @10, telling SAS to go to column 10. Then it tells SAS to print the words `Candy sales report for` followed by the variable NAME. The variables NAME, CLASS, and QUANTITY are printed in list style whereas PROFIT is printed using formatted style and the DOLLAR6.2 format. A slash line pointer tells SAS to skip to the next line; two slashes skips two lines. You could use multiple PUT statements instead of slashes to skip lines because SAS goes to a new line every time there is a new PUT statement. The statement PUT _PAGE_ inserts a page break after each student's report. When the program is run, the log will contain these notes:

```
NOTE: 10 records were read from the infile 'candy.dat'.
NOTE: 30 records were written to the file 'student.rep'.
```

The first three pages of the report look like this:

```
Candy sales report for Adriana from classroom 21

Congratulations!  You sold 7 boxes of candy
and earned  $8.75 for our field trip.
```

```
Candy sales report for Nathan from classroom 14

Congratulations!  You sold 19 boxes of candy
and earned $23.75 for our field trip.
```

```
Candy sales report for Matthew from classroom 14

Congratulations!  You sold 14 boxes of candy
and earned $17.50 for our field trip.
```

FILE statement
PUT statement

5.9 Summarizing Your Data Using PROC MEANS

One of the first things people usually want to do with their data, after reading it and making sure it is correct, is look at some simple statistics. Statistics such as the mean value, standard deviation, and minimum and maximum values give you a feel for your data. These types of information can also alert you to errors in your data (98 runs scored in a baseball game, for example, is suspect). The MEANS procedure provides simple statistics on numeric variables.

The MEANS procedure starts with the keywords PROC MEANS, followed by options listing the statistics you want printed:

```
PROC MEANS options;
```

If you do not specify any options, MEANS will print the number of non-missing values, the mean, the standard deviation, and the minimum, and maximum values for each variable. The following is a list of options you can request with the PROC MEANS statement:

N	number of non-missing values
NMISS	number of missing values
MIN	the minimum value
MAX	the maximum value
RANGE	the range
SUM	the sum
SUMWGT	sum of weight variables
MEAN	the mean
USS	uncorrected sum of squares
VAR	the variance
STD	the standard deviation
STDERR	the standard error of the mean
CV	the coefficient of variation
SKEWNESS	skewness
KURTOSIS	kurtosis
T	Student's t
PRT	probability for t-value above

If you use the PROC MEANS statement with no other statements, then you will get statistics for all observations and all numeric variables in your data set. Here are some of the optional statements that can be used with PROC MEANS:

BY *variable-list*; The BY statement performs separate analyses for each level of the variables in the list. The data must first be sorted in same order as the variable-list. (You can use PROC SORT to do this).

CLASS *variable-list*; The CLASS statement performs separate analyses for each level of the variables in the list; but its output is more compact than with the BY statement, and the data do not have to be sorted first.

VAR *variable-list*; The VAR statement specifies which numeric variables to use in the analysis. If it is absent then all numeric variables are used.

Example A wholesale nursery is selling garden flowers, and they want to summarize their sales figures by month. The data file which follows contains the customer ID, date of sale, and number of petunias, snapdragons, and marigolds sold:

```
756-01   05/04/97 120  80 110
834-01   05/12/97  90 160  60
901-02   05/18/97  50 100  75
834-01   06/01/97  80  60 100
756-01   06/11/97 100 160  75
901-02   06/19/97  60  60  60
756-01   06/25/97  85 110 100
```

The following program reads the data; computes a new variable, MONTH, which is the month of the sale; sorts the data by MONTH using PROC SORT; then summarizes the data by MONTH using PROC MEANS with a BY statement:

```
DATA sales;
   INFILE 'flowers.dat';
   INPUT custid $ @9 saledate MMDDYY8. petunia snapdrag marigold;
   month = MONTH(saledate);
PROC SORT;
   BY month;
* Calculate means by month for flower sales;
PROC MEANS;
   BY month;
   VAR petunia snapdrag marigold;
   TITLE 'Summary of Flower Sales by Month';
RUN;
```

Here are the results of the PROC MEANS:

```
                   Summary of Flower Sales by Month                  1

------------------------------ MONTH=5 ------------------------------

    Variable  N        Mean         Std Dev       Minimum       Maximum
    ------------------------------------------------------------------
    PETUNIA   3    86.6666667    35.1188458    50.0000000    120.0000000
    SNAPDRAG  3   113.3333333    41.6333200    80.0000000    160.0000000
    MARIGOLD  3    81.6666667    25.6580072    60.0000000    110.0000000
    ------------------------------------------------------------------


------------------------------ MONTH=6 ------------------------------

    Variable  N        Mean         Std Dev       Minimum       Maximum
    ------------------------------------------------------------------
    PETUNIA   4    81.2500000    16.5201897    60.0000000    100.0000000
    SNAPDRAG  4    97.5000000    47.8713554    60.0000000    160.0000000
    MARIGOLD  4    83.7500000    19.7378655    60.0000000    100.0000000
    ------------------------------------------------------------------
```

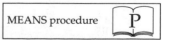

MEANS procedure

5.10 Writing Summary Statistics to a SAS Data Set

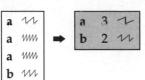

Sometimes you want to save summary statistics to a SAS data set for further analysis, or to merge with other data. For example, you might want to plot the hourly temperature in your office to show how it heats up every afternoon, causing you to fall asleep. But the instrument you have records data for every minute. The MEANS procedure can condense the data by computing the mean temperature for each hour and then writing the results to a SAS data set so it can be plotted using PROC PLOT.

Use the OUTPUT statement in PROC MEANS to save the summary statistics to a SAS data set. The OUTPUT statement has the following form:

```
OUTPUT OUT = data-set output-statistic-list;
```

Here, *data-set* is the name of the SAS data set which will contain the results (this can be either temporary or permanent), and *output-statistic-list* defines which statistics you want and the associated variable names. You can have more than one OUTPUT statement and multiple output statistic lists. The following is one of the possible forms for *output-statistic-list*:

```
statistic(variable-list) = name-list
```

Here, *statistic* can be any of the statistics available in PROC MEANS (SUM, N, MEAN, for example), *variable-list* defines which of the variables in the VAR statement you want to output, and *name-list* defines the new variable names for the statistics. The new variable names must be in the same order as their corresponding variables in *variable-list*. For example, the following PROC MEANS statements produce a new data set called ZOOSUM, which contains one observation with the variables LIONWGT, the mean of the lions' weights, and BEARWGT, the mean of the bears' weights:

```
PROC MEANS NOPRINT;
   VAR lions tigers bears;
   OUTPUT OUT = zoosum MEAN(lions bears) = lionwgt bearwgt;
RUN;
```

The NOPRINT option on the PROC MEANS statement tells SAS there is no need to produce any printed results since we are saving the results to a SAS data set.

The SAS data set created in the OUTPUT statement will contain all the variables defined in *output statistic list*; any variables listed in a BY or CLASS statement; plus two new variables, _TYPE_ and _FREQ_. If there is no BY or CLASS statement, then the data set will have just one observation. If there is a BY statement, then the data set will have one observation for each level of the BY group. CLASS statements produce one observation for each level of interaction of the class variables. The value of the _TYPE_ variable is dependent on the level of interaction. The observation where _TYPE_ has a value of zero is the grand total[1].

---

[1] For a complete explanation of the _TYPE_ variable, see the *SAS Procedures Guide*.

Example The following are sales data for a wholesale nursery with the customer ID; date of sale; and the number of petunias, snapdragons, and marigolds sold:

```
756-01  05/04/97 120  80 110
834-01  05/12/97  90 160  60
901-02  05/18/97  50 100  75
834-01  06/01/97  80  60 100
756-01  06/11/97 100 160  75
901-02  06/19/97  60  60  60
756-01  06/25/97  85 110 100
```

You want to summarize the data so that you have only one observation per customer containing the sum and mean of the number of plant sets sold, and you want to save the results in a SAS data set for further analysis. The following program reads the data from the file; sorts by the customer ID, CUSTID; and then uses the MEANS procedure with the NOPRINT option to calculate the sums and means by CUSTID. The results are saved in a SAS data set named TOTALS in the OUTPUT statement. The sums are given the original variable names PETUNIA, SNAPDRAG, and MARIGOLD, and the means are given new variable names MP, MS, and MM. A PROC PRINT is used to show the TOTALS data set:

```
DATA sales;
   INFILE 'flowers.dat';
   INPUT custid $ @9 saledate MMDDYY8. petunia snapdrag marigold;
PROC SORT;
   BY custid;
* Calculate means by custid, output sum and mean to new data set;
PROC MEANS NOPRINT;
   BY custid;
   VAR petunia snapdrag marigold;
   OUTPUT OUT = totals  MEAN(petunia snapdrag marigold) = mp ms mm
      SUM(petunia snapdrag marigold) = petunia snapdrag marigold;
PROC PRINT;
   TITLE 'Sum of Flower Data over Customer ID';
   FORMAT mp ms mm 3.;
RUN;
```

Here are the results:

```
              Sum of Flower Data over Customer ID                 1

    OBS CUSTID _TYPE_ _FREQ_  MP  MS  MM PETUNIA SNAPDRAG MARIGOLD

     1  756-01    0      3   102 117  95   305      350      285
     2  834-01    0      2    85 110  80   170      220      160
     3  901-02    0      2    55  80  68   110      160      135
```

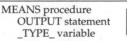

MEANS procedure
OUTPUT statement
TYPE variable

5.11 Using PROC FREQ to Examine Your Data

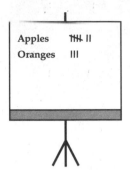

A frequency table is a simple list that answers the question "How many are there of each kind?" A cross-tabulation is the same thing but for two or more variables in combination. The most obvious reason for using PROC FREQ is to create tables showing the distribution of a variable. However, there are a few other reasons: to calculate statistics such as chi-square, to create a summary data set, or to find irregularities in your data. This last reason, while extremely helpful, is often overlooked. You could get dizzy proofreading a large data set, but data entry errors are often glaringly obvious in a frequency table.

The basic form of PROC FREQ is

```
PROC FREQ;
     TABLES variable-combinations;
```

To produce a one-way frequency table, just list the variable name. This statement produces a frequency table listing the number of observations for each sex:

```
TABLES sex;
```

To produce a cross-tabulation, list the variables separated by an asterisk. This statement produces a cross-tabulation showing the number of observations for each combination of sex by years of education:

```
TABLES sex * yrsed;
```

You can specify any number of table requests in a single TABLES statement, and you can have as many TABLES statements as you wish. Be careful though; reading cross-tabulations of three or more levels is like playing three-dimensional tic-tac-toe without the benefit of a three-dimensional board.

Options, if any, appear after a slash in the TABLES statement. The statement below, for instance, requests chi-square statistics and then tells SAS to put the results into a new data set named NEWDATA:

```
TABLES sex * yearsed / CHISQ OUT = newdata;
```

Example The police in a small town have received a lot of reports of unidentified flying objects, or UFOs. They want to see if there is any kind of pattern, so they keep a log of the reports and then use PROC FREQ. Below is a copy of the log with one line for each sighting. For each incident, the investigating police officer records the report number, the time (AM or PM), zone of the town (residential or commercial), and a short description:

```
85845 AM R white with long tail
85776 PM z bright white light
85873 PM R white and red flashing lights
85879 AM R little green men carrying boomboxes
86790 PM C throbbing purple light
86823 PM R giant toads
```

Here is the program:

```
DATA ufos;
     INFILE 'ufo.dat' PAD;
     INPUT repnum time $ zone $ descrip $ 12-46;
```

```
* Print tables for zone and time by zone;
PROC FREQ;
   TABLES zone  time * zone;
   TITLE 'UFO Reports';
RUN;
```

The output contains two tables:

```
                     UFO Reports                       1

                                    Cumulative   Cumulative
       ZONE     Frequency   Percent  Frequency     Percent
     ------------------------------------------------------
        C          1        16.7        1          16.7
        R          4        66.7        5          83.3
        z          1        16.7        6         100.0
```

The first table is a one-way frequency table for the variable ZONE. For each value of ZONE, SAS lists the frequency, percent, and then cumulative frequency and percent. Notice that there is one observation with a value of z for ZONE. Valid values for ZONE are C or R, so z is a data entry error.

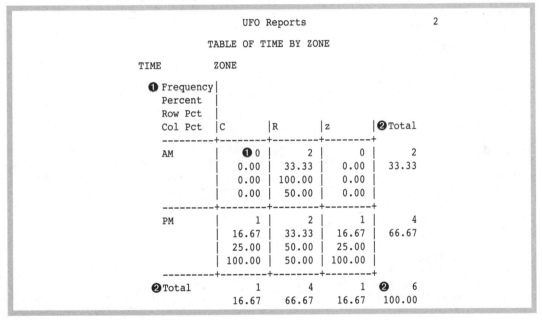

```
                          UFO Reports                        2

                      TABLE OF TIME BY ZONE

             TIME          ZONE

          ❶ Frequency|
            Percent  |
            Row Pct  |
            Col Pct  |C       |R       |z       |❷Total
            ---------+--------+--------+--------+
            AM       |  ❶ 0   |    2   |    0   |    2
                     |  0.00  |  33.33 |  0.00  |  33.33
                     |  0.00  | 100.00 |  0.00  |
                     |  0.00  |  50.00 |  0.00  |
            ---------+--------+--------+--------+
            PM       |    1   |    2   |    1   |    4
                     |  16.67 |  33.33 |  16.67 |  66.67
                     |  25.00 |  50.00 |  25.00 |
                     | 100.00 |  50.00 | 100.00 |
            ---------+--------+--------+--------+
          ❷Total         1        4        1   ❷     6
                       16.67    66.67    16.67   100.00
```

The second table is a two-way cross-tabulation of TIME by ZONE. Note that

❶ In each cell, SAS prints the frequency, percent, percent for that row, and percent for that column.

❷ The cumulative frequencies and percents appear along the right side and bottom.

FREQ procedure

5.12 Using PROC PLOT to Visualize Your Data

If a picture is worth a thousand words, then PROC PLOT is worth volumes. There are times when trying to see relationships in a table full of abstract numbers can leave you scratching your head. That is when you need PROC PLOT. The scatter plots produced by this procedure are simple, but they provide an easy, intuitive way to get a feel for your data. The basic form of PROC PLOT is

```
PROC PLOT;
    PLOT vertical-variable * horizontal-variable;
```

The PLOT statement tells SAS which variables to plot and how. SAS plots the first variable on the vertical axis and the second on the horizontal. You can have any number of PLOT statements and any number of plot requests in a single PLOT statement. The statement below requests two plots: one for HEIGHT by WEIGHT and another for HEIGHT by AGE:

```
PLOT height * weight  height * age;
```

By default, SAS uses letters to mark the points on your plots: A for a single observation, B for two observations at the same point, C for three, and so on. To substitute a different character, such as an asterisk, specify it this way:

```
PLOT height * weight = '*';
```

You can also use a third variable as the plot character, making a convenient label for each point. This statement tells SAS to use the first letter from the variable NAME to mark each point:

```
PLOT height * weight = name;
```

Example To help visualize the value of PROC PLOT, here are data about the Walla Walla Sweets, a local minor league baseball team. For each home game, the variables are name of visiting team, onion ring sales at concession stands and in the bleachers, number of hits for the home team, hits for the visiting team, runs for the home team, and runs for the visiting team:

```
Columbia Peaches     102  67  1 10 2 1
Plains Peanuts       210  54  2  5 0 1
Gilroy Garlics        15 335 12 11 7 6
Sacramento Tomatoes  124 185 15  4 9 1
Boise Spuds          162  75  5  6 2 3
Orlando Tangelos     144  86  9  3 4 2
Des Moines Corncobs   73 210 10  5 9 3
```

The ballpark owners suspect that in games with a lot of hits and runs, more onion rings are sold in the bleachers. To investigate this, the DATA step below reads the raw data and adds together all the runs and hits to create a variable named ACTION. Then PROC PLOT plots sales in the bleachers by ACTION:

```
DATA sales;
    INFILE 'onions.dat';
    INPUT vteam $ 1-20 csales bsales ourhits vhits ourruns vruns;
    action = ourhits + vhits + ourruns + vruns;
```

```
* Plot action by bsales;
PROC PLOT;
   PLOT bsales * action = vteam;
   TITLE 'Onion Ring Sales';
RUN;
```

The output looks like this:

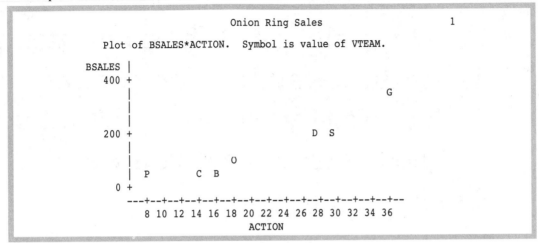

```
                        Onion Ring Sales                        1

           Plot of BSALES*ACTION.   Symbol is value of VTEAM.

     BSALES |
        400 +
            |                                          G
            |
            |
            |
        200 +                              D  S
            |
            |                    O
            |  P        C  B
          0 +
            ---+--+--+--+--+--+--+--+--+--+--+--+--+--+--+--
               8 10 12 14 16 18 20 22 24 26 28 30 32 34 36
                                ACTION
```

Looking at this plot, it appears that the ballpark owners are right. As ACTION increases, BSALES do tend to increase.

You can plot more than one variable on the vertical axis by using the OVERLAY option. For example, in the preceding program you could rewrite the PLOT statement as shown below. Notice that the plot character is no longer VTEAM because you need to distinguish the points for CSALES from the points for BSALES:

```
PLOT    csales * action = 'C'  bsales * action = 'B' / OVERLAY;
```

If you add a BY statement, SAS will produce a separate plot for each value of the BY variable. Remember, though, that your data must already be sorted by the variables in the BY statement.

PROC PLOT does not require a special graphics monitor or graphics printer, but because of that the plots are rather crude looking. To get presentation-quality plots, use PROC GPLOT, which is part of SAS/GRAPH software and is licensed separately from Base SAS. PROC GPLOT uses the same statements and options as PROC PLOT plus a whole lot more.

PLOT procedure

6

" I usually say, 'The computer is the dumbest thing on campus. It does exactly what you tell it to; not necessarily what you want. Logic is up to you.' "

NECIA A. BLACK, R.N., PH.D., SAS® USER SINCE 1987

From the SAS L listserv, May 6, 1994. Reprinted by permission of the author.

CHAPTER 6

Modifying and Combining SAS® Data Sets

6.1 Modifying a Data Set Using the SET Statement

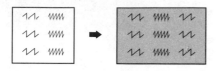

The SET statement in the DATA step allows you to read a SAS data set so you can add new variables, create a subset, or otherwise modify the data set. If you were short on disk space, for example, you might not want to store your calculated variables in a permanent SAS data set. Instead, you might want to calculate them as needed for analysis. Likewise, to save processing time, you might want to create a subset of a SAS data set when you only want to look at a small portion of a large data set. The SET statement brings a SAS data set, one observation at a time, into the DATA step for processing.

To read a SAS data set, start with the DATA statement specifying the name of the new SAS data set. Then follow with the SET statement specifying the name of the old SAS data set you want to read. If you don't want to create a new SAS data set, you can specify the same name in the DATA and SET statements. Then the results of the DATA step will overwrite the old data set named in the SET statement.[1] The following shows the general form of the DATA and SET statements:

```
DATA new-data-set;
   SET data-set;
```

Any assignment, subsetting IF, or other DATA step statements usually follow the SET statement. For example, the following creates a new data set, FRIDAY, which is a replica of the SALES data set, except FRIDAY has only the observations for Fridays, and it has an additional variable, TOTAL:

```
DATA friday;
   SET sales;
   IF day = 'F';
   total = popcorn + peanuts;
RUN;
```

Example The Fun Times Amusement Park is collecting data about their train ride. They can add more cars on the train during peak hours to shorten the wait, or take them off when they're not needed to save fuel costs. The raw data file contains data for the time of day, the number of cars on the train, and the total number of people on the train:

```
10:10   6 21
12:15  10 56
15:30  10 25
11:30   8 34
13:15   8 12
10:45   6 13
20:30   6 32
23:15   6 12
```

---

[1] By default, SAS will not overwrite a data set in a DATA step that has errors.

The data are read into a permanent SAS data set stored on the park's central computer with the following program:

```
* Define library name for permanent SAS data set trains;
LIBNAME mylib 'c:\mydir';
DATA mylib.trains;
   INFILE 'train.dat';
   INPUT time TIME5. cars people;
RUN;
```

Each train car holds a maximum of six people. After collecting the data, the Fun Times management decides they want to know the average number of people per car on each ride. This number was not calculated in the original DATA step which created the permanent SAS data set, but can be calculated with the following program:

```
* Read the SAS data set mylib.trains with a SET statement;
LIBNAME mylib 'c:\mydir';
DATA avgtrain;
   SET mylib.trains;
   avgpeopl = people / cars;
PROC PRINT;
   TITLE 'Average Number of People per Train Car';
   FORMAT time TIME5.;
RUN;
```

The DATA statement defines the new SAS data set AVGTRAIN. The SET statement reads the permanent SAS data set MYLIB.TRAINS creating a copy of the data in the temporary data set AVGTRAIN. An assignment statement follows the SET statement, creating the new variable AVGPEOPL. Here are the results of the PROC PRINT:

```
            Average Number of People per Train Car        1

            OBS     TIME     CARS    PEOPLE    AVGPEOPL

             1      10:10      6       21       3.50000
             2      12:15     10       56       5.60000
             3      15:30     10       25       2.50000
             4      11:30      8       34       4.25000
             5      13:15      8       12       1.50000
             6      10:45      6       13       2.16667
             7      20:30      6       32       5.33333
             8      23:15      6       12       2.00000
```

SET statement

6.2 Stacking Data Sets Using the SET Statement

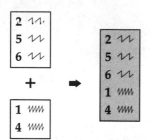

The SET statement with one SAS data set allows you to read and modify the data. With two or more data sets, in addition to reading and modifying the data, the SET statement concatenates or stacks the data sets one on top of the other. This is useful when you want to combine data sets with all or most of the same variables but different observations. You might, for example, have data from two different locations or data taken at two separate times, but you need the data together for analysis.

In a DATA step, first specify the name of the new SAS data set in the DATA statement, then list the names of the old data sets you want to combine in the SET statement:

```
DATA new-data-set;
   SET data-set-1 data-set-n;
```

The number of observations in the new data set will equal the sum of the number of observations in the old data sets. The order of observations is determined by the order of the list of old data sets. If one of the data sets has a variable not contained in the other data sets, then the observations from the other data sets will have missing values for that variable.

Example   The Fun Times Amusement Park has two entrances where they collect data about their customers. The data file for the south entrance has an S (for south) followed by the customers' Fun Times pass numbers, the sizes of their parties, and their ages. The file for the north entrance has a N (for north), the same data as the south entrance, plus one more column for the parking lot where they left their cars (the south entrance only has one lot). The following shows parts of the two data files:

Data for South Entrance	Data for North Entrance
S 43 3 27	N 21 5 41 1
S 44 3 24	N 87 4 33 3
S 45 3 2	N 65 2 67 1
	N 66 2 7 1

The first two parts of the following program read the raw data for the south and north entrances into SAS data sets and print them to make sure they are correct. The third part combines the two SAS data sets using a SET statement. The same DATA step creates a new variable, PAID, which tells how much each customer paid based on their age. This final data set is printed using PROC PRINT:

```
DATA sentr;
   INFILE 'south.dat';
   INPUT enter $ passnum prtysize age;
PROC PRINT;
   TITLE 'South Entrance Data';

DATA nentr;
   INFILE 'north.dat';
   INPUT enter $ passnum prtysize age lot;
PROC PRINT;
   TITLE 'North Entrance Data';
```

```
* Create a data set, both, combining nentr and sentr;
* Create a variable, paid, based on value of variable age;
DATA both;
    SET sentr nentr;
    IF age = . THEN paid = .;
        ELSE IF age < 3  THEN paid = 0;
        ELSE IF age < 65 THEN paid = 17;
        ELSE paid = 12;
PROC PRINT;
    TITLE 'Both Entrances';
RUN;
```

The following are the results of the three PRINT procedures in the program. Notice that the final data set has missing values for the variable LOT for all the observations which came from the south entrance. This is because the variable LOT was not in the SENTR data set. SAS assigns missing values to those observations.

```
                          South Entrance Data                      1

              OBS     ENTER     PASSNUM     PRTYSIZE     AGE

               1        S          43           3         27
               2        S          44           3         24
               3        S          45           3          2

                          North Entrance Data                      2

          OBS     ENTER     PASSNUM     PRTYSIZE     AGE     LOT

           1        N          21           5         41       1
           2        N          87           4         33       3
           3        N          65           2         67       1
           4        N          66           2          7       1

                          Both Entrances                           3

      OBS     ENTER     PASSNUM     PRTYSIZE     AGE     LOT     PAID

       1        S          43           3         27       .       17
       2        S          44           3         24       .       17
       3        S          45           3          2       .        0
       4        N          21           5         41       1       17
       5        N          87           4         33       3       17
       6        N          65           2         67       1       12
       7        N          66           2          7       1       17
```

SET statement
SAS data sets, concatenating

6.3 Interleaving Data Sets Using the SET Statement

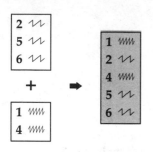

The previous section explained how to stack data sets that have all or most of the same variables but different observations. However, if you have data sets that are already sorted by some important variable, then simply stacking the data sets may unsort the data sets. You could stack the two data sets and then resort them using PROC SORT. But if your data sets are already sorted, it is more efficient to preserve that order, than to stack and resort. All you need to do is use a BY statement with your SET statement. Here's the general form:

```
DATA new-data-set;
   SET data-set-1 data-set-n;
   BY variable-list;
```

In a DATA statement, you specify the name of the new SAS data set you want to create. In a SET statement, you list the data sets to be interleaved. Then in a BY statement, you list one or more variables that SAS should use for ordering the observations. The number of observations in the new data set will be equal to the sum of the number of observations in the old data sets. If one of the data sets has a variable not contained in the other data sets, then values of that variable will be set to missing for observations from the other data sets.

Before you can interleave observations, the data sets must be sorted by the BY variables. If one or the other of your data sets is not already sorted, then use PROC SORT to do the job.

Example   To show how this is different from stacking data sets, we'll use the amusement park data again. There are two data sets, one for the south entrance and one for the north. For every customer, the park collects the following data: the entrance (S or N), the customer's Fun Times pass number, size of that customer's party, and age. For customers entering from the north, the data set also includes parking lot number. Here is a sample of the data:

Data for South Entrance	Data for North Entrance
S 43 3 27	N 21 5 41 1
S 44 3 24	N 87 4 33 3
S 45 3 2	N 65 2 67 1
	N 66 2 7 1

Notice that the data for the south entrance is already sorted by pass number, but the data for the north entrance is not.

Instead of stacking the two data sets, this program interleaves the data sets by pass number. This program first reads the data for the south entrance and prints it to make sure it is correct. Then the program reads the data for the north entrance, sorts it, and prints it. Then in the final DATA step, SAS combines the two data sets, NENTR and SENTR, creating a new data set named INTRLEAV. The BY statement tells SAS to combine the data sets by PASSNUM:

```
DATA sentr;
   INFILE 'south.dat';
   INPUT enter $ passnum prtysize age;
PROC PRINT;
   TITLE 'South Entrance Data';
```

```
DATA nentr;
   INFILE 'north.dat';
   INPUT enter $ passnum prtysize age lot;
PROC SORT;
   BY passnum;
PROC PRINT;
   TITLE 'North Entrance Data';

* Interleave observations by passnum;
DATA intrleav;
   SET nentr sentr;
   BY passnum;
PROC PRINT;
   TITLE 'Both Entrances, By Pass Number';
RUN;
```

Here are the results of the three PRINT procedures. Notice how the observations have been interleaved so that the new data set is sorted by PASSNUM:

```
                        South Entrance Data                    1

           OBS      ENTER     PASSNUM     PRTYSIZE     AGE

            1         S          43          3          27
            2         S          44          3          24
            3         S          45          3           2

                        North Entrance Data                    2

       OBS      ENTER     PASSNUM     PRTYSIZE     AGE     LOT

        1         N          21          5          41      1
        2         N          65          2          67      1
        3         N          66          2           7      1
        4         N          87          4          33      3

                   Both Entrances, By Pass Number             3

       OBS      ENTER     PASSNUM     PRTYSIZE     AGE     LOT

        1         N          21          5          41      1
        2         S          43          3          27      .
        3         S          44          3          24      .
        4         S          45          3           2      .
        5         N          65          2          67      1
        6         N          66          2           7      1
        7         N          87          4          33      3
```

SET statement
   SAS data sets, interleaving

6.4 Combining Data Sets Using a One-to-One Match Merge

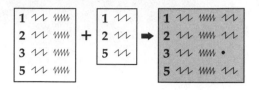

When you have two SAS data sets with related data and you want to combine them, use the MERGE statement in the DATA step. If you know the two data sets are in EXACTLY the same order you don't have to have any common variables between the data sets. Typically, however, you will want to have, for matching purposes, a common variable or several variables which taken together uniquely identify each observation. This is important. Having a common variable to merge by, ensures that the observations in the data sets are properly matched. For example, to merge patient data with billing data, you would use the patient ID as a matching variable. Otherwise you risk getting Mary Smith's visit to the obstetrician mixed up with Matthew Smith's visit to the optometrist.

Merging SAS data sets is a simple process. First, if the data are not already sorted, use the SORT procedure to sort all data sets by the common variables. Then, in the DATA statement, name the new SAS data set to hold the results and follow with a MERGE statement listing the data sets to be combined. Use a BY statement to indicate the common variables:

```
DATA new-data-set;
   MERGE data-set-1 data-set-2;
   BY variable-list;
```

If you merge two data sets, and they have variables with the same names—besides the BY variables—then variables from the second data set will overwrite any variables having the same name in the first data set.

Example   The owners of Fun Times Amusement Park want to know if the number of people in a party is related to screaming on the roller coaster ride. Data for the size of the party is collected at the park's entrance. The entrance data file shown below has data for the entrance (N or S), Fun Times pass number, party size, and age. Data for screaming is collected after the ride by noting each person's Fun Times pass number and asking if he or she screamed (1 if yes, 0 if no). The pass number is used as a common variable to merge the two data sets. Here are samples from the two raw data files:

Entrance data				Screaming data	
N	21	5	41	21	1
S	43	3	27	43	0
S	44	3	24	44	1
S	45	3	2	66	0
N	65	2	67	87	0
N	66	2	7		
N	87	4	41		

The first two parts of the following program read the raw entrance and screaming data. In both cases, the data are already sorted by PASSNUM, so we don't need to use PROC SORT. (If you attempt to merge data which are not sorted, SAS will refuse and give you this error message: `ERROR: BY variables are not properly sorted.`)

```
DATA entrance;
   INFILE 'enter.dat';
   INPUT enter $ passnum prtysize age;

DATA screams;
   INFILE 'scream.dat';
   INPUT passnum scream;

* Merge data sets by passnum;
DATA all;
   MERGE entrance screams;
   BY passnum;
PROC PRINT;
   TITLE 'SAS Data Set All';
   TITLE2 'Merge of Entrance Data and Screaming Data';
RUN;
```

The final part of the program creates a data set named ALL by merging the entrance data set, ENTRANCE, and the screaming data set, SCREAMS. The common variable PASSNUM in the BY statement is used for matching purposes. The following output shows the final data set after merging:

```
                      SAS Data Set All                        1
            Merge of Entrance Data and Screaming Data

        OBS    ENTER    PASSNUM    PRTYSIZE    AGE    SCREAM

         1       N         21          5        41       1
         2       S         43          3        27       0
         3       S         44          3        24       1
         4       S         45          3         2       .
         5       N         65          2        67       .
         6       N         66          2         7       0
         7       N         87          4        41       0
```

Notice that the final data set has missing values for SCREAM in the forth and fifth observations. This is because pass numbers 45 and 65 did not appear in the screaming data. All observations from both data sets were included in the final data set whether they had a match or not.

| MERGE statement |
| one-to-one merging |

6.5 Combining Data Sets Using a One-to-Many Match Merge

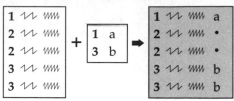

Sometimes you need to combine two data sets by matching one observation from one data set with more than one observation in another. Suppose you had data for every state in the U.S. and wanted to combine it with data for every county. This would be a one-to-many match merge because each state observation matches with many county observations.

The statements for a one-to-many match merge are identical to the statements for a one-to-one match merge:

```
DATA new-data-set;
   MERGE data-set-1 data-set-2;
   BY variable-list;
```

The order of the data sets in the MERGE statement does not matter to SAS. In other words, a one-to-many merge is the same as a many-to-one merge.

Before you merge two data sets, they must be sorted by one or more common variables. If your data sets are not already sorted in the proper order, then use PROC SORT to do the job.

You cannot do a one-to-many merge without a BY statement. SAS uses the variables listed in the BY statement to decide which observations belong together. Without any BY variables for matching, SAS simply joins together the first observation from each data set, then the second observation from each data set, and so on. In other words, SAS performs a one-to-one unmatched merge.

If you merge two data sets, and they have variables with the same names—besides the BY variables—then variables from the second data set will overwrite any variables having the same name in the first data set. For example, if you merge two data sets by a variable named ID, and both data sets contain a variable named SCORE, then the final data set will contain only one variable named SCORE. The values for SCORE will come from the second data set. You can fix this by renaming the variables (perhaps SCORE1 and SCORE2) so that they will not overwrite each other.[1]

Example   A distributor of exercise video tapes is putting all its tapes on sale at 20–30% off the regular price. The distributor has two data files, one with information about each video and one with the discount factors. The first file contains three variables: title, type of exercise (aerobics, step, or weights), and regular price. The second file contains two variables: type of exercise and discount. Here are samples from the two raw data files:

Videos data				Discount data	
Adorable Abs		aerobics	12.99	aerobics	.20
Aerobic Childcare for Parents	aerobics	13.99	step	.30
Judy Murphy's Fun Fitness	step	12.99	weights	.25
Lavonnes' Low Impact Workout	aerobics	13.99		
Muscle Makers		weights	15.99		
Rock N Roll Step Workout	step	12.99		

---

[1] The RENAME= data set option is discussed in section 6.9.

To find the sale price, the following program combines the two data files:

```
DATA videos;
   INFILE 'vid.dat';
   INPUT name $ 1-29 extype $ regprice;
PROC SORT DATA = videos;
   BY extype;

DATA discount;
   INFILE 'disc.dat';
   INPUT extype $ adjust;

* Perform many-to-one match merge;
DATA prices;
   MERGE videos discount;
   BY extype;
   newprice = ROUND(regprice - (regprice * adjust), .01);
PROC PRINT DATA = prices;
   TITLE 'Price List for May 21-27';
RUN;
```

The first DATA step reads the regular prices, creating a data set named VIDEOS. That data set is then sorted by EXTYPE using PROC SORT. The second DATA step reads the price adjustments, creating a data set named DISCOUNT. This data set is already arranged by EXTYPE, so PROC SORT is not needed. The third DATA step creates a data set named PRICES, merging the first two data sets by EXTYPE, and computes a variable called NEWPRICE. The output looks like this:

```
                  Price List for May 21-27                    1

     OBS NAME                         EXTYPE   REGPRICE ADJUST NEWPRICE

       1 Adorable Abs                 aerobics  12.99   0.20    10.39
       2 Aerobic Childcare for Parents aerobics 13.99   0.20    11.19
       3 Lavonnes' Low Impact Workout aerobics  13.99   0.20    11.19
       4 Judy Murphy's Fun Fitness    step      12.99   0.30     9.09
       5 Rock N Roll Step Workout     step      12.99   0.30     9.09
       6 Muscle Makers                weights   15.99   0.25    11.99
```

Notice that the values for ADJUST from the DISCOUNT data set are repeated for every observation in the VIDEOS data set with the same value of EXTYPE.

```
┌──────────────────────────┐
│ MERGE statement          │  [L]
│ match-merging            │
└──────────────────────────┘
```

6.6 Merging Summary Statistics with the Original Data

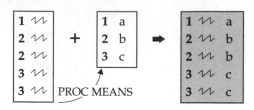

Once in a while you need to combine summary statistics with your data, such as when you want to compare each observation to the group mean, or when you want to calculate a percentage using the group total. To do this, you summarize your data using PROC MEANS, writing the results in a new data set. Then merge the summarized data back with the original data using a one-to-many match merge.

Example A distributor of exercise videos is considering doing a special promotion for the top selling titles. The vice-president of marketing has asked you to produce a report. The report should be divided by type of exercise (aerobic, step, or weights) and show the percentage of sales for each title within its type. The raw data file contains three variables—video title, type of exercise, and total sales for the last quarter:

```
Adorable Abs                      aerobics 1930
Aerobic Childcare for Parents aerobics 2250
Judy Murphy's Fun Fitness        step     4150
Lavonnes' Low Impact Workout  aerobics 1130
Muscle Makers                     weights  2230
Rock N Roll Step Workout         step     1190
```

Here is the program:

```
DATA videos;
   INFILE 'vidsales.dat';
   INPUT title $ 1-29 extype $ sales;
PROC SORT DATA = videos;
   BY extype;

* Summarize sales by extype and print;
PROC MEANS NOPRINT;
   VAR sales;
   BY extype;
   OUTPUT OUT = sumdata SUM(sales) = total;
PROC PRINT DATA = sumdata;
   TITLE 'Summary Data Set';

* Merge totals with the original data set;
DATA videosum;
   MERGE videos sumdata;
   BY extype;
   percent = sales / total * 100;
PROC PRINT DATA = videosum;
   BY extype;
   ID extype;
   VAR title sales total percent;
   TITLE 'Sales Share by Type of Exercise';
RUN;
```

This program is long but straightforward. It starts by reading the raw data in a DATA step and sorting it with PROC SORT. Then it summarizes the data with PROC MEANS by the variable EXTYPE. The OUTPUT statement tells SAS to create a new data set named SUMDATA, containing a variable named TOTAL, which equals the sum of SALES. The NOPRINT option tells SAS not to print the standard PROC MEANS report. Instead, the summary data set is printed by PROC PRINT:

```
                        Summary Data Set                        1

          OBS    EXTYPE      _TYPE_    _FREQ_     TOTAL

           1     aerobics      0         3        5310
           2     step          0         2        5340
           3     weights       0         1        2230
```

In the last part of the program, the original data set, VIDEOS, is merged with SUMDATA to make a new data set, VIDEOSUM. This DATA step computes a new variable called PERCENT. Then the last PROC PRINT writes the final report with percent of sales by EXTYPE for each title. Using a BY and an ID statement together gives this report a little different look:

```
              Sales Share by Type of Exercise                 2

     EXTYPE     TITLE                       SALES   TOTAL   PERCENT

     aerobics   Adorable Abs                 1930    5310    36.347
                Aerobic Childcare for Parents 2250   5310    42.373
                Lavonnes' Low Impact Workout 1130    5310    21.281

     step       Judy Murphy's Fun Fitness    4150    5340    77.715
                Rock N Roll Step Workout     1190    5340    22.285

     weights    Muscle Makers                2230    2230   100.000
```

| MEANS procedure | P |

6.7 Combining a Grand Total with the Original Data

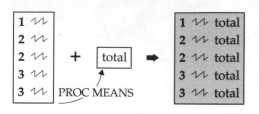

You can use the MEANS procedure to create a data set containing a grand total rather than BY group totals. But you cannot use a MERGE statement to combine a grand total with the original data because there is no common variable to merge by. If you try merging them anyway, SAS will combine the grand total with the first observation of the original data, and then set the variables for the grand total data set to missing for all other observations. Luckily, there is a better way. You can use two SET statements like this:

```
DATA new-data-set;
   IF _N_ = 1 THEN SET summary-data-set;
   SET original-data-set;
```

In this DATA step, `original-data-set` is the data set with more than one observation, the original data, and `summary-data-set` is the data set with a single observation, the grand total. SAS reads `original-data-set` in a normal SET statement, simply reading the observations in a straightforward way. SAS also reads `summary-data-set` with a SET statement but only in the first iteration of the DATA step (when _N_ equals 1). SAS then retains the values of variables from `summary-data-set` for all observations in `new-data-set`.

This works because variables read with a SET statement are automatically retained. Normally you don't notice this because the retained values are overwritten by the next observation. But in this case the variables from `summary-data-set` are read once at the first iteration of the DATA step and then retained for all other observations. The effect is similar to a RETAIN statement.

Example   To show how this is different from merging BY group summary statistics with original data, we'll use the same data as in the previous section. A distributor of exercise videos is considering doing a special promotion for the top-selling titles. The vice-president of marketing asks you to produce a report. The report should show the percentage of total sales for each title. The raw data file contains three variables—video title, type of exercise, and sales for the last quarter:

```
Adorable Abs                   aerobics 1930
Aerobic Childcare for Parents  aerobics 2250
Judy Murphy's Fun Fitness      step     4150
Lavonne's Low Impact Workout   aerobics 1130
Muscle Makers                  weights  2230
Rock N Roll Step Workout       step     1190
```

Here is the program:

```
DATA videos;
   INFILE 'vidsales.dat';
   INPUT title $ 1-29 extype $ sales;

* Find the grand total for sales;
* Output total to a data set and print;
PROC MEANS NOPRINT;
   VAR sales;
   OUTPUT OUT = sumdata SUM(sales) = grandtot;
PROC PRINT DATA = sumdata;
   TITLE 'Summary Data Set';

* Combine the grand total with the original data;
DATA videosum;
   IF _N_ = 1 THEN SET sumdata;
   SET videos;
   percent = sales / grandtot * 100;
PROC PRINT DATA = videosum;
   VAR title extype sales grandtot percent;
   TITLE 'Overall Sales Share';
RUN;
```

This program starts with a DATA step to input the raw data. Then PROC MEANS creates an output data set named SUMDATA with one observation containing a variable named GRANDTOT, which is equal to the sum of SALES. This will be a grand total because there is no BY or CLASS statement. The second DATA step combines the original data with the grand total using two SET statements and then computes the variable PERCENT using the grand total data. This technique can be used any time you want to combine a single observation with many observations, without a common variable.

The output looks like this:

```
                      Summary Data Set                    1

            OBS    _TYPE_    _FREQ_    GRANDTOT

             1        0         6       12880


                     Overall Sales Share                  2

OBS  TITLE                         EXTYPE    SALES  GRANDTOT  PERCENT

 1   Adorable Abs                  aerobics   1930   12880   14.9845
 2   Aerobic Childcare for Parents aerobics   2250   12880   17.4689
 3   Judy Murphy's Fun Fitness     step       4150   12880   32.2205
 4   Lavonne's Low Impact Workout  aerobics   1130   12880    8.7733
 5   Muscle Makers                 weights    2230   12880   17.3137
 6   Rock N Roll Step Workout      step       1190   12880    9.2391
```

| SET statement | L | | MEANS procedure | P |

6.8 Updating a Master Data Set with Transactions

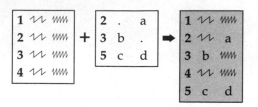

The UPDATE statement is used far less than the MERGE statement, but it is just right for those times when you have a master data set that must be updated with bits of new information. A bank account is a good example of this type of transaction-oriented data, since it is regularly updated with credits and debits.

The UPDATE statement is similar to the MERGE statement, because both combine data sets by matching observations on common variables. However, there are critical differences:

▶ First, with UPDATE the resulting master data set has only one observation for each unique value of the common variables, even though the transaction data set may have more than one such observation. That way, you don't get a new observation for your bank account every time you deposit a pay check.

▶ Second, data values that are missing in the transaction data set do not overwrite existing values in the master data set. That way, you are not obliged to enter your address and tax ID number every time you make a withdrawal.

The basic form of the UPDATE statement is

```
DATA master-data-set;
   UPDATE master-data-set transaction-data-set;
   BY variable-list;
```

Here are a few points to remember about the UPDATE statement. You can only specify two data sets: one master and one transaction. Both data sets must be sorted by their common variables. Also, the values of those BY variables must be unique in the master data set. Using the bank example, you could have many transactions for a single account, but only one observation per account on the master data set.

Example A hospital maintains a master database with current information for all patients. A sample from the master database appears below. It contains seven variables: account number, last name, address, date of birth, sex, insurance code, and the date that patient's information was last updated:

```
620135 Smith    234 Aspen St.     12-21-75 m CBC 02-16-93
645722 Miyamoto 65 3rd Ave.       04-03-36 f MCR 05-30-94
645739 Jensvold 505 Glendale Ave. 06-15-60 f HLT 09-23-88
874329 Kazoyan  .                 .        . MCD 01-15-94
```

Whenever a patient is admitted to the hospital, the admissions staff check the data for that patient. They create a transaction record for every new patient and for any returning patients whose status has changed. The transaction data set contains the same variables as the master data set:

```
620135 .                          .        . HLT 06-15-94
874329 Kazoyan  76-C La Vista     04-24-54 m .   06-15-94
235777 Harman   5656 Land Way     01-18-60 f MCD 06-15-94
```

There are three transactions. The first is for a returning patient whose insurance has changed. The second transaction fills in missing information for a returning patient. The last transaction is for a new patient who must be added to the database.

Since master data sets are updated frequently, they are usually saved as permanent SAS data sets. To make this example realistic, this program puts the master data into a permanent data set named PERM.PATIENTS in the MYSASLIB directory on the C drive (DOS, OS/2, Windows). The LIBNAME statement may differ on your operating system.

```
LIBNAME perm 'c:\mysaslib';
DATA perm.patients;
   INFILE 'admit.dat';
   INPUT acctno lastname $ 8-16 address $ 17-34
      bdate MMDDYY8. sex $ inscode $ 46-48 @50 lastdate MMDDYY8.;
RUN;
```

The next program reads the transaction data and sorts them with PROC SORT. Then it adds the transactions to PERM.PATIENTS with an UPDATE statement. The master data set is already sorted by ACCTNO and, therefore, doesn't need to be sorted again:

```
LIBNAME perm 'c:\mysaslib';
DATA trans;
   INFILE 'newadmit.dat';
   INPUT acctno lastname $ 8-16 address $ 17-34
         bdate MMDDYY8. sex $ inscode $ 46-48 @50 lastdate MMDDYY8.;
PROC SORT DATA = trans;
   BY acctno;

* Update patient data with transactions;
DATA perm.patients;
   UPDATE perm.patients trans;
   BY acctno;
PROC PRINT DATA = perm.patients;
   FORMAT bdate lastdate MMDDYY8.;
   TITLE 'Admissions Data';
RUN;
```

The output of PROC PRINT looks like this:

```
                         Admissions Data                        1

OBS   ACCTNO   LASTNAME   ADDRESS             BDATE    SEX  INSCODE  LASTDATE

 1    235777   Harman     5656 Land Way       01/18/60  f    MCD     06/15/94
 2    620135   Smith      234 Aspen St.       12/21/75  m    HLT     06/15/94
 3    645722   Miyamoto   65 3rd Ave.         04/03/36  f    MCR     05/30/94
 4    645739   Jensvold   505 Glendale Ave.   06/15/60  f    HLT     09/23/88
 5    874329   Kazoyan    76-C La Vista       04/24/54  m    MCD     06/15/94
```

UPDATE statement

6.9 Using SAS Data Set Options

In this book, you have already seen a lot of options. It may help to keep them straight if you realize that the SAS language has three basic types of options: system options, statement options, and data set options. System options have the most global influence, followed by statement options, with data set options having the most limited effect.

System options are those that stay in effect for the duration of your job or session. These options affect how SAS operates. Options are usually issued when you invoke SAS or via the OPTIONS statement. System options include the CENTER option, which tells SAS to center all output, and the LINESIZE option setting the maximum line length for output.[1]

Statement options appear in individual statements and influence how SAS runs that particular DATA or PROC step. DATA=, for example, is a statement option you can use in any procedure that reads a SAS data set. This option tells SAS which data set to use. Without it, SAS defaults to the most recently created data set.

In contrast, data set options only affect how SAS reads or writes an individual data set. You can use data set options in DATA steps (in DATA, SET, MERGE, or UPDATE statements) or in PROC steps (with a DATA= statement option). To use a data set option, you simply put it between parentheses directly following the data set name. These are the most frequently used data set options:

KEEP = *variable-list*	tells SAS which variables to keep.
DROP = *variable-list*	tells SAS which variables to drop.
RENAME = (*oldvar* = *newvar*)	tells SAS to rename certain variables.
FIRSTOBS = *n*	tells SAS to start reading at observation *n*.
OBS = *n*	tells SAS to stop reading at observation *n*.
IN = *new-var-name*	creates a temporary variable for tracking whether that data set contributed to the current observation.

Selecting and renaming variables   Here are examples of the KEEP=, DROP=, and RENAME= data set options:

```
DATA small;
   SET animals (KEEP = cat mouse rabbit);
DATA big (DROP = cat mouse rabbit);
   SET animals;
DATA animals (RENAME = (cat = feline dog = canine));
   SET animals;
```

---

[1] Other system options are discussed in section 2.10.

You could probably get by without these options, but they play an important role in fine tuning SAS programs. Data sets, for example, have a way of accumulating unwanted variables. Dropping unwanted variables will make your program run faster and use less disk space. Often when you read a large data set you need only a few variables. By using the KEEP= option, you can avoid reading a lot of variables you don't intend to use.

The DROP=, KEEP=, and RENAME= options are similar to the DROP, KEEP, and RENAME statements. However, the statements are more limited than the options since they can be used only in DATA steps and apply only to the data set being created. In contrast, the data set options can be used in DATA or PROC steps and can apply to input or output data sets. Please note that these options do not change input data sets; they only change what is read from input data sets.

Selecting observations by observation number   You can use the FIRSTOBS= and OBS= data set options together to tell SAS which observations to read from a data set. The options in this statement tell SAS to read just 20 observations:

```
PROC PRINT DATA = animals (FIRSTOBS = 101 OBS = 120);
```

If you use large data sets, you can save development time by testing your programs with a subset of your data with the FIRSTOBS= and OBS= options.

The FIRSTOBS= and OBS= data set options are similar to statement and system options with the same name. The statement options apply only to raw data files being read with an INFILE statement, whereas the data set options apply only to SAS data sets. The system options apply to all files and data sets. If you use similar system and data set options, the data set option will override the system option for that particular data set.

Tracking observations   The IN= option is somewhat different from other options covered here. While the other options affect existing variables, IN= creates a new variable. That new variable is temporary and has the name you specify in the option. In this example, SAS would create two temporary variables, one named INA and the other named INH:

```
DATA animals;
   MERGE animals (IN = INA) habitat (IN = INH);
   BY species;
```

These variables exist only for the duration of the current DATA step and are not added to the data set being created. SAS gives IN= variables a value of 0 if that data set did not contribute to the current observation and a value of 1 if it did. You can use the IN= variable to track, select, or eliminate observations based on the data set of origin. The next section contains a complete explanation of the IN= option.

data set options

6.10 Tracking and Selecting Observations with the IN= Option

Select matching observations

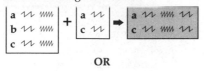

OR

Select non-matching observations

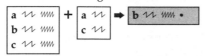

When you combine two data sets, you can use IN= options to track which of the original data sets contributed to each observation in the new data set. You can think of the IN= option as a sort of tag. Instead of saying "Product of Canada," the tag says something like "Product of data set one." Once you have that information, you can use it in many ways including selecting matching or non-matching observations during a merge.

The IN= data set option can be used any time you read a SAS data set in a DATA step—with SET, MERGE, or UPDATE—but is most often used with MERGE. To use the IN= option, you simply put the option in parentheses directly following the data set you want to track, and specify a name for the IN= variable. The names of IN= variables must follow standard SAS naming conventions—start with a letter or underscore; be eight characters or fewer in length; and contain letters, numerals, or underscores.

The DATA step below creates a data set named BOTH by merging two data sets named STATE and COUNTY. Then the IN= options create two variables named IN_S and IN_C:

```
DATA both;
   MERGE state (IN = in_s) county (IN = in_c);
   BY statname;
```

Unlike most variables, IN= variables are temporary, existing only during the current DATA step. SAS gives the IN= variables a value of 0 or 1. A value of 1 means that data set did contribute to the current observation, and a value of 0 means the data set did not contribute. Suppose the COUNTY data set above contained no data for Louisiana. (Louisiana has parishes, not counties.) In that case, the BOTH data set would contain one observation for Louisiana, and it would have a value of 1 for the variable IN_S and a value of 0 for IN_C because the STATE data set contributed to that observation, but the COUNTY data set did not.

You can use this variable like any other variable in the current DATA step, but it is most often used in subsetting IF or IF-THEN statements such as these:

```
Subsetting IF:    IF in_s = 1;
                  IF in_c = 0;
                  IF in_s = 1 AND in_c = 0;

IF-THEN:    IF in_c = 1 THEN origin = 1;
            IF in_s = 1 THEN state = 'Idaho';
```

Example A sporting goods manufacturer wants to send a sales rep to contact all customers who did not place any orders during the third quarter of the year. The company has two data files, one that contains all customers and one that contains all orders placed during the third quarter. To compile a list of customers without orders, you merge the two data sets using the IN= option, and then select customers who had no observations in the orders data set. The customer data file contains three variables: customer number, name, and address. The orders data file contains two variables: customer number and total price, with one observation for every order placed during the third quarter. Here is a sample of the two data files:

Customer data		Orders data
101 Murphy's Sports	115 Main St.	102 562.01
102 Sun N Ski	2106 Newberry Ave.	104 254.98
103 Sports Outfitters	19 Cary Way	104 1642.00
104 Cramer & Johnson	4106 Arlington Blvd.	101 3497.56
105 Sports Savers	2708 Broadway	102 385.30

Here is the program that finds customers who did not place any orders:

```
DATA customer;
   INFILE 'address.dat' PAD;
   INPUT custno name $ 5-21 address $ 23-42;
DATA orders;
   INFILE 'ordersq3.dat';
   INPUT custno total;
PROC SORT DATA = orders;
   BY custno;

* Combine the data sets using the IN= option;
DATA noorders;
   MERGE customer orders (IN = recent);
   BY custno;
   IF recent = 0;
PROC PRINT;
   TITLE 'Customers with No Orders in the Third Quarter';
RUN;
```

The customer data are already sorted by customer number and so does not need to be sorted with PROC SORT. The orders data however are in the order received and must be sorted by customer number before merging. In the final DATA step, the IN= option creates a variable named RECENT, which equals 1 if the ORDERS data set contributed to that observation and 0 if it did not. Then a subsetting IF statement, keeps only the observations where RECENT is equal to 0—those observations with no orders data. Notice that there is no IN= option on the CUSTOMER data set. Only one IN= option was needed to identify customers who did not place any orders. Here is the list that can be given to sales reps:

```
          Customers with No Orders in the Third Quarter          1

     OBS     CUSTNO       NAME            ADDRESS        TOTAL

      1       103     Sports Outfitters  19 Cary Way       .
      2       105     Sports Savers      2708 Broadway     .
```

The values for the variable TOTAL are missing because these customers did not have observations in the ORDERS data set. The variable RECENT does not appear in the output because, as a temporary variable, it was not added to the NOORDERS data set.

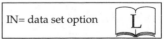
IN= data set option

6.11   Writing Multiple Data Sets Using the OUTPUT Statement

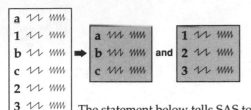

Up to this point, all the DATA steps in this book have created a single data set, except for DATA _NULL_ statements which produce no data set at all. Normally you only want to make one data set in each DATA step. However, there may be times when it is more efficient or more convenient to create multiple data sets in a single DATA step. You can do this by simply putting more than one data set name in your DATA statement. The statement below tells SAS to create three data sets named LIONS, TIGERS, and BEARS:

```
DATA lions tigers bears;
```

If that is all you do, then SAS will write all the observations to all the data sets, and you will have three identical data sets. Normally, of course, you want to create different data sets. You can do that with an OUTPUT statement.

Every DATA step has an implied OUTPUT statement at the end which tells SAS to write the current observation to the output data set before returning to the beginning of the DATA step to process the next observation. You can override this implicit OUTPUT statement with your own OUTPUT statement. The basic form of the OUTPUT statement is

```
OUTPUT data-set-name;
```

If you leave out the data set name, using just the word OUTPUT, then the observation will be written to all data sets named in the DATA statement. OUTPUT statements can be used alone or in IF-THEN or DO-loop processing.

```
IF family = 'Ursidae' THEN OUTPUT bears;
```

Example   Administrators at a local zoo are conducting a survey to find out which animals are the most popular. As visitors leave they are asked to check all the animals they saw that day and then vote for their favorite animal. A portion of the survey results appears below. Each observation includes the type of animal, its class, the number of people who saw the animal, and the number of people who selected that animal as their favorite:

```
bears      Mammalia   254 15
elephants  Mammalia   542 65
flamingos  Aves       434  8
frogs      Amphibian  120  3
kangaroos  Mammalia   332 12
lions      Mammalia   450 53
parrots    Aves       345  6
snakes     Reptilia   120 14
tigers     Mammalia   449 42
zebras     Mammalia   409 15
```

The administrators have asked you to analyze the data starting by separating the data for the mammals from the data for other animals. You can do this with the following program:

```
DATA mammals others;
   INFILE 'zoo.dat';
   INPUT animal $ 1-10 class $ 12-20 viewed favorite;
   IF class = 'Mammalia' THEN OUTPUT mammals;
      ELSE OUTPUT others;
PROC PRINT DATA = mammals;
   TITLE 'Survey Results for Mammals';
PROC PRINT DATA = others;
   TITLE 'Survey Results for Non-mammals';
RUN;
```

This DATA step creates two data sets named MAMMALS and OTHERS. Then the IF-THEN/ELSE statements tell SAS which observations to put in each data set. The log contains these notes telling you that one input file was read and two data sets were written:

```
NOTE: 10 records were read from the infile 'zoo.dat'.
NOTE: The data set WORK.MAMMALS has 6 observations and 4 variables.
NOTE: The data set WORK.OTHERS has 4 observations and 4 variables.
```

Here are the two reports, one for each data set:

```
                    Survey Results for Mammals                    1

        OBS     ANIMAL       CLASS        VIEWED      FAVORITE
         1      bears        Mammalia      254           15
         2      elephants    Mammalia      542           65
         3      kangaroos    Mammalia      332           12
         4      lions        Mammalia      450           53
         5      tigers       Mammalia      449           42
         6      zebras       Mammalia      409           15

                  Survey Results for Non-mammals                  2

        OBS     ANIMAL       CLASS        VIEWED      FAVORITE

         1      flamingos    Aves          434            8
         2      frogs        Amphibian     120            3
         3      parrots      Aves          345            6
         4      snakes       Reptilia      120           14
```

OUTPUT statements have other uses besides writing multiple data sets in a single data step and can be used any time you want to explicitly control when SAS writes observations to a data set.

OUTPUT statement

6.12 Using the OUTPUT Statement to Make Several Observations from One

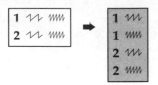

Usually SAS writes an observation to a data set at the end of the DATA step, but you can change this using the OUTPUT statement. If you want to write several observations for each pass through the DATA step, you can put an OUTPUT statement in a DO loop or just use several OUTPUT statements. The OUTPUT statement gives you control over when an observation is written to a SAS data set. If your DATA step doesn't have an OUTPUT statement, then it is implied at the end. Once you put an OUTPUT statement in your DATA step, it is no longer implied, and SAS only writes an observation when it encounters an OUTPUT statement.

Example The following program demonstrates how you can use an OUTPUT statement in a DO loop to generate data. Here we have a mathematical equation (y=x2) and we want to generate data points for later plotting:

```
* Create data for variables x and y;
DATA generate;
   DO x = 1 TO 6;
      y = x ** 2;
      OUTPUT;
   END;
PROC PRINT;
   TITLE 'Generated Data';
RUN;
```

This program has no INPUT or SET statement, so it only goes through the DATA step once. But it has a DO loop with six iterations. Because the OUTPUT statement is inside the DO loop, an observation is created each time through the loop. Without the OUTPUT statement, SAS would have written only one observation at the end of the DATA step when it reached the implied OUTPUT. The following are the results of the PROC PRINT:

```
                        Generated Data          1

                        OBS   X    Y

                         1    1    1
                         2    2    4
                         3    3    9
                         4    4   16
                         5    5   25
                         6    6   36
```

Example Here's how you can use OUTPUT statements to create several observations from a single pass through the DATA step. The following data are for ticket sales at three movie theaters. After the month are the theaters' names and sales for all three theaters:

```
Jan Varsity 56723 Downtown 69831 Super-6 70025
Feb Varsity 62137 Downtown 43901 Super-6 81534
Mar Varsity 49982 Downtown 55783 Super-6 69800
```

For the analysis you want to do, you need to have the theater name as one variable and the ticket sales as another variable. The month should be repeated three times, once for each theater.

The following program has three INPUT statements all reading from the same raw data file. The first INPUT statement reads MONTH, LOCATION, and TICKETS then holds the data line using the trailing at sign (@). The OUTPUT statement that follows writes an observation. The next INPUT statement reads the second set of data for LOCATION and TICKETS and again holds the data line. Another OUTPUT statement writes another observation. MONTH still has the same value because it isn't in the second INPUT statement. The last INPUT statement reads the last values for LOCATION and TICKETS, this time releasing the data line for the next iteration through the DATA step. The final OUTPUT statement writes the third observation for that iteration of the DATA step. The program has three OUTPUT statements for the three observations per iteration of the DATA step:

```
* Create three observations for each data line read
*    using three OUTPUT statements;
DATA theaters;
   INFILE 'movies.dat';
   INPUT month $ location $ tickets @;
   OUTPUT;
   INPUT location $ tickets @;
   OUTPUT;
   INPUT location $ tickets;
   OUTPUT;
PROC PRINT;
   TITLE 'Ticket Sales';
RUN;
```

The following are the results of the PROC PRINT. Notice that there are three observations in the data set for each line in the raw data file and that the value for MONTH is repeated:

```
                         Ticket Sales                          1

          OBS    MONTH    LOCATION    TICKETS

           1      Jan     Varsity      56723
           2      Jan     Downtown     69831
           3      Jan     Super-6      70025
           4      Feb     Varsity      62137
           5      Feb     Downtown     43901
           6      Feb     Super-6      81534
           7      Mar     Varsity      49982
           8      Mar     Downtown     55783
           9      Mar     Super-6      69800
```

OUTPUT statement
DO statement, iterative

6.13 Changing Observations to Variables Using PROC TRANSPOSE

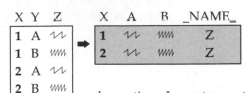

We have already seen ways to combine data sets, create new variables, and sort data. Now, using PROC TRANSPOSE, we will flip data—so get your spatulas ready.

The TRANSPOSE procedure transposes SAS data sets, turning observations into variables or variables into observations. In most cases, to convert observations into variables, you can use the following statements:

```
PROC TRANSPOSE DATA = oldname OUT = newname;
   BY variable-list;
   ID variable;
   VAR variable-list;
```

In the PROC TRANSPOSE statement, OLDNAME refers to the SAS data set you want to transpose, and NEWNAME is the name of the newly transposed data set.

BY statement   You can use the BY statement if you have any grouping variables that you want to keep as variables. These variables are included in the transposed data set, but they are not themselves transposed. The transposed data set will have one observation for each BY level per variable transposed. For example, in the figure above, the variable X is the BY variable. The data set must be sorted by these variables before transposing.

ID statement   The ID statement names the variable whose formatted values will become the new variable names. The ID values must occur only once in the data set; or if a BY statement is present, then the values must be unique within BY-groups. If the ID variable is numeric, then the new variable names have an underscore for a prefix (_1, or _2, for example). If you don't use an ID statement, then the new variables will be named COL1, COL2, and so on. In the figure above, the variable Y is the ID variable. Notice how its values are the new variable's names in the transposed data set.

VAR statement   The VAR statement names the variables whose values you want to transpose. In the figure above, the variable Z is the VAR variable. SAS creates a new variable, _NAME_, which has as values the names of the variables in the VAR statement. If there are more than one VAR variables, then _NAME_ will have more than one value.

Example   Suppose you have the following data about players for minor league baseball teams. You have the team name, player's number, the type of data (salary or batting average), and the entry:

```
Garlics 10 salary 43000
Peaches  8 salary 38000
Garlics 21 salary 51000
Peaches 10 salary 47500
Garlics 10 batavg .281
Peaches  8 batavg .252
Garlics 21 batavg .265
Peaches 10 batavg .301
```

You want to look at the relationship between batting average and salary using PROC PLOT. To do this, salary and batting average must be variables. The following program reads the raw data into a SAS data set and sorts the data by team and player. Then the data are transposed using PROC TRANSPOSE

```
DATA baseball;
   INFILE 'transpos.dat';
   INPUT team $ player type $ entry;
PROC SORT;
   BY team player;
PROC PRINT;
   TITLE 'Baseball Data After Sorting and Before Transposing';

* Transpose data so salary and batavg are variables;
PROC TRANSPOSE DATA = baseball OUT = flipped;
   BY team player;
   ID type;
   VAR entry;
PROC PRINT;
   TITLE 'Baseball Data After Transposing';
RUN;
```

In the PROC TRANSPOSE step, the BY variables are TEAM and PLAYER. You want those variables to remain in the data set, and they define the new observations (you only want one observation for each team and player combination). The ID variable is TYPE, whose values (salary and batavg) will be the new variable names. The variable to be transposed, ENTRY, is given in the VAR statement. Notice that its name, ENTRY, now appears as a value under the variable _NAME_. The TRANSPOSE procedure automatically generates the _NAME_ variable, but in this application it is not very meaningful and could be dropped.

Here are the results:

```
          Baseball Data After Sorting and Before Transposing        1

             OBS     TEAM      PLAYER     TYPE        ENTRY

              1      Garlics      10      salary     43000.00
              2      Garlics      10      batavg         0.28
              3      Garlics      21      salary     51000.00
              4      Garlics      21      batavg         0.27
              5      Peaches       8      salary     38000.00
              6      Peaches       8      batavg         0.25
              7      Peaches      10      salary     47500.00
              8      Peaches      10      batavg         0.30

                 Baseball Data After Transposing                    2

       OBS     TEAM      PLAYER    _NAME_    SALARY    BATAVG

        1      Garlics      10     ENTRY     43000     0.281
        2      Garlics      21     ENTRY     51000     0.265
        3      Peaches       8     ENTRY     38000     0.252
        4      Peaches      10     ENTRY     47500     0.301
```

| TRANSPOSE procedure | P |

6.14 Using SAS Automatic Variables

In addition to the variables you create in your SAS data set, there are a few more variables that SAS creates called automatic variables. You don't ordinarily see these variables because they are temporary and are not saved with your data. But they are available in the DATA step, and you can use them just like you use any variable that you create yourself.

_N_ and _ERROR_   The _N_ and _ERROR_ variables are always available to you in the DATA step. _N_ indicates the number of times SAS has looped through the DATA step. This is not necessarily equal to the observation number, since a simple subsetting IF statement can change the relationship between observation number and the number of iterations of the DATA step. The _ERROR_ variable has a value of 1 if there is a data error for that observation and 0 if there isn't. Things that can cause data errors include invalid data (such as characters in a numeric field), conversion errors (like division by zero), and illegal arguments in functions (including log of zero).

FIRST.*variable* and LAST.*variable*   Other automatic variables are available only in special circumstances. The FIRST.*variable* and LAST.*variable* automatic variables are available when you are using a BY statement in a DATA step. The FIRST.*variable* will have a value of 1 when SAS is processing an observation with the first occurrence of a new value for that variable and a value of 0 for the other observations. The LAST.*variable* will have a value of 1 for an observation with the last occurrence of a value for that variable and the value 0 for the other observations.

Example   Your hometown is having a walk around the town square to raise money for the library. You have the following data: entry number, age group, and finishing time. (Notice that there are more than one observation per line of data.)

```
54 youth  35.5 21 adult  21.6  6 adult  25.8 13 senior 29.0
38 senior 40.3 19 youth  39.6  3 adult  19.0 25 youth  47.3
11 adult  21.9  8 senior 54.3 41 adult  43.0 32 youth  38.6
```

The first thing you want to do is create a new variable for overall finishing place and print the results. The first part of the following program reads the raw data, and sorts the data by finishing time (TIME). Then in another DATA step, the _N_ variable creates the new PLACE variable. The PRINT procedure produces the list of finishers:

```
DATA walkers;
   INFILE 'walk.dat';
   INPUT entry agegrp $ time @@;
PROC SORT;
   BY time;
* Create a new variable, place;
DATA ordered;
   SET walkers;
   place = _N_;
PROC PRINT;
  TITLE 'Results of Walk';
```

```
PROC SORT;
   BY agegrp time;
* Set the data by agegrp and keep the first
  observation in each group;
DATA winners;
   SET ordered;
   BY agegrp;
   IF FIRST.agegrp = 1;
PROC PRINT;
   TITLE 'Winners in Each Age Group';
RUN;
```

The second part of this program produces a list of the top finishers in each age category. The ORDERED data set containing the new PLACE variable is sorted by AGEGRP and TIME. In the DATA step, the SET statement reads the ORDERED data set. The BY statement in the DATA step generates the FIRST.*agegrp* and LAST.*agegrp* temporary variables. The subsetting IF statement, IF FIRST.*agegrp* = 1, keeps only the first observation in the BY-group. Since the WINNERS data set is sorted by AGEGRP and TIME, the first observation in each BY-group is the top finisher of that group.

Here are the results of the two PRINT procedures. The first page shows the data after sorting by TIME and including the new variable PLACE. Notice that the _N_ temporary variable does not appear in the print out. The second page shows the results of the second part of the program—the winners for each age category and their overall place:

```
                    Results of Walk                          1

          OBS    ENTRY    AGEGRP    TIME    PLACE

           1       3      adult     19.0      1
           2      21      adult     21.6      2
           3      11      adult     21.9      3
           4       6      adult     25.8      4
           5      13      senior    29.0      5
           6      54      youth     35.5      6
           7      32      youth     38.6      7
           8      19      youth     39.6      8
           9      38      senior    40.3      9
          10      41      adult     43.0     10
          11      25      youth     47.3     11
          12       8      senior    54.3     12

                 Winners in Each Age Group                   2

          OBS    ENTRY    AGEGRP    TIME    PLACE

           1       3      adult     19.0      1
           2      13      senior    29.0      5
           3      54      youth     35.5      6
```

| automatic variables
 BY-group processing | |

7

> "33⅓ % of the mice used in the experiment were cured by the test drug; 33⅓% of the test population were unaffected by the drug and remained in a moribund condition; the third mouse got away."

ERWIN NETER

From "How to Write a Scientific Paper" by Robert A. Day, *ASM News*, vol 41, no. 7, pp 486-494, July 1975. Reprinted by permission of publisher and author. Also appears in *How to Write and Publish a Scientific Paper* 4th edition by Robert A. Day, copyright 1994 by Oryx Press.

CHAPTER 7

Using Basic Statistical Procedures

7.1 Examining the Distribution of Data with PROC UNIVARIATE

When you are doing statistical analysis, you usually have a goal in mind, a question you are trying to answer, a hypothesis that you want to test. But before you jump into testing your major hypotheses, it is a good idea to pause and do a little exploration. A good procedure to use at this point is the UNIVARIATE procedure.

PROC UNIVARIATE, which is part of Base SAS software, produces statistics describing the distribution of a single variable. These statistics include the mean, median, mode, standard deviation, skewness and kurtosis.[1]

Using PROC UNIVARIATE is fairly simple. After the PROC statement, you specify one or more numeric variables in a VAR statement:

```
PROC UNIVARIATE;
    VAR variable-list;
```

Without a VAR statement, SAS will calculate statistics for all numeric variables in your data set. You can specify other options in the PROC statement, if you wish, such as PLOT or NORMAL:

```
PROC UNIVARIATE  PLOT  NORMAL;
```

The NORMAL option produces a test of normality while the PLOT option produces three plots of your data (stem-and-leaf plot, box plot, and normal probability plot). You can use a BY statement to obtain separate analyses for BY groups. (Just remember to use PROC SORT first if your data are not already sorted by your BY variables.)

Example The following data from a fictitious statistics class contain just one variable, test score:

```
56 78 84 73 90 44 76 87 92 75
85 67 90 84 74 64 73 78 69 56
87 73 100 54 81 78 69 64 73 65
```

The program below reads the raw data from a file called SCORES.DAT and then runs PROC UNIVARIATE:

```
DATA class;
    INFILE 'scores.dat';
    INPUT score @@;
PROC UNIVARIATE;
    VAR score;
    TITLE;
RUN;
```

---

[1] Many of the statistics produced by UNIVARIATE can also be produced by specifying options on PROC MEANS. However, PROC UNIVARIATE produces some statistics that MEANS does not including median, mode, quartiles, a test of normality, and plots.

Here is the output:

```
                        Univariate Procedure                    1
            Variable=SCORE
                              Moments
    ❶ N               30          Sum Wgts        30
    ❷ Mean       74.63333          Sum          2239
    ❸ Std Dev    12.58484          Variance   158.3782
    ❹ Skewness   -0.34951      ❺ Kurtosis   0.103858
      USS          171697          CSS        4592.967
      CV         16.86222          Std Mean   2.297667
      T:Mean=0   32.48223          Pr>|T|       0.0001
      Num ^= 0         30          Num > 0          30
      M(Sign)          15          Pr>=|M|      0.0001
      Sgn Rank      232.5          Pr>=|S|      0.0001

                        Quantiles(Def=5)
    ❻ 100% Max      100           99%         100
       75% Q3        84           95%          92
    ❼  50% Med     74.5           90%          90
       25% Q1        67           10%          56
    ❽   0% Min       44            5%          54
                                   1%          44

           Range         56
           Q3-Q1         17
    ❾ Mode             73

                            Extremes
        Lowest     Obs      Highest      Obs
           44(      6)          87(      21)
           54(     24)          90(       5)
           56(     20)          90(      13)
           56(      1)          92(       9)
           64(     28)         100(      23)
```

Highlights of the output are

❶ N   number of observations
❷ Mean   arithmetic mean
❸ Std dev   standard deviation
❹ Skewness   measures how symmetrical the distribution is, whether it is more spread out on one side than the other
❺ Kurtosis   measures how flat or peaked the distribution is
❻ Max   maximum, highest value in the data set
❼ Med   median, the value half-way between the maximum and minimum
❽ Min   minimum, lowest value in the data set
❾ Mode   most frequently occurring value.

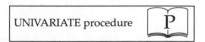

UNIVARIATE procedure

7.2 Examining Correlations with PROC CORR

The CORR procedure, which comes with Base SAS, computes correlations. A correlation coefficient measures the relationship between two variables, or how co-related they are. The basic statements for PROC CORR are rather simple:

```
PROC CORR;
```

With these two words SAS computes correlations between all the numeric variables in the most recently created data set. You can use the VAR and WITH statements to tell SAS which variables to use:

```
VAR variable-list;
WITH variable-list;
```

Variables listed in the VAR statement appear across the top of the table of correlations, while variables listed in the WITH statement appear down the side of the table. If you use a VAR statement but no WITH statement, then all the variables appear along the top and the side.

By default, PROC CORR computes Pearson product-moment correlation coefficients. You can add options to the PROC statement to request nonparametric correlation coefficients. The SPEARMAN option in the statement below tells SAS to compute Spearman's rank correlations instead of Pearson's correlations:

```
PROC CORR  SPEARMAN;
```

Other options include HOEFFDING (for Hoeffding's D statistic) and KENDALL (for Kendall's tau-b coefficients). Many other options are available with PROC CORR including options for saving statistics in an output data set.

Example   For each student in a fictitious statistics class, there are three variables: test score, the number of hours spent studying statistics in the week prior to the test, and the number of hours spent exercising during the same week. Here are the raw data:

```
56 6 2    78 7 4    84 5 5    73 4 2    90 6 4
44 2 0    76 5 1    87 6 3    92 6 7    75 8 3
85 7 1    67 4 2    90 5 5    84 6 5    74 5 2
64 4 1    73 8 5    78 5 2    69 6 1    56 4 1
87 8 4    73 8 3   100 5 6    54 8 0    81 5 4
78 5 2    69 4 1    64 7 1    73 7 3    65 4 4
```

Notice that each line contains data for five students. The following program reads the raw data from a file called STUDY.DAT and then uses PROC CORR to compute the correlations for hours of studying, hours of exercising, and test score:

```
DATA class;
   INFILE 'study.dat';
   INPUT score study exercise @@;
PROC CORR;
   VAR study exercise;
   WITH score;
   TITLE 'Correlations for Test Scores';
   TITLE2 'With Hours of Studying and Exercise';
RUN;
```

Here is the report from PROC CORR:

```
                    Correlations for Test Scores              1
                  With Hours of Studying and Exercise

                         Correlation Analysis

                   1 'WITH' Variables:  SCORE
                   2 'VAR' Variables:   STUDY      EXERCISE


                         Simple Statistics
                     ❶      ❷        ❸         ❹         ❺          ❻
        Variable     N      Mean    Std Dev    Sum     Minimum    Maximum

        SCORE        30    74.6333  12.5848    2239    44.0000   100.0000
        STUDY        30     5.6667   1.5388  170.0000   2.0000     8.0000
        EXERCISE     30     2.8000   1.8270   84.0000        0     7.0000

                         Correlation Analysis
        ❼Pearson Correlation Coefficients /❽Prob > |R|  under Ho: Rho=0 / N=30

                                     STUDY           EXERCISE

                     SCORE         ❼0.25879         ❼0.73907
                                   ❽0.1673          ❽0.0001
```

This report includes two tables, one containing descriptive statistics for each variable and one containing the correlations. Highlights of the output are

❶ N	number of observations
❷ Mean	arithmetic mean
❸ Std Dev	standard deviation
❹ Sum	sum of all values
❺ Minimum	lowest value
❻ Maximum	highest value
❼ Correlation	correlation coefficient (in this case, Pearson)
❽ Prob > |R|	probability of getting a larger absolute value for the correlation.

In this example, the correlation between test score and time spent exercising is much higher than the correlation between score and studying.

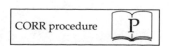

CORR procedure

7.3 Using PROC REG for Simple Regression Analysis

The REG procedure fits linear regression models by least-squares and is one of several SAS procedures which perform regression analysis. PROC REG is part of the SAS/STAT product, which is licensed separately from Base SAS. We will focus on simple regression analysis using continuous numeric variables with only one regressor variable. However, PROC REG is capable of analyzing models with many regressor variables using a variety of model-selection methods including stepwise regression, forward selection, and backward elimination.

The REG procedure has only two required statements. It must start with the PROC REG statement and have a MODEL statement specifying the analysis model. The following shows the general form of the REG procedure:

```
PROC REG;
   MODEL dependent = independent;
```

In the MODEL statement, the dependent variable is listed on the left side of the equal sign and the independent or regressor variable on the right.

The PLOT statement is one of many optional statements in the REG procedure. You can use the PLOT statement to generate scatter plots of your data, including some of the statistics generated by the regression analysis. The PLOT statement has the following general form:

```
PLOT yvariable * xvariable = 'symbol';
```

The *yvariable* goes on the vertical axis, and the *xvariable* goes on the horizontal axis. The *symbol* specifies what symbol to use to represent the data point. If you don't specify a symbol, SAS will use numbers indicating how many observations fall in that location on the plot.

To specify a statistic in a PLOT statement, use the statistic's name followed by a period. The following is a partial list of statistics and their names:

P	predicted values
R	residuals
STUDENT	studentized residuals
U95	upper bounds of a 95% confidence interval for an individual prediction
L95	lower bounds.

If, for example, you want to plot the predicted versus the actual batting averages of the baseball players based on the regression analysis, you could use the following PLOT statement:

```
PLOT P. * batavg;
```

You can have several PLOT statements per MODEL statement, and you can specify several plots per PLOT statement. If you want to overlay one plot on top of the other, list the plot specifications after the PLOT keyword, follow with a slash (/), and put the keyword OVERLAY. For example, if you want to plot the baseball player's batting average versus their salaries and overlay that with the predicted batting average based on the regression analysis, then the PLOT statement would look like

```
PLOT batavg * salary P. * salary / OVERLAY;
```

Example   At your young neighbor's T-ball game (that's where the players hit the ball from the top of a tee instead of having the ball pitched to them), he said to you, "You can tell how far they'll hit the ball by how tall they are." To give him a little practical lesson in statistics, you decide to test his hypothesis. You gather data from 30 players, measuring their height in inches and their longest of three hits in feet. The following are the data. Notice that data for five players are listed on one line:

```
50 110   49 135   48 129   53 150   48 124
50 143   51 126   45 107   53 146   50 154
47 136   52 144   47 124   50 133   50 128
50 118   48 135   47 129   45 126   48 118
45 121   53 142   46 122   47 119   51 134
49 130   46 132   51 144   50 132   50 131
```

The following program reads the data and performs the regression analysis:

```
DATA hits;
   INFILE 'baseball.dat';
   INPUT height distance @@;
* Perform regression analysis, plot observed and predicted values;
PROC REG;
   MODEL distance = height;
   PLOT distance * height = '*' P. * height = 'p' / OVERLAY;
   TITLE 'Results of Regression Analysis';
RUN;
```

In the MODEL statement, DISTANCE is the dependent variable, and HEIGHT is the independent variable. The PLOT statement plots the observed values (using an * to mark the points) overlaid with the predicted values (using a p). The PLOT statement is a convenient way to get a rough idea of what your data look like. The results are rather crude printer plots. If you want more refined plots, you can save the predicted values in a SAS data set using the OUTPUT statement, then use PROC GPLOT[1] to obtain a high quality plot. The output from the above program is shown and discussed in the next section.

| REG procedure | S |

---

[1] GPLOT is part of the SAS/GRAPH product which is licensed separately.

7.4 Reading the Output of PROC REG

The output from each REG procedure has at least two parts, the analysis of variance section and the parameter estimates. These sections usually print on the same page. Some optional statements, like PLOT, produce additional output on separate pages.

The output shown in this section is the result of the following PROC REG statements from the preceding section:

```
PROC REG;
    MODEL distance = height;
    PLOT distance * height = '*' P. * height ='p' / OVERLAY;
    TITLE 'Results of Regression Analysis';
RUN;
```

The first section of output is the analysis of variance section, which gives information about how well the model fits the data:

```
                      Results of Regression Analysis                        1

         Model: MODEL1
         Dependent Variable: DISTANCE

                             Analysis of Variance

                          ❸ Sum of      ❹ Mean
     ❶ Source      ❷ DF    Squares       Square      ❺ F Value    ❻ Prob>F

       Model        1    1365.50831    1365.50831     16.855       0.0003
       Error       28    2268.35836     81.01280
       C Total     29    3633.86667

          ❼ Root MSE      9.00071    ❿ R-square      0.3758
          ❽ Dep Mean    130.73333    ⓫ Adj R-sq      0.3535
          ❾ C.V.          6.88479
```

❶ Source	source of variation
❷ DF	degrees of freedom associated with the source
❸ Sum of Squares	sum of squares for the term
❹ Mean Square	mean square (sum of squares divided by the degrees of freedom)
❺ F value	F value for testing the null hypothesis (all parameters are zero except intercept)
❻ Prob>F	significance probability
❼ Root MSE	root mean square error
❽ Dep Mean	sample mean of the dependent variable
❾ C.V.	The coefficient of variation
❿ R-square	The R-square value
⓫ Adj R-sq	The R-square value adjusted for degrees of freedom.

The parameter estimates follow the analysis of variance section and give the parameters for each term in the model, including the intercept:

❶ Variable	❷ DF	❸ Parameter Estimate	❹ Standard Error	❺ T for H0: Parameter=0	❻ Prob > |T|
		Parameter Estimates			
INTERCEP	1	-11.008591	34.56363192	-0.319	0.7525
HEIGHT	1	2.894661	0.70506219	4.106	0.0003

Highlights of the output are

❶ Variable	regressor variable and the intercept
❷ DF	degrees of freedom for the variable
❸ Parameter Estimate	parameter estimate for the variable
❹ Standard Error	standard error
❺ T for H0:	*t* test for the parameter equal to zero
❻ Prob > |T|	two-tailed significance probability.

The following section shows the results of the PLOT statement. Here, two plots are overlaid: a plot of the observed values (indicated by *) and a plot of the predicted values (indicated by p). Where you see question marks (?) there are both predicted and actual values. You can see that the P's and ?'s do not produce a perfectly straight line. That is because this rather crude plot has only a few discrete print positions:

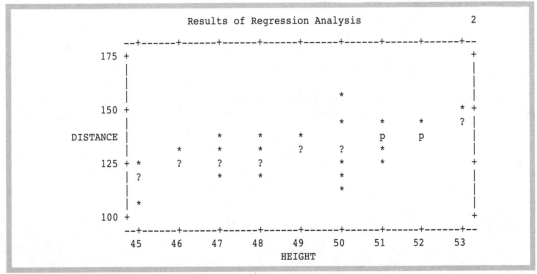

In this example, the distance the ball was hit did increase with the player's height, but the relationship was not very strong (R-square = 0.3758). Perhaps age or years of experience are better predictors of how far the ball will go.

REG procedure
printed output

7.5 Using PROC ANOVA for One-Way Analysis of Variance

The ANOVA procedure is one of several in the SAS System for performing analysis of variance. PROC ANOVA is part of SAS/STAT software, which is licensed separately from Base SAS. PROC ANOVA is specifically designed for balanced data—data where there are equal numbers of observations in each classification. If your data are not balanced, then you should use the GLM procedure, whose statements are almost identical to those of PROC ANOVA. Although we are only discussing simple one-way analysis of variance in this section, PROC ANOVA can handle multiple classification variables and models that include nested and crossed effects as well as repeated measures.

The ANOVA procedure has two required statements: the CLASS and MODEL statements. The following is the general form of the ANOVA procedure:

```
PROC ANOVA;
    CLASS variable-list;
    MODEL dependent = effects;
```

The CLASS statement must come before the MODEL statement and defines the classification variables. For one-way analysis of variance, only one variable is listed. The MODEL statement defines the dependent variable and the effects. For one-way analysis of variance, the effect is the classification variable.

As you might expect, there are many optional statements for PROC ANOVA. One of the most useful is the MEANS statement, which calculates means of the dependent variable for any of the main effects in the MODEL statement. In addition, the MEANS statement can perform several types of multiple comparisons tests including Bonferroni t-tests (BON), Duncan's multiple-range test (DUNCAN), Scheffe's multiple-comparison procedure (SCHEFFE), pairwise t-tests (T), and Tukey's studentized range test (TUKEY). The MEANS statement has the following general form:

```
MEANS effects / options;
```

The effects can be any main effect in the MODEL statement (no crossed or nested effects), and options include the name of the desired multiple comparisons test (SCHEFFE for example).

Example Your friend says his daughter complains that it seems like the girls on all the other softball teams are taller than her team. You decide to test her hypothesis by getting the heights for all the girls and performing analysis of variance to see if there are any differences among teams. You have the team name and girl's height for players on five different teams. Notice that there are data for six girls on each line:

```
red  55 red  48 red  53 red  47 red  51 red  43
red  45 red  46 red  55 red  54 red  45 red  52
blue 46 blue 56 blue 48 blue 47 blue 54 blue 52
blue 49 blue 51 blue 45 blue 48 blue 55 blue 47
gray 55 gray 45 gray 47 gray 56 gray 49 gray 53
gray 48 gray 53 gray 51 gray 52 gray 48 gray 47
pink 53 pink 53 pink 58 pink 56 pink 50 pink 55
pink 59 pink 57 pink 49 pink 55 pink 56 pink 57
gold 53 gold 55 gold 48 gold 45 gold 47 gold 56
gold 55 gold 46 gold 47 gold 53 gold 51 gold 50
```

Because each team has exactly 12 girls, the data are balanced and you can use the ANOVA procedure. You want to know which, if any, teams are taller than the rest, so you use the MEANS statement in your program and choose Scheffe's multiple-comparison procedure to compare the means. Here is the program to read the data and perform the analysis of variance:

```
DATA soft;
   INFILE 'softball.dat';
   INPUT team $ height @@;
* Use ANOVA to run one-way analysis of variance;
PROC ANOVA;
   CLASS team;
   MODEL height = team;
   MEANS team / SCHEFFE;
   TITLE "Girls' Heights on Softball Teams";
RUN;
```

In this case, TEAM is the classification variable and also the effect in the MODEL statement. HEIGHT is the dependent variable. The MEANS statement will produce means of the girls' heights for each team, and the SCHEFFE option will test which teams are different from the others. The output from the above program is shown and discussed in the next section.

ANOVA procedure	S

7.6 Reading the Output of PROC ANOVA

PROC ANOVA has at least two parts to its output. First it prints a table giving information about the classification variables: number of levels, values, and number of observations. Next it prints the analysis of variance table. If you use optional statements like MEANS, then their output would follow.

The example from the previous section, where we wanted to test to see if there were differences in the heights among softball teams, used the following PROC ANOVA statements:

```
PROC ANOVA;
   CLASS team;
   MODEL height = team;
   MEANS team / SCHEFFE;
   TITLE "Girls' Heights on Softball Teams";
RUN;
```

The first page of the output gives information about the classification variable:

```
                    Girls' Heights on Softball Teams                 1

                       Analysis of Variance Procedure
                          Class Level Information

               Class     Levels     Values

               TEAM          5       blue gold gray pink red

               Number of observations in data set = 60
```

Here the CLASS variable is TEAM. It has 5 levels with values blue, gold, gray, pink, and red representing the 5 teams. There are a total of 60 observations in the data set.

The second part of the output is the analysis of variance table:

```
                    Girls' Heights on Softball Teams                 2

                       Analysis of Variance Procedure

     Dependent Variable: HEIGHT
                                   ❸Sum of        ❹Mean
         ❶Source            ❷DF     Squares        Square    ❺F Value    ❻Pr > F

           Model             4     228.000000    57.000000     4.14       0.0053

           Error            55     758.000000    13.781818

           Corrected Total  59     986.000000

                    ❼R-Square          ❽C.V.      ❾Root MSE      ❿HEIGHT Mean

                     0.231237        7.279190      3.71239           51.0000

         Source              DF     Anova SS    Mean Square   F Value    Pr > F
         TEAM                 4    228.000000    57.000000     4.14       0.0053
```

Highlights of the output are

❶ Source   source of variation
❷ DF   degrees of freedom for the model, error and total
❸ Sum of Squares   sum of squares for the portion attributed to the model, error, and the
                   total
❹ Mean Square   mean square (sum of squares divided by the degrees of freedom)
❺ F value   F value (mean square for the model divided by the mean square for the
                   error)
❻ Pr > F   significance probability associated with the F statistic
❼ R-Square   R-square
❽ C.V.   coefficient of variation
❾ Root MSE   root mean square error
❿ HEIGHT mean   mean of the dependent variable.

The SCHEFFE option on the MEANS statement produces the following results. Letters are used to group means, and means with the same letters are not significantly different from each other (at the 0.05 level). This shows that the PINK team is significantly taller than the BLUE and RED teams because the PINK team only has the letter A and the BLUE and RED teams only have the letter B. The PINK team is not taller than GOLD and GRAY, according to Scheffe's test, because all three teams have the letter A. Your friend's daughter was partially correct—one team (PINK) was taller than her team (RED) but not all the teams were taller.

```
                Girls' Heights on Softball Teams                3
                   Analysis of Variance Procedure
                 Scheffe's test for variable: HEIGHT

    NOTE: This test controls the type I experimentwise error rate but
          generally has a higher type II error rate than REGWF for
          all pairwise comparisons

                Alpha= 0.05  df= 55  MSE= 13.78182
                   Critical Value of F= 2.53969
                Minimum Significant Difference= 4.8306

        Means with the same letter are not significantly different.

           Scheffe Grouping          Mean     N  TEAM

                          A        54.833    12  pink
                          A
                  B       A        50.500    12  gold
                  B       A
                  B       A        50.333    12  gray
                  B
                  B                49.833    12  blue
                  B
                  B                49.500    12  red
```

ANOVA Procedure
printed output

8

"Problems that go away by themselves come back by themselves."

MARCY E. DAVIS

CHAPTER 8

Debugging Your SAS® Programs

8.1 ▶ Writing SAS Programs that Work

It's not always easy to write a program that works the first time you run it. Even experienced SAS programmers will tell you it's a delightful surprise when their programs run on the first try. The longer and more complicated the program, the more likely it is to have syntax or logic errors. But don't despair, there are a few guidelines you can follow that can make your programs run correctly sooner and help you discover errors more easily.

Make programs easy to read One simple thing you can do is develop the habit of writing programs in a neat and consistent manner. Programs that are easy to read are easier to debug and will save you time in the long run. The following are suggestions on how to write your programs:

▶ Put only one SAS statement on a line. SAS allows you to put as many statements on a line as you wish, which may save you some space in your program, but the saved space is rarely worth the sacrifice in readability.

▶ Use indention to show the different parts of the program. Indent all statements within the DATA and PROC steps. This way you can tell at a glance how many DATA and PROC steps there are in a program and which statement belongs to which step. It's also helpful to further indent any statements between a DO statement and its END statement.

▶ Use comment statements generously to document your programs. This takes some discipline but is important, especially if anyone else is likely to read or use your program. Everyone has a different programming style, and it is often impossible to figure out what someone else's program is doing and why. Comment statements take the mystery out of the program.

Test each part of the program You can increase your programming efficiency tremendously by making sure each part of your program is working before moving on to write the next part. If you were building a house, you would make sure the foundation was level and square before putting up the walls. You would test the plumbing before finishing the bathroom. You are, by law, required to have each stage of the house inspected before moving on to the next. The same should be done for your SAS program. But you don't have to wait for the inspector to come out; you can do it yourself.

If you are reading data from a file, use PROC PRINT to print the SAS data set at least once to make sure it is correct before moving on. Sometimes, even though there are no errors or even suspicious notes in your SAS log, the SAS data set is not correct. This could happen because SAS did not read the data the way you imagined (after all it only does what you say not what you're thinking) or because the data had some peculiarities you did not realize. For example, a researcher who received two data files from Taiwan wanted to merge them together by date. She could not figure out why they refused to merge correctly until she printed both data sets and realized one of the files used Taiwanese dates, which are offset by 11 years.

It's a good habit to print all the SAS data sets you create in a program at least once to make sure they are correct. As with reading raw data files, sometimes merging and setting data sets can produce the wrong result even though there were no error messages. So when in doubt, use PROC PRINT.

Test programs with small data sets Sometimes it's not practical to test your program with your entire data set. If your data files are very large, you may not want to print all the data and it may take a long time for your programs to run. In these cases, you can test your program with a subset of your data.

If you are reading data from a file, you can use the OBS= option on the INFILE statement to tell SAS to stop reading when it gets to that line in the file. This way you can read only the first 50 or 100 lines of data or however many it takes to get a good representation of your data. The following statement will only read the first 100 lines of the data file MYDATA.DAT:

```
INFILE 'mydata.dat' OBS = 100;
```

You can also use the FIRSTOBS= option to start reading from the middle of the data file. So, if the first 100 data lines are not a good representation of your data but 100 through 200 are, you can use the following statement to just read those lines:

```
INFILE 'mydata.dat' FIRSTOBS = 100 OBS = 200;
```

Here *FIRSTOBS* and *OBS* relate to the lines of data in the file, not necessarily observations. If, for example, you are reading two lines of data for each observation, then you would need to read 200 lines of data to get 100 observations.

If you are reading a SAS data set instead of a raw data file, you can use the OBS= and FIRSTOBS= data set options on the SET, MERGE, or UPDATE statements.[1] This controls which observations are processed in the DATA step. For example, the following DATA step will read the first 50 observations in the CATS data set. Note that when reading SAS data sets OBS and FIRSTOBS truly do correspond to the observations and not to data lines:

```
DATA smcats;
   SET cats (OBS = 50);
```

Test with representative data   Using OBS= and FIRSTOBS= is an easy way to test your programs, but sometimes it is difficult to get a good representation of your data this way. You may need to create a small test data set by extracting representative parts of the larger data set. Or you may want to make up representative data for testing purposes. Making up data has the advantage that you can simplify the data and make sure you have every possible combination of values to test.

Sometimes you may want to make up data and write a small program just to test one aspect of your larger program. This can be extremely useful for narrowing down possible sources of error in a large complicated program.

---

[1]Data set options are discussed in section 6.9.

8.2 Fixing Programs that Don't Work

In spite of your best efforts, sometimes programs just don't work. More often than not, programs don't run the first time. Even with simple programs it is easy to forget a semicolon or misspell a keyword—everyone does sometime. If your program doesn't work, the source of the problem may be obvious like an error message with the offending part of your program underlined, or not so obvious as when you have no errors but still don't have the expected results. Whatever the problem, here are a few guidelines you can follow to help fix your program.

Read the SAS log   The SAS log has a wealth of information about your program. In addition to listing the program statements, it tells you things like how many lines were read from your raw data file and what were the minimum and maximum line lengths. It gives the number of observations and variables in each SAS data set you create. Information like this may seem inconsequential at first but can be very helpful in finding the source of your errors.

The SAS log has three types of messages about your program: errors, warnings, and notes.

Errors are hard to ignore. Not only do they come up in red on your screen, but your program will not run with errors. Usually errors are some kind of syntax or spelling mistake. The following shows the error message when you accidentally add a slash between the PROC MEANS and DATA= keywords. SAS underlines the problem (the slash) and tells you it doesn't recognize the symbol.

```
1    PROC MEANS / DATA = one;
               -
               200
ERROR 200-322: The symbol is not recognized.
```

The location of the error is easy to find, because it is usually underlined, but the source of the error can sometimes be tricky. Sometimes what is wrong is not what is underlined but something else earlier in the program.

Warnings are less serious than errors because your program will run with warnings. But beware, a warning may mean that SAS has done something you have not intended. For example, SAS will attempt to correct your spelling of certain keywords. If you misspell INPUT as IMPUT you will get the following message in your log:

```
WARNING 1-322: Assuming the symbol INPUT was misspelled as IMPUT.
```

Usually you would think, "SAS is so smart—it knows what I meant to say," but occasionally that may not be what you meant at all. Make sure that you know what all the warnings are about and that you agree with them.

Notes are less straightforward than either warnings or errors. Sometimes notes just give you information, like telling you the execution time of each step in your program. But sometimes notes can indicate a problem. Suppose, for example, that you have the following note in your SAS log:

```
NOTE: SAS went to a new line when INPUT statement reached past the end of a line.
```

This could mean that SAS did exactly what you wanted, or it could indicate a problem with either your program or your data. Make sure that you know what each note means and why it is there.

Start at the beginning   Whenever you read the SAS log, start at the beginning. This seems like a ridiculous statement—why wouldn't you start at the beginning? Well, if you are using the SAS Display Manager System, the SAS log rolls by in the window. When the program is finished, you are left looking at the end of the log. If you happen to see an error at the end of the log it is natural to try to fix that error first—the first one you see. Avoid this temptation. Often errors at the end of the log are caused by earlier ones. If you fix the first error, often most or all of the other errors will disappear. If your lawnmower is out of gas and won't start, it's probably better to add gas before trying to figure out why it won't start. The same logic applies to debugging SAS programs, fixing one problem will often fix others.

Look for common mistakes first   More often than not there is a simple reason why your program doesn't work. Look for the simple reason before trying to find something more complicated. The remainder of this chapter consists of sections discussing the most common errors encountered in SAS programming. When you see this little bug in the upper right corner of a section, you'll know that the material deals with how to debug your program. Some programming errors produce error messages, some just notes. If your SAS log contains an error or a suspicious note, look in this chapter for a section which discusses your error or note.

Sometimes error messages just don't make any sense. For example, you may get an error message saying the INPUT statement is not valid. This doesn't make much sense because you know INPUT is a valid SAS statement. In cases like these, look for missing semicolons in the statements before the error. If SAS has underlined an item, be sure to look not only at the underlined item but also at the previous few statements.

Finally, if you just can't figure out why you are not getting the results you expect, make sure you add PROC PRINT statements everywhere you create a new SAS data set. This can really help you discover errors in your logic, and sometimes uncover surprising details about your data.

8.3 Searching for the Missing Semicolon

DATA toads ;

Missing semicolons are the most common source of errors in SAS programs. For whatever reason, we humans can't seem to remember to put a semicolon at the end of all our statements. (Maybe we all have rebellious right pinkies—who knows.) This is unfortunate because, while it is easy to forget the semicolon, it is not always easy to find the missing semicolon. The error messages produced are often misleading, making it difficult to find the error.

SAS reads statements from one semicolon to the next without regard to the layout of the program. If you leave off a semicolon, you in effect concatenate two SAS statements. Then SAS gets confused because it seems as though you are missing statements, or it tries to interpret entire statements as options to the previous statement. This can produce some very puzzling messages. So, if you get an error message that just doesn't make sense, look for missing semicolons.

Example   The following program is missing a semicolon on the comment statement before the DATA statement:

```
* Read the data file toadjump.dat using list input
DATA toads;
   INFILE 'toadjump.dat';
   INPUT toadname $ weight jump1 jump2 jump3;
RUN;
```

Here is the SAS log after running the program:

```
1    * Read the data file toadjump.dat using list input
2    DATA toads;
3        INFILE 'toadjump.dat';
     ------
     180

ERROR 180-322: Statement is not valid or it is used out of proper
               order.

4        INPUT toadname $ weight jump1 jump2 jump3;
     -----
     180

ERROR 180-322: Statement is not valid or it is used out of proper order.

5    RUN;
```

In this case, DATA toads becomes part of the comment statement. Because there is now no DATA statement, SAS underlines the INFILE and INPUT keywords and says, "Hey these statements are in the wrong place; they have to be part of a DATA step." This doesn't make much sense to you because you know INFILE and INPUT are valid statements, and you did put them in a DATA step (or so you thought). That's when you should suspect a missing semicolon.

Example The next example shows the same program, but now the semicolon is missing from the DATA statement. The INFILE statement becomes part of the DATA statement, and SAS doesn't recognize 'toadjump.dat' as a valid part of the DATA statement. It also gives you an error saying that there is no CARDS or INFILE statement. In addition, you get some warnings about the data set being incomplete. This is a good example of how one simple mistake can produce a lot of confusing messages:

```
1    * Read the data file toadjump.dat using list input;
2    DATA toads
3       INFILE 'toadjump.dat';
             ------------
                200
4       INPUT toadname $ weight jump1 jump2 jump3;
5    RUN;

ERROR 200-322: The symbol is not recognized.

ERROR: No CARDS or INFILE statement.
NOTE: The SAS System stopped processing this step because of errors.
WARNING: The data set WORK.TOADS may be incomplete.  When this step was stopped there were
         0 observations and 5 variables.
WARNING: The data set WORK.INFILE may be incomplete.  When this step was stopped there were
         0 observations and 5 variables.
NOTE: The DATA statement used 1.69 seconds.
```

Missing semicolons can produce a variety of error messages. Usually the messages say that either a statement is not valid, or an option or parameter is not valid or recognized. Sometimes you don't get an error message, but the results are still not right. If you leave off the semicolon from the last RUN statement when using display manager mode, you won't get an error. But SAS won't run the last part of your program either.

Note: INPUT Statement Reached Past the End of the Line

The note "SAS went to a new line when INPUT statement reached past the end of a line" is rather innocent looking, but its presence can indicate a problem. This note often goes unnoticed. It doesn't come up in red or even yellow lettering. It doesn't cause your program to stop. But look for it in your SAS log because it is a common note that usually means there is a problem.

This message means that as SAS was reading your data, it got to the end of the data line before it read all the variables in your INPUT statement. When this happens, SAS goes by default to the next line of data to get values for the remaining variables. Sometimes this is exactly what you want SAS to do, but if it's not, take a good look at your SAS log and output to be sure you know why this is happening.

Look in your SAS log where it tells you the number of lines it read from the data file and the number of observations in the SAS data set. If you have fewer observations than lines read, and you planned on having one observation per line, then you know you have a problem. Print the SAS data set using PROC PRINT. This can be very helpful in determining the source of the problem.

Example   The following shows what can happen if you are using list input, and you don't have periods for missing values. You have the following data from the toad-jumping contest, where the toad's number is followed by its weight and distances for each of three jumps. When a toad was disqualified from a jump, no entry was made for that jump:

```
13   65 1.9 3.0
25 131 2.5 3.1 .5
10 202 3.8
8  128 3.2 1.9 2.6
3  162
21  99 2.4 1.7 3.0
```

The following is the SAS log from a program that reads the raw data using list input and prints the results using PROC PRINT:

```
1    DATA toads;
2       INFILE 'toadjmp2.dat';
3       INPUT toadnum weight jump1 jump2 jump3;

NOTE: The infile 'toadjmp2.dat' is:
      FILENAME=toadjmp2.dat,
      RECFM=V,LRECL=132
```

❶ NOTE: 6 records were read from the infile 'toadjmp2.dat'.
      The minimum record length was 6.
      The maximum record length was 18.
❸ NOTE: SAS went to a new line when INPUT statement reached past the
      end of a line.
❷ NOTE: The data set WORK.TOADS has 3 observations and 5 variables.
  NOTE: The DATA statement used 4.78 seconds.

```
4    PROC PRINT;
5        TITLE 'SAS Data Set Toads';
```

❶ Notice that there were six records read from the raw data file.

❷ But, there are only three observations in the SAS data set.

❸ The note `INPUT statement reached past the end of a line` should alert you that there may be a problem.

A look at the results of the PROC PRINT confirms that there is a problem since the numbers don't look at all correct. (Can a toad jump 128 feet?)

```
                          SAS Data Set Toads                        1

          OBS    TOADNUM    WEIGHT    JUMP1    JUMP2    JUMP3

           1        13         65      1.9       3      25.0
           2        10        202      3.8       8     128.0
           3         3        162     21.0      99       2.4
```

Here SAS went to a new line when you didn't want it to. To fix this problem, the simplest thing to do is use the MISSOVER option of the INFILE statement. MISSOVER instructs SAS to assign missing values to any variables for which there were no data instead of going to the next line for data. The INFILE statement would look like this:

```
INFILE 'toadjmp2.dat' MISSOVER;
```

There are several other reasons why you might get the message informing you that the INPUT statement reached past the end of the line:

▶ You planned on SAS going to the next data line when it ran out of data.

▶ Blank lines in your data file, usually at the beginning or end, can cause this message. Look at the minimum line length in the SAS log. If it is zero, then you have blank lines. Edit out the blank lines and re-run your program.

▶ If you are using list input and you do not have a space between every value, you can get this message. For example, if you try to read the following data using list input, SAS will run out of data for the Gilroy Garlics because there is no space between the 15 and the 1035. SAS will read it as one number, then read the 12 where it should have been reading the 1035, and so on. To correct this problem, either add a space between the two numbers, or use column or formatted input.

```
Columbia Peaches      35  67  1 10  2  1
Gilroy Garlics       151035 12 11  7  6
Sacramento Tomatoes  124  85 15  4  9  1
```

▶ If you have some data lines which are shorter than the rest, and you are using column or formatted input, this can cause a problem. If you try to read a name, for example, in columns 60–70 when some of the names only extend to column 68, and you didn't add spaces at the end of the line to fill it out to column 70, then SAS will go to the next line to read the name. To avoid this problem, add the PAD option in the INFILE statement to add spaces to the ends of the data lines:

```
INFILE 'names.dat' PAD;
```

INFILE statement
MISSOVER option
PAD option

Note: Lost Card

Lost card? You thought you were writing SAS programs, not playing a card game. This message makes more sense if you remember that computer programs and data used to be punched out on computer cards. A lost card means that SAS was expecting another line (or card) of data and didn't find it.

If you are reading multiple lines of data for each observation, then a lost card could mean you have missing or duplicate lines of data. If you are reading two data lines for each observation, then SAS will expect an even number of lines in the data file. If you have an odd number, then you will get the lost-card message. It can often be difficult to locate the missing or duplicate lines, especially with large data files. Printing the SAS data set as well as careful proofreading of the data file can be helpful in identifying problem areas.

Example The following example shows what can happen if you have a missing data line. The raw data show the normal high and low temperatures and the record high and low for the month of July for each city. The last city is missing the last data line:

```
Nome AK
55 44
88 29
Miami FL
90 75
97 65
Raleigh NC
88 68
```

The following shows the SAS log from a program which reads the data, three lines per observation:

```
1    DATA highlow;
2        INFILE 'temps.dat';
3        INPUT city $ state $ / normhigh normlow / rechigh reclow;

NOTE: The infile 'temps.dat' is:
      FILENAME=temps.dat,
      RECFM=V,LRECL=132

NOTE: LOST CARD.
CITY=Raleigh STATE=NC NORMHIGH=88 NORMLOW=68 RECHIGH=. RECLOW=.
_ERROR_=1 _N_=3
NOTE: 8 records were read from the infile 'temps.dat'.
      The minimum record length was 5.
      The maximum record length was 10.
NOTE: The data set WORK.HIGHLOW has 2 observations and 6 variables.
NOTE: The DATA statement used 2.29 seconds.
```

In this case, you get the lost-card message, and SAS prints the values of the variables it read for the observation with the lost card. The observation is not included in the SAS data set. You can see from the log that SAS read eight records from the file (it should have been a multiple of three) but the SAS data set only has two observations. The last partial observation was not included.

Example It is very common to get other messages along with the lost-card note. Invalid data is a common byproduct of the lost card. If the second line were missing from the temperature data, then you would get invalid data as well as a lost card because SAS will try to read Miami FL as the record high and low. The following shows the invalid data note from the SAS log:

```
Nome AK
88 29
Miami FL
90 75
97 65
Raleigh NC
88 68
105 50
```

```
NOTE: Invalid data for RECHIGH in line 3 1-5.
NOTE: Invalid data for RECLOW in line 3 7-8.
RULE:    ----+----1----+----2----+----3----+----4----+----5----+----6
3       Miami FL
CITY=Nome STATE=AK NORMHIGH=88 NORMLOW=29 RECHIGH=. RECLOW=. _ERROR_=1 _N_=1
```

Example In addition to getting the lost-card note, it is also common to get a note indicating that the INPUT statement reached past the end of a line. If you forgot the last number in the file, as in the following example, then you would get these two notes together:

```
Nome AK
55 44
88 29
Miami FL
90 75
97 65
Raleigh NC
88 68
105
```

Because the program uses list input, SAS will try to go to the next line to get the data for the last variable. Since there isn't another line of data, you get the lost-card message. The following is part of the SAS log showing these two messages together:

```
NOTE: LOST CARD.
CITY=Raleigh STATE=NC NORMHIGH=88 NORMLOW=68 RECHIGH=105 RECLOW=.
_ERROR_=1 _N_=3
NOTE: 9 records were read from the infile 'temps.dat'.
      The minimum record length was 3.
      The maximum record length was 10.
NOTE: SAS went to a new line when INPUT statement reached past the
      end of a line.
NOTE: The data set WORK.HIGHLOW has 2 observations and 6 variables.
NOTE: The DATA statement used 0.88 seconds.
```

For this example, the solution is to add the missing data to the raw data file and rerun the program.

Note: Invalid Data

The typical new SAS user, upon seeing the invalid data message, will ignore it, hoping perhaps that it will simply go away by itself. That's rather ironic considering that the message is explicit and easy to interpret once you know how to read it.

Interpreting the message   The invalid-data message appears when SAS is unable to read from a raw data file because the data are inconsistent with the INPUT statement. This message almost always indicates a problem. For example, one common mistake is typing in the letter O instead of the number 0. If the variable is numeric, then SAS is unable to interpret the letter O. In response, SAS does two things; it sets the value of this variable to missing and prints out a message like this for the problematic observation:

```
❶NOTE: Invalid data for ID in line 8 1-6.
❷RULE:       ----+----1----+----2----+----3----+----4
❷8           007   James Bond    SA341
❸ID=. NAME=James Bond CLASS=SA Q1=3 Q2=4 Q3=1 _ERROR_=1 _N_=8
```

❶ The first line of the message is the NOTE telling you where the problem occurred. Specifically, it states the name of the variable SAS got stuck on and the line number and columns of the raw data file that SAS was trying to read. In this example, the error occurred while SAS was trying to read a variable named ID from line 8 in columns 1–6 of the input file.

❷ The next line, labeled RULE, is a sort of ruler with columns as the increments. The 1 marks the 10th column, 2 marks the 20th, and so on. Immediately below the ruler, SAS dumps the actual line of raw data so you can see the little troublemaker for yourself. Using the ruler as a guide, you can count over to the column in question. At this point you can compare the actual raw data to your INPUT statement, and the error is usually obvious. The value of ID should be zero-zero-seven, but looking at the line of actual data you can see that a careless typist has typed zero-letter O-seven. Such an error may seem minor to you, but you'll soon learn that computers are hopelessly persnickety.

❸ As if this weren't enough, SAS prints one more piece of information: the values of each variable for that observation as SAS read it. In this case, you can see that ID equals missing, NAME equals James Bond, and so on. Two automatic variables appear at the end of the line: _ERROR_ and _N_. The _ERROR_ variable has a value of 1 if there is a data error for that observation, and 0 if there is not. In an invalid-data message, _ERROR_ always equals 1. _N_ is the number of times SAS has looped through the DATA step.

Unprintable characters   Occasionally invalid data contain unprintable characters such as a form-feed. Typically this happens when data are entered into some other software such as a spread sheet or word processor and then transferred to SAS without being properly written to a text file. In such cases, SAS also prints the raw data in hexadecimal format in two lines labeled ZONE and NUMR.

This invalid data message contains unprintable characters:

```
NOTE: Invalid data for ID in line 11 1-6.
RULE:      ----+----1----+----2----+----3----+----4

10  CHAR   ..   Indiana Jones PI83.
    ZONE   0122224666666246667254332222222222222222
    NUMR   DB00009E491E10AFE5300983E000000000000000

ID=. NAME=Indiana Jones CLASS=PI Q1=8 Q2=3 Q3=5 _ERROR_=1 _N_=10
```

You needn't understand hexadecimal values to be able to read this. SAS prints the data this way because the normal 10 numerals and 26 letters don't provide enough values to represent all computer symbols uniquely. Hexadecimal uses two characters to represent each symbol. To read hexadecimal, take a digit from the ZONE line together with the corresponding digit from the NUMR line. In this case, a form-feed and a carriage-return-line-feed slipped into columns 1–2 and appear as two harmless-looking periods in the CHAR line. In hexadecimal, however, the periods are translated as 0D and 1B, while a real period in column 25 is 2E in hex.[1]

Possible causes   Common reasons for receiving the invalid data message include

- using the letter O instead of the number zero
- forgetting to specify that a variable is character (SAS assumes it is numeric)
- incorrect column specifications producing embedded spaces in numeric data
- list-style data with two periods in a row and no space in between
- a missing period for free format-style input causing SAS to read the next data value
- special characters such as carriage-return-line-feed and form-feed
- invalid dates (such as September 31) read with a date informat.

---

[1] The codes for form-feed and carriage-return-line-feed vary among operating systems, so yours may be different.

The missing-values message appears when SAS is unable to compute the value of a variable because of pre-existing missing values in your data. This is not necessarily a problem. It is possible that your data contain legitimate missing values and that setting a new variable to missing is a desirable response. But it is also possible that the missing values result from an error and that you need to fix your program or your data. A good rule is to think of the missing-values message as a flag telling you to check for an error.

Example The SAS log below shows a program marred by the missing-values message. The program reads data about a toad-jumping contest and computes the average distance jumped by each toad. The raw data file appears below and contains four variables—the toad's name and the distance jumped in each of three trials:

```
Lucky   1.9  .   3.0
Spot    2.5 3.1 0.5
Tubs     .   .  3.8
Hop     3.2 1.9 2.6
Noisy   1.3 1.8 1.5
Winner   .   .   .
```

Notice that several of the toads have missing values for one or more jumps. To compute the average distance jumped, the program in the following SAS log reads the raw data, adds together the values for the three jumps, and divides by 3:

```
1    DATA toads;
2       INFILE 'jump.dat';
3       INPUT toadname $ jump1 jump2 jump3;
4       avgjump = (jump1 + jump2 + jump3) / 3;
5    RUN;

NOTE: The infile 'jump.dat' is:
      FILENAME=\jump.dat,
      RECFM=V,LRECL=132

NOTE: 6 records were read from the infile 'jump.dat'.
      The minimum record length was 18.
      The maximum record length was 18.

NOTE: ❶Missing values were generated as a result of performing an
      operation on missing values.
      ❷Each place is given by: (Number of times) at (Line):(Column)
        3 at 4:21   3 at 4:29   3 at 4:38

NOTE: The data set WORK.TOADS has 6 observations and 5 variables.
NOTE: The DATA statement used 5.21 seconds.
```

Because of missing values in the data, SAS was unable to compute AVGJUMP for some of the toads. In response, SAS printed the missing-values message which has two parts:

❶ The first part of the message is a NOTE saying that SAS was forced to set some values to missing.

❷ The second part is a bit more cryptic. SAS lists the number of times values were set to missing. This generally corresponds to the number of observations that generated missing values, unless the problem occurs within a DO-loop. Next SAS states where in the program it encountered the problem. In the preceding example, SAS set three values to missing: at line 4, column 21; then at line 4, column 29; and again at line 4, column 38. Looking at the program, you can see that line 4 is the line which calculates AVGJUMP. In column 21, the variable JUMP1 is added to the variable JUMP2; in column 29, the variable JUMP2 is added to the variable JUMP3; and in column 38 the sum of the jumps is divided by 3. Looking at the raw data, you can see that three observations have missing values for JUMP1, JUMP2, or JUMP3. Those observations are the three times mentioned in the missing-values message.

Finding the missing values In this case it was easy to find the observations with missing values. But if you had a data set with hundreds, or millions, of observations, then you couldn't just glance at the data. In that case, you could subset the problematic observations with a subsetting IF statement, and print them with a program like this:

```
DATA missing;
   INFILE 'jump.dat';
   INPUT toadname $ jump1 jump2 jump3;
   avgjump = (jump1 + jump2 + jump3) / 3;
   IF avgjump = .;

PROC PRINT;
   TITLE 'Observations with Missing Values Generated';
RUN;
```

Your output would look like this:

```
            Observations with Missing Values Generated        1

   OBS    TOADNAME    JUMP1    JUMP2    JUMP3    AVGJUMP

    1      Lucky       1.9       .       3.0        .
    2      Tubs         .        .       3.8        .
    3      Winner       .        .        .         .
```

Using the SUM and MEAN functions
It is possible to circumvent this problem when you are computing a sum or mean—just use the SUM or MEAN function instead of an arithmetic expression. In the preceding program, you could remove this line:

```
avgjump = (jump1 + jump2 + jump3) / 3;
```

And substitute this line:

```
avgjump = MEAN(jump1, jump2, jump3);
```

The SUM and MEAN functions exclude missing values from the computation. This means that SAS successfully computes a nonmissing value for the new variable and does not print the missing-values message.

8.8 Note: Numeric Values Have Been Converted to Character (or Vice Versa)

Even with only two data types, numeric and character, SAS programmers sometimes get their variables mixed up. When you accidentally mix numeric and character variables, SAS tries to patch together your program by converting variables from numeric to character or vice versa, as needed. Programmers sometimes try to ignore this message, but that is not a good idea. SAS is quite generous to try to fix your program, but a SAS solution may not be what you want. If you ignore this message, it may come back to haunt you as you find new incompatibilities resulting from the fix. If, indeed, a variable needs to be converted, you should do it yourself, explicitly, so you know what your variables are doing.

Example   To show how SAS handles this kind of incompatibility, here is the log from a program that mixes the two types of data:

```
1    DATA numchar;
2        a = 5;
3        b = '5';
4        c = a * b;
5        d = 98;
6        e = SUBSTR(d, 2, 1);
7    RUN;
NOTE: Character values have been converted to numeric
      values at the places given by: (Line):(Column).
      4:12
NOTE: Numeric values have been converted to character
      values at the places given by: (Line):(Column).
      6:15
NOTE: The data set WORK.NUMCHAR has 1 observations and 5 variables.
NOTE: The DATA statement used 1.42 seconds.
```

In this program the variable A is numeric because it is equal to the number 5; B is character because it is equal to 5 enclosed in quotes. The variable C is the product of A and B. Since character variables cannot be used in arithmetic expressions, SAS converts B to numeric and prints the values-have-been-converted message. This note tells you where in your program SAS found an incompatibility. In this case, the problem occurred at line 4, column 12. The variable name, B, appears at line 4, column 12, so you know that SAS converted B from character to numeric.

The variable D is numeric because it is equal to the number 98. However, in line 6 of the program, D is used in the SUBSTR function, which requires a character variable. To rectify the problem, SAS converts D to character and prints a note saying that numeric values were converted to character at line 6, column 15.

Converting variables   To convert variables from character to numeric, you use the INPUT function. To convert from numeric to character, you use the PUT function. Most often, you would use these functions in an assignment statement with the following syntax:

Character to Numeric	**Numeric to Character**
newvar = INPUT(*oldvar, informat*);	*newvar* = PUT(*oldvar, format*);

These two slightly eccentric functions are first cousins of the PUT and INPUT statements. Just as an INPUT statement uses informats, the INPUT function uses informats; and just as PUT statements use formats, the PUT function uses formats. These functions can be confusing because they are similar but different. In the case of the INPUT function, the informat must be the type you are converting to—numeric. In contrast, the format for the PUT function must be the type you are converting from—numeric.[1] To convert the troublesome variables in the program that mixes character and numeric variables, you would use these statements:

Character to Numeric

```
newb = INPUT(b, 1.);
```

Numeric to Character

```
newd = PUT(d, 2.);
```

If you rerun the preceding program with functions added to convert the variables, you will receive a log like this:

```
10    DATA numchar;
11       a = 5;
12       b = '5';
13       newb = INPUT(b, 1.);
14       c = a * newb;
16       d = 98;
17       newd = PUT(d, 2.);
18       e = SUBSTR(newd, 2, 1);
19    RUN;

NOTE: The data set WORK.CHARNUM has 1 observations and 7 variables.
NOTE: The DATA statement used 1.1 seconds.
```

Notice that this version of the program runs without any suspicious messages, and uses slightly less CPU time.

---

[1] In this discussion, we are talking about converting variables from numeric to character or vice versa, but you can also use the PUT function to change one character value to another character value. When you do this, *oldvar* and *newvar* would be character variables, and the format would be a character format.

Some of the hardest errors to debug aren't errors at all, at least not to SAS. If you do complex programming, you may write a DATA step that runs just fine—with no errors or suspicious notes—but produces the wrong results. The more complex your programs are, the more likely you are to get this kind of error. Sometimes it seems like a DATA step is a black box. You know what goes in, and you know what comes out, but what happens in the middle is a mystery. This problem is actually a logic error; somewhere along the way SAS got the wrong instruction.

Example Here is a program that illustrates this problem and how to debug it. The raw data file below contains five variables—student's name, scores from three tests, and score from homework:

```
Derek     72 64  56 39
Kathy     98 82 100 48
Linda     53 60  66 42
Michael 80 55  95 50
```

This program is supposed to select students whose average score is below 70, but it doesn't work. Here is the log from the wayward program:

```
1     * Keep only students with mean below 70;
2     DATA lowscore;
3        INFILE 'class.dat';
4        INPUT name $ score1 score2 score3 hmwk;
5        hmwk = hmwk * 2;
6        avgscore = MEAN(score1 + score2 + score3 + hmwk);
7        IF avgscore < 70;
8     RUN;

NOTE: The infile 'class.dat' is:
      FILENAME=class.dat,
      RECFM=V,LRECL=132

NOTE: 4 records were read from the infile 'class.dat'.
      The minimum record length was 20.
      The maximum record length was 20.
NOTE: The data set WORK.LOWSCORE has 0 observations and 6
      variables.
NOTE: The DATA statement used 9.76 seconds.
```

First, the DATA step reads the raw data from a file called CLASS.DAT. The highest possible score on homework is 50. To make the homework count the same as a test, the program doubles the value of HMWK. Then the program computes the mean of the three test scores and homework, and subsets the data by selecting only observations with a mean score below 70. Unfortunately, something went wrong. The LOWSCORE data set contains no observations. A glance at the raw data confirms that there should be students whose mean scores are below 70.

Using the PUT statement to debug To debug a problem like this, you have to figure out exactly what is happening inside the DATA step. A good way to do this is with PUT statements. Elsewhere in this book, PUT statements are used along with FILE statements to write raw data files and custom reports. If you use a PUT statement without a FILE statement, then SAS writes the data in the SAS log. That is just fine for debugging. PUT statements can take many forms, but for debugging, a handy style of PUT statement is

```
PUT _ALL_;
```

SAS will print all the variables in your data set: first the variable name, then the actual data value, with an equal sign in between. If you have a lot of variables, you can print just the relevant ones this way:

```
PUT varname = varname = ;
```

Without the equal signs, SAS would print just the data values. Adding the equal sign tells SAS to label the data so that you know which data values are which.

The DATA step below is identical to the one shown earlier except that a PUT statement was added. In a longer DATA step, you might choose to have more than one PUT statement. In this case, one will suffice. This PUT statement is placed before the subsetting IF, since in this particular program the subsetting IF eliminates all observations:

```
9     * Keep only students with mean below 70;
10    DATA lowscore;
11       INFILE 'class.dat';
12       INPUT name $ score1 score2 score3 hmwk;
13       hmwk = hmwk * 2;
14       avgscore = MEAN(score1 + score2 + score3 + hmwk);
15       PUT name= score1= score2= score3= hmwk= avgscore=;
16       IF avgscore < 70;
17    RUN;

NOTE: The infile 'class.dat' is:
      FILENAME=class.dat,
      RECFM=V,LRECL=132

NAME=Derek SCORE1=72 SCORE2=64 SCORE3=56 HMWK=78 AVGSCORE=270
NAME=Kathy SCORE1=98 SCORE2=82 SCORE3=100 HMWK=96 AVGSCORE=376
NAME=Linda SCORE1=53 SCORE2=60 SCORE3=66 HMWK=84 AVGSCORE=263
NAME=Michael SCORE1=80 SCORE2=55 SCORE3=95 HMWK=100 AVGSCORE=330

NOTE: 4 records were read from the infile 'class.dat'.
      The minimum record length was 20.
      The maximum record length was 20.
NOTE: The data set WORK.LOWSCORE has 0 observations and 6
      variables.
NOTE: The DATA statement used 5.16 seconds.
```

Looking at the the log, you can see the result of the PUT statement. The data listed in the middle of the log show that the variables are being input properly, and the variable HMWK is being adjusted properly. However, something is wrong with the values of AVGSCORE; they are much too high. There is a syntax error in the line that computes AVGSCORE. Instead of commas separating the three score variables in the MEAN function, there are addition signs. Since functions can contain arithmetic expressions, SAS simply added the four variables together, as instructed, and computed the mean of a single number.

8.10 Error: Invalid Option, Error: The Option is Not Recognized, or Error: Statement Is Not Valid

If SAS cannot make sense out of one of your statements, it stops executing the current DATA or PROC step and prints one of these messages:

```
ERROR 22-7: Invalid option name.
ERROR 202-322: The option or parameter is not recognized.
ERROR 180-322: Statement is not valid or it is used out of proper order.
```

The invalid-option message and its cousin, the option-is-not-recognized message, tell you that you have a valid statement, but SAS can't make sense out of an apparent option. The statement-is-not-valid message, on the other hand, means that SAS can't understand the statement at all. Thankfully, with all three messages SAS underlines the point at which it got confused.

Example The SAS log below contains an invalid option:

```
1    DATA class (ROP = score1);
              ---
              22
2        INFILE 'scores.dat';
3        INPUT score1 score2;

ERROR 22-7: Invalid option name ROP.

NOTE: The SAS System stopped processing this step because of errors.
NOTE: The DATA statement used 2.52 seconds.
```

In this DATA step, the word DROP was misspelled as ROP. Since SAS cannot interpret this, it underlines the word ROP, prints the invalid-option message, and stops processing the DATA step.

Example The following log contains an option-not-recognized message:

```
1    PROC PRINT
2        VAR score2;
         --- ------
         202 202
3    RUN;

ERROR 202-322: The option or parameter is not recognized.

NOTE: The SAS System stopped processing this step because of errors.
NOTE: The PROCEDURE PRINT used 1.42 seconds.
```

SAS underlined the VAR statement. This message may seem puzzling since VAR is not an option, but a statement, and a valid statement at that. But if you look at the previous statement, you will see that the PROC statement is missing one of those pesky semicolons. As a result, SAS tried to interpret the words VAR and SCORE2 as options for the PROC statement. Since no options exist with those names, SAS stopped processing the step and printed the option-not-recognized message.

Example   Here is a log with the statement-is-not-valid message:

```
4    PROC PRINT;
5       SET class;
        ---
        180
6    RUN;

ERROR 180-322: Statement is not valid or it is used out of proper order.

NOTE: The SAS System stopped processing this step because of errors.
NOTE: The PROCEDURE PRINT used 0.27 seconds.
```

In this case, a SET statement was used in a PROC step. Since SET statements can only be used in DATA steps, SAS underlines the word SET and prints the statement-is-not-valid message.

Possible causes   Generally, with these error messages, the cause of the problem is easy to detect. You should check the underlined item and the previous statement for possible errors. Possible causes include

- a misspelled keyword
- a missing semicolon
- a DATA step statement in a PROC step (or vice versa)
- the correct option with the wrong statement
- an unmatched quote.

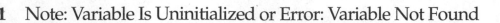

8.11 Note: Variable Is Uninitialized or Error: Variable Not Found

If you find one of these messages in your SAS log, then SAS is telling you that the variable named in the message does not exist:

```
NOTE: Variable X is uninitialized.

ERROR: Variable X not found.
```

Generally, the first time you get one of these messages, it is quite a shock. You may be sure that the variable does exist. After all, you remember creating it. Fortunately, the problem is usually easy to fix once you understand what SAS is telling you.

If the problem happens in a DATA step, then SAS prints the note above, initializes the variable, and continues to execute your program. Normally variables are initialized when they are read (via an INPUT, SET, MERGE, or UPDATE statement) or when they are created via an assignment statement. If you use a variable for the first time in a way that does not assign a value to the variable (such as on the right side of an assignment statement, in the condition of an IF statement, or in a DROP or KEEP option) then SAS tries to fix the problem by assigning a value of missing to the variable for all observations. This is very generous of SAS, but it almost never fixes the problem; you probably don't want the variable to have missing values for all observations.

When the problem happens in a PROC step, the results are more grave. SAS prints the error message above and does not execute the step.

Example Here is the log from a program with both types of missing variable problems:

```
1    DATA highscor (KEEP = name total);
2       INPUT name $ score1 score2;
3       IF scor1 > 5;
4       total = score1 + score2;
5       CARDS;

NOTE: Variable SCOR1 is uninitialized.
NOTE: The data set WORK.HIGHSCOR has 0 observations and 2 variables.
NOTE: The DATA statement used 6.04 seconds.

6    PROC PRINT;
7       VAR name score2 total;

ERROR: Variable SCORE2 not found.

8    RUN;

NOTE: The SAS System stopped processing this step because of errors.
NOTE: The PROCEDURE PRINT used 0.93 seconds.
```

In this DATA step, the INPUT statement reads three variables: NAME, SCORE1, and SCORE2. But a misspelling in the subsetting IF statement causes SAS to initialize a new variable named SCOR1. Because SCOR1 has missing values, none of the observations satisfy the subsetting IF, and the data set HIGHSCOR is left with zero observations.

In the PROC PRINT, the VAR statement requests three variables: NAME, SCORE2, and TOTAL. SCORE2 did exist but was dropped from the data set by the KEEP option in the DATA statement. That KEEP option kept only two variables, NAME and TOTAL. As a result, SAS prints the variable-not-found error message and does not execute the PROC PRINT.

Possible causes Common ways to "lose" variables include

- misspelling a variable name
- using a variable that was dropped at some earlier time
- using the wrong data set
- a logic error, such as using a variable before it is created.

If the source of the problem is not immediately obvious, PROC CONTENTS can often help you figure out what is going on. PROC CONTENTS, which is discussed in section 3.11, gives you information about what is in a SAS data set including variable names.

Sometimes you may notice that some, or all, of the values of a character variable are truncated. You may be expecting "peanut butter" and get "peanut b" or "chocolate ice cream" and get "chocolate ice." This usually happens when you use IF statements to create a new character variable, or when you are using list-style input and you have values longer than eight characters.

chocolate ice
peanut b

All character variables have a fixed length. The length is determined by one of the following methods.

INPUT statement If a variable is read from a raw data file, then the length is determined by the INPUT statement. If you are using list-style input, then the length defaults to 8. If you are using column or formatted input, then the length is determined by the number of columns, or informat. The following shows examples of INPUT statements that read the FOOD variable and the resulting lengths of FOOD:

INPUT statement	Length of FOOD
INPUT food;	8
INPUT food $ 1-10;	10
INPUT food $15.;	15

Assignment statement If you are creating the variable in an assignment statement, then the length is determined by the first occurrence of the new variable name. For example, the following program creates a variable, STATUS, whose values are determined by the TEMP variable:

```
DATA summer;
   SET temps;
   IF temp > 100 THEN status = 'HOT';
      ELSE status = 'COLD';
RUN;
```

Because the word HOT has three characters and that is the first statement which uses the variable, STATUS has a length of 3. Any other values for that variable would be truncated to three characters (COL instead of COLD for example).

LENGTH statement The LENGTH statement in a DATA step defines variable lengths and, if it comes before the INPUT or assignment statement, will override either of the previous two methods of determining length. The following LENGTH statement sets the length of the STATUS variable to 4 and the FOOD variable to 15:

```
LENGTH status $4 food $15;
```

ATTRIB statement You can also assign variable lengths in an ATTRIB statement in a DATA step where you can associate formats, informats, labels, and lengths to variables in a single statement. For example, the following statement assigns the character variable STATUS a length of 4 and the label Hot or Cold:

```
ATTRIB status LENGTH = $4 LABEL = 'Hot or Cold';
```

Example The following example shows what can happen if you let SAS determine the length of a character variable (in this case, using the assignment statement method). You have the following data for a consumer survey of car color preferences. The person's age is followed by their sex (coded as 1 for male and 2 for female), annual income, and preferred car color (yellow, gray, blue, or white):

```
19 1 14000 Y
45 1 65000 G
72 2 35000 B
31 1 44000 Y
58 2 83000 W
```

You want to create a new variable, AGEGROUP, which has these values: Teen for customers under 20, Adult for ages 20-64, and Senior for those 65 and over. In the following program, a series of IF-THEN/ELSE statements create AGEGROUP:

```
DATA carsurv;
    INFILE 'cars.dat';
    INPUT age sex income color $;
    IF age < 20 THEN agegroup = 'Teen';
        ELSE IF age < 65 THEN agegroup = 'Adult';
        ELSE agegroup = 'Senior';
PROC PRINT;
    TITLE 'Car Color Survey Results';
RUN;
```

The following results of the PROC PRINT show how the values of AGEGROUP are truncated to 4 characters—the number of characters in Teen.

```
                        Car Color Survey Results                1

            OBS    AGE    SEX    INCOME    COLOR    AGEGROUP

             1      19     1      14000      Y        Teen
             2      45     1      65000      G        Adul
             3      72     2      35000      B        Seni
             4      31     1      44000      Y        Adul
             5      58     2      83000      W        Adul
```

The addition of a LENGTH statement in the program, as follows, would eliminate the truncation problem:

```
* Use the LENGTH statement to set the length of agegroup;
DATA carsurv;
    INFILE 'cars.dat';
    INPUT age sex income color $;
    LENGTH agegroup $7;
    IF age < 20 THEN agegroup = 'Teen';
        ELSE IF age < 65 THEN agegroup = 'Adult';
        ELSE agegroup = 'Senior';
RUN;
```

LENGTH statement
ATTRIB statement

8.13   SAS Stops in the Middle of a Job

One of the most disconcerting errors encountered by SAS users is having SAS stop in the middle of a job. It's as if your program has suddenly dropped dead without so much as an error message to act as a smoking gun. Without an error message, you are left to sleuth this problem on your own. Often the problem has nothing to do with SAS. Instead the operating system may have stopped your program in its tracks. Other times the problem results from programming errors that prevent SAS from seeing the entire job.

A number of completely unrelated reasons can cause SAS to stop in the middle of a job. They are listed below, starting with the most general problems and ending with the ones that are specific to certain execution modes or operating systems.

An unmatched quote   Unmatched quotation marks wreak havoc with SAS programs, including making SAS stop in the middle of a job. In this case, SAS stops because, in effect, it thinks the remainder of the job is part of a quote. In batch or noninteractive mode, the solution is simple enough. Insert the missing quotation mark and resubmit the program. In display manager you can't just resubmit the program because SAS is still waiting for the other quote. The solution is to submit a sacrificial quote like this:

```
';
RUN;
```

Then recall your program, correct the problem (remembering to delete the extra quote and RUN statement at the end), and rerun the program. Some people prefer to exit SAS and start over. If you do, just remember to recall and save your program before exiting.

An unmatched comment   Unmatched comments can cause SAS to stop in the middle of a program, much like unmatched quotes. The problem is that SAS can't read the entire program because part of it is accidentally stuck in a comment. This isn't so likely to happen if you use the kind of comment that starts with an asterisk and ends with a semicolon since programs contain so many semicolons, and any semicolon will do to end a comment. But if you use the style of comments that starts with /* and ends with */, and forget to include the last */, then SAS will assume that the remainder of your job is one long comment. The solution, in batch or noninteractive mode is to insert the missing end-of-comment and resubmit the program. In display manager, the solution is to submit a lone end-of-comment like this:

```
*/;
RUN;
```

Then recall your program, correct the problem (remembering to delete the extra end of comment and RUN statement at the end), and rerun the program. Some people prefer to exit SAS and start over. If you do, just remember to recall and save your program before exiting.

No RUN statement at the end of a program   This problem occurs only in dispay manager. In noninteractive or in batch mode there is an implicit RUN at the end of every SAS job. The problem is that in interactive mode SAS has no way of knowing when it is time to execute your last step unless you tell it with a RUN statement. The solution is to submit the wayward statement.

```
RUN;
```

Out of time Batch systems often have time limits, measured in CPU seconds, for computer jobs. These limits are set locally by your system programmers. And these limits are helpful because they allow small jobs to be submitted to a special queue with a higher priority. That way your short job doesn't have to wait for some mega-job to finish processing. Time limits may also be set to stop jobs that accidentally get into an infinite loop. If your job stops in the middle, and you are running in batch mode, and you can find no unmatched quotes or comments, then you should consider whether your job might have stopped because it ran into a time limit. To find out how to fix this problem, talk to your local SAS Software Consultant or systems programmer.

/* in the first column under MVS Under MVS there is a unique hazard. Recall that one style of SAS comment starts with a slash-asterisk (/*). Batch jobs under MVS use Job Control Language (JCL). In JCL a /* starting in column one signals the end of your program file. So if SAS programmers start a comment with a /* in column one, they inadvertently instruct MVS to stop right then and there. SAS never even sees the remainder of the job. The solution, of course, is to move the comment out of column one or to change to a comment starting with an asterisk (*) and ending with a semicolon (;).

8.14 SAS Runs Out of Memory or Disk Space

What do you do when you finally get your program running, and you get a message that your computer is out of memory or disk space? Well, you could petition to buy a bigger computer, which isn't really such a bad idea, but there are a few things you can try before resorting to spending money. Because this issue is very system dependent, it is not possible to cover everything you might be able to do in this section. However, this section describes a few universal actions you can take to remedy the situation. If none of these things work, then seek out your site's SAS Software Consultant for advice.

It is helpful, in trying to solve the problem, to know why it happens. Usually when you run out of memory, it's when you are doing some pretty intensive computations or sorting data sets with lots of variables. The GLM procedure (General Linear Models), for example, can use lots of memory when your model is complicated and there are many levels for each classification variable. You run out of disk space because SAS uses disk to store all its temporary working files, including temporary SAS data sets, and the SAS log and output. If you are creating many large temporary SAS data sets during the course of a SAS session, this can quickly fill up your disk space.

Memory and disk space   One thing you can do to help decrease disk storage is decrease the number of bytes needed to store data. This can also help memory problems that arise when sorting data sets with character data. Since all numbers are expanded to the fullest precision while SAS is processing data, changing storage requirements for numeric data will not help memory problems. Both character, if using list input, and numeric variables have a default storage requirement of 8 bytes. This works for most situations. But if memory or disk space is at a premium, you can usually find some variables which require fewer bytes.

For character data, each character requires one byte of storage. The length of a character variable is determined by either the INPUT statement, the LENGTH or ATTRIB statement, or, if it is created in an assignment statement, the length of the first value. If you are using list input, then variables are given a length of 8. If your data are only one character long, Y or N for example, then you are using 8 times the storage space you actually need. You can use the LENGTH statement before the INPUT statement to change the default length. For example, the following gives the character variable ANSWER a length of one byte:

```
LENGTH answer $1;
```

If you are using column input, then the length is equal to the number of columns you are reading; if you are using formatted input, then the length is equal to the width of the format. You can change the lengths of variables in existing SAS data sets by using a LENGTH statement between a DATA statement and a SET, MERGE, or UPDATE statement.

Disk space   If you are running out of disk space, in addition to shortening the lengths of character variables, you may also be able to decrease the lengths of numeric variables. Numeric data are a little trickier than character when it comes to length. All numbers can be safely stored in 8 bytes, and that's why 8 is the default. Some numbers can be safely stored in fewer bytes, but which numbers depends on your operating system. The SAS Companion documentation for your operating system gives information on which numbers can be stored in how many bytes. In general, if your numbers contain decimal values, then you must use 8 bytes. If you have small integer values, then you can use 4 bytes (on some operating systems 2 or 3 bytes). Use the LENGTH statement to change the lengths of numeric data:

```
LENGTH tigers 4;
```

This statement changes the length of the numeric variable TIGERS to 4 bytes. If your numbers are categorical, like 1 for male and 2 for female, then you can read them as character data with a length of 1 and save even more space.

Another thing you can try if you are running out of disk space, is to decrease the number and size of SAS data sets created during a SAS session. If you are only going to use a fraction of your data for analysis, then subset your data as soon as possible using the subsetting IF statement. For example, if you only needed observations for females, then use the following statement in your DATA step:

```
IF sex = 'female';
```

If you only need to look at a few of the variables in your data set, then use the KEEP= (or DROP=) data set option to decrease the number of variables. For example, if you had a data set containing information about all the zoo animals, but you only wanted to look at the lions and tigers, then you could use the following statements to create a data set with only the LIONS and TIGERS variables:

```
DATA partial;
    SET zooanmls (KEEP = lions tigers);
```

The SAS log and output also take up disk space. If you are using display manager, then clear the SAS log and output often.

If you have more than one disk on your system, then you might be able to have SAS store its working files in a different location where there is more space. See the SAS Companion documentation for your operating system, or check with your site's SAS Software Consultant for more information on how to do this.

Memory   If memory is your problem, then do what you can to eliminate other programs that are using your computer's memory. If you are using display manager to run your SAS programs, try running in batch or noninteractive mode instead. The display manager takes quite a lot of memory, and on a personal computer it can be a significant fraction of the total available memory. Also, see the SAS Companion documentation for your operating system for potential ways to make more memory available on your system.

If you have tried all of the above, and you are still running out of memory or disk space, then you can always try finding a bigger computer. One of the nice things about SAS is that the language is the same for all operating systems. To move your program to another operating system, you would only need to change a few statements like INFILE, which deal directly with the operating system. If you are using permanent SAS data sets, you would also need to transport them to be able to use them on a different operating system. Section 3.15 discusses transporting SAS data sets.

DROP= data set option
KEEP= data set option
LENGTH statement

> "The riders in a race do not stop short when they reach their goal. There is little finishing canter before coming to a standstill. There is time to hear the kind voice of friends and to say to one's self: 'The work is done.' But just as one says that, the answer comes: 'The race is over, but the work never is done while the power to work remains.'

JUSTICE OLIVER WENDELL HOLMES, JR.

From a radio address on the occasion of his 90th birthday, March 8, 1931. *Bartlett's Familiar Quotations* 13th edition, by John Bartlett, copyright 1955 by Little, Brown and Company. Fair use consent by the publisher.

APPENDICES

Appendix A   Where to Go from Here

The goal of this book is to get you started using SAS and to teach you basic principles of SAS programming. For some of you, this book may be all you need. Others, however, may need to go beyond this book. This section lists sources for other training and information about the SAS System. Contact SAS Institute for more information on any of the following items. You may also have additional sources of information, developed locally, at your site. Check with your site's SAS Software Consultant for more information.

SAS Manuals   SAS Institute publishes many manuals about their software. They fall into several general categories: Getting Started, Reference, Usage, Syntax, Examples, and Technical Reports. The Getting Started series of manuals is designed to get you started using a particular piece of SAS software. The Reference series is for looking up information about SAS procedures and statements. All statements are discussed in the reference manuals, and the syntax is given. The Usage series is designed to be more instructive than the Reference series—giving many examples and explanations. The Syntax guides are small books giving just syntax, and the Examples series is designed for people who learn best by example. The Technical Reports either deal with specific topics or document changes and enhancements to the SAS System for a given release of the software.

Books by Users   There are many titles in the Books by Users series offered by SAS Institute. These books are written by users of SAS software, and thus offer a different perspective from the SAS manuals. Topics range from very general and introductory to very specific.

SAS/TUTOR   SAS/TUTOR is a product of SAS Institute and is licensed separately. These online courses are highly interactive and cover a broad range of topics from general introduction to specialized areas. You can license each course individually or the whole library.

HELP Window   The HELP window in the SAS Display Manager System provides useful information on the SAS System. Help is provided on SAS windows, statements, host information, report writing, data management, and much more.

SAS Institute Training Courses   The Institute offers courses on SAS software taught by instructors at regional offices. These courses cover many topics and vary in length and cost. You can also arrange to have on-site training for many of the courses. In addition to the instructor-based courses, SAS also offers video-based courses. Contact the Institute for more information about either of these training opportunities.

SAS Users Groups

SAS has a network of users groups which spans the globe. There are in-house groups, local groups, and regional and international groups. The regional and international groups generally meet once a year for several days. Talks are given by users and SAS employees; there are workshops and training opportunities and usually vendor exhibits. SAS Users Group International (SUGI) is the largest users group. Local and in-house groups usually meet more frequently for a shorter duration. These user-group meetings can be a great source of information about SAS software.

SAS Communications and Observations

These two magazines published by SAS Institute are good sources of information. *SAS Communications* is available to all SAS users at no extra cost. It covers news items like capabilities of new releases of SAS software, has articles of general interest, and has some technical information. *Observations* is a technical journal for SAS software users and is available at an additional cost.

SAS L

SAS L is an electronic mailing list of SAS users all over the world. (With electronic mailing lists, you send a message to the list, and a copy is sent to each person on the list.) This group of people helps each other solve SAS problems, discuss SAS philosophy, post announcements, and discuss whatever else seems related to SAS. Contact your site's SAS Software Consultant for information on how to subscribe to this high-volume list.

SAS Technical Support

If you are really stuck on a SAS problem, you should contact your site's SAS Software Consultant for help. If the consultant is unable to help you, then he or she can call SAS Technical Support for help. Technical Support keeps answers to many questions online, so often you are able to get an answer to your question right away. If not, they will assign your problem to a support person, and you will usually get a response in a day or so. You may also get help using SAS Technical Support's electronic services. Contact SAS Institute for more information.

Appendix B   An Overview of SAS Products

SAS Institute licenses many different products. This book covers elements from Base SAS software and SAS/STAT software. You can see from the following list that there is much more to SAS than just these two products. Fortunately, most of the products are integrated, so you don't have to convert data sets or start up another program to use the other products. The following is a partial list of SAS products with brief descriptions. Since the number of SAS products is constantly changing, check the most recent *SAS Communications* for a current list. You must have Base SAS installed on your system to run most of these products. Not all products are available for all operating systems. Contact SAS Institute for more information on any of their products:

Base SAS	must be installed on your system to run most of the other SAS products. Base SAS includes the DATA step for manipulating your data and simple statistical and utilitarian procedures.
SAS/ACCESS	allows you access to data used by other software packages. You can read and, in some cases, write data in their native formats without having to leave the SAS System. Most of the popular database software is supported, and each has its own SAS/ACCESS product.
SAS/AF	allows you to write your own interactive SAS applications. Applications written with SAS/AF allow users quick-and-easy access to information without knowing the SAS language.
SAS/ASSIST	is a menu-driven front end to SAS. You make choices from menus, and SAS writes the program for you. Programs can be stored for later use.
SAS/CALC	is a spreadsheet application.
SAS/CONNECT	connects computers running the SAS System. Data can be shared between the computers, and programs developed on one computer or operating system can be transferred to another for processing.
SAS/CPE	is for computer performance evaluation, capacity planning, tuning, and problem determination. This product allows you to access, analyze, and produce reports of your computer's or network's performance data.
SAS/EIS	allows you to develop and use custom executive information systems. Managers can use the EIS interfaces to SAS to quickly get the information they need by simply pointing and clicking (with a mouse of course).
SAS/ENGLISH	provides a natural language interface for accessing data stored in the SAS System. A Knowledge Base is used to associate words and concepts with your data.
SAS/ETS	has many procedures for analysis of time series data, forecasting, and business planning.

SAS/FSP	are full screen products that provide interactive methods for data entry, editing, and retrieval. Custom data entry screens can be developed with error checking built in.
SAS/GIS	is a geographic information system for analyzing data with spatial relationships.
SAS/GRAPH	produces high-resolution plots, charts, and maps.
SAS/IML	Interactive Matrix Language is a programming language with an extensive set of mathematical and matrix operators.
SAS/INSIGHT	is a tool for visual analysis of your data. Statistical results are displayed graphically whenever possible and interactive manipulation of data is possible.
SAS/LAB	is for guided statistical analysis. This product is good for people who need to analyze data but do not have a background in statistics.
SAS/NVISION	offers high-end, three-dimensional graphics capabilities.
SAS/OR	provides procedures for project management and operations research. Included in its capabilities are linear programming, Gantt charts, activity networks, and decision analysis.
SAS/PH-Clinical	has tools for pharmaceutical industries involved with drug research and development.
SAS/QC	provides procedures for statistical quality improvement, including methods for experimental design, improved process, and statistical control.
SAS/SHARE	provides concurrent access to data by multiple users.
SAS/SPECTRAVIEW	is a tool for analysis and visualization of three-dimensional data.
SAS/STAT	has procedures for most types of statistical analyses including many forms of regression and analysis of variance.
SAS/TOOLKIT	gives you the capability of writing your own SAS procedures, functions, formats, informats, and engines.
SAS/TUTOR	is an online tool for learning the SAS software. There are lessons covering many different aspects of the SAS System.

SAS Institute has other products which are not integrated into the SAS System. These products include the following. Not all of these products are available for all operating systems:

JMP	provides interactive data analysis for the Macintosh.
SAS/C	is a C compiler and library products.
SYSTEM 2000	is data management software with multi-user capabilities.

Appendix C   Coming to SAS from SPSS

More often than not, the first question asked by people who know SPSS and want to learn SAS is "How do the two software packages compare?" No simple answer is possible. Two facts make it difficult to draw hard-and-fast comparisons between SAS and SPSS. First, both products are continually evolving, with new releases introducing new capabilities. Second, SPSS varies significantly among operating systems in both style and function. For example, some advice for SPSS users under Windows would be irrelevant to SPSS users under MVS, and vice versa. Nonetheless, general comparisons can be drawn.

SAS and SPSS are very similar. Compared to other statistical software, these two products (plus a few others) are similar because they are languages. Most other statistical packages are extremely rigid, lacking the flexibility of a language. Compared to other computer languages, SAS and SPSS are similar because of their powerful, built-in data handling and statistical capabilities.

Despite their fundamental similarities, SAS and SPSS have different styles. SAS is more diverse, especially when you consider the entire family of SAS products. "Appendix B" contains a listing of SAS Institute products at the time this book was written. Most of these products are integrated, so they can be used seamlessly with Base SAS. SAS has more options. More options mean more power to get exactly what you want. People who do really complex programming find they can do things with SAS that would be impossible to do with SPSS.

Terminology   Some vocabulary differences exist between SAS and SPSS. To help you translate from one language to the other, here is a brief dictionary of analogous terms:

SPSS term	Analogous SAS term
active file	*no analogous term*
no analogous term	temporary SAS data set
case	observation
command	statement
display file	log file
display file	listing or output file
file handle	libref
function	function
input format	informat
numeric data	numeric data
output format	format
portable file	SAS transport data set
system file	permanent SAS data set
string data	character data
value label	user-defined format
variable	variable
variable label	label
no analogous term	DATA step
no analogous term	PROC step

Active files   The concept of an active file in SPSS has no equivalent in SAS. When you read data in an SPSS program, SPSS creates an active system file. This active file is similar to a temporary SAS data set because it exists only for the duration of the SPSS session, just as temporary SAS data sets exist only for the duration of a SAS session. However, SPSS has only one active file at a time, while SAS can have any number of temporary or permanent data sets. When you run an analysis in SPSS, the data must come from the active file. When you run an analysis in SAS, by default SAS will use the data set most recently created. But you can easily use any other SAS data set including the permanent SAS data set you created last week and haven't touched since. All SAS data sets are always active.

DATA and PROC steps   The SAS language has some concepts that have no parallel in SPSS, such as DATA and PROC steps. All SAS programs are divided into these two types of steps. Basically, DATA steps read and modify data while PROC (short for procedure) steps perform specific analyses or functions such as sorting, writing reports, regression or factor analysis. SPSS programs do the same types of operations but without distinct steps.

Interactive and batch modes   Both SAS and SPSS give you a choice of modes. You can create your program in a menu-driven interactive system, or you can write your program with an editor and submit it noninteractively or in batch. SAS works basically the same on all operating systems. SPSS, however, differs from one operating system to another. To make the following examples apply to as many SPSS users as possible, they were run in batch mode on the VMS operating system.

Examples   To provide a comparison, the following two programs perform the same operations in SPSS and SAS. A radio station commissioned a market research company to survey listeners. Respondents are asked to listen to songs and rate them on a scale of 1 to 5, with 1 being "dislike very much" and 5 being "like very much." Here is a sample of the raw data. The variables are first name, age, sex, and the ratings for five songs:

```
Gail     14 1 5 3 1 3 5
Jim      56 2 3 2 2 3 2
Susan    34 1 4 2 1 1 5
Barbara  45 1 3 3 1 2 4
Steve    13 2 5 4 1 4 5
```

The two programs below read the same raw data file and produce the same types of reports:

SPSS Program

```
DATA LIST FILE=survey.dat
   /name 1-8 (A) age 9-10
   sex 12 song1 TO song5 13-22.
VARIABLE LABELS
   song1 'Black Water/DB'
   song2 'Bennie and the Jets/EJ'
   song3 'Stayin Alive/BG'
   song4 'Fire and Rain/JT'
   song5 'Country Roads/JD'.
VALUE LABELS
   sex 1 'female' 2 'male'.
TITLE 'Music Market Survey'.
LIST.
FREQUENCIES
   VARIABLES = song1.
CROSSTABS
   /TABLES = sex BY song1.
SAVE OUTFILE = 'survey.sav'.
```

SAS program

```
LIBNAME mydir '[]';
DATA mydir.survey;
   INFILE 'survey.dat';
   INPUT name $ 1-8 age
         sex song1-song5;
   LABEL song1 = 'Black Water/DB'
         song2 = 'Bennie and the Jets/EJ'
         song3 = 'Stayin Alive/BG'
         song4 = 'Fire and Rain/JT'
         song5 = 'Country Roads/JD';
PROC FORMAT;
   VALUE sex 1 = 'female'
             2 = 'male';
TITLE 'Music Market Survey';
PROC PRINT;
PROC FREQ;
   TABLE song1 sex * song1;
   FORMAT sex sex.;
RUN;
```

The following table shows which SPSS commands and SAS statements perform the same operations:

SPSS command	SAS statement
DATA LIST	INFILE and INPUT
VARIABLE LABELS	LABEL
VALUE LABELS	PROC FORMAT
TITLE	TITLE
LIST	PROC PRINT
FREQUENCIES and CROSSTABS	PROC FREQ
SAVE OUTFILE	LIBNAME and DATA

SPSS display file   Here are the reports from the SPSS display file. To make the output easier to read, the program commands and system notes have been deleted:

```
NAME      AGE SEX SONG1 SONG2 SONG3 SONG4 SONG5

Gail       14  1    5     3     1     3     5
Jim        56  2    3     2     2     3     2
Susan      34  1    4     2     1     1     5
Barbara    45  1    3     3     1     2     4
Steve      13  2    5     4     1     4     5


SONG1     Black Water/DB

                                            Valid    Cum
  Value Label    Value  Frequency  Percent  Percent  Percent

                   3        2       40.0     40.0     40.0
                   4        1       20.0     20.0     60.0
                   5        2       40.0     40.0    100.0
                                   -------  -------  -------
                Total        5      100.0    100.0

Valid cases      5      Missing cases      0


SEX   by  SONG1  Black Water/DB

                    SONG1           Page 1 of 1
             Count |
                   |
                   |                      Row
                   |    3|    4|    5| Total
  SEX        -------+------+------+------+
               1 |    1|    1|    1|    3
       female    |     |     |     | 60.0
             +------+------+------+
               2 |    1|     |    1|    2
       male      |     |     |     | 40.0
             +------+------+------+
           Column    2     1     2     5
            Total   40.0  20.0  40.0 100.0

Number of Missing Observations:   0
```

SAS output The following SAS output looks similar to the SPSS display file. One difference is that the results of SAS procedures are written to a separate file, so you don't have to wade through the program statements and notes from the computer to find your results the way you normally do with SPSS:

```
                        Music Market Survey                    1

     OBS   NAME     AGE   SEX   SONG1   SONG2   SONG3   SONG4   SONG5

      1    Gail      14    1      5       3       1       3       5
      2    Jim       56    2      3       2       2       3       2
      3    Susan     34    1      4       2       1       1       5
      4    Barbara   45    1      3       3       1       2       4
      5    Steve     13    2      5       4       1       4       5


                        Music Market Survey                    2

                        Black Water/DB

                                      Cumulative   Cumulative
     SONG1   Frequency   Percent      Frequency    Percent
     -------------------------------------------------------
       3         2         40.0           2          40.0
       4         1         20.0           3          60.0
       5         2         40.0           5         100.0


                     TABLE OF SEX BY SONG1

        SEX          SONG1(Black Water/DB)

        Frequency|
        Percent  |
        Row Pct  |
        Col Pct  |      3|      4|      5|  Total
        ---------+-------+-------+-------+
        female   |    1  |    1  |    1  |    3
                 | 20.00 | 20.00 | 20.00 | 60.00
                 | 33.33 | 33.33 | 33.33 |
                 | 50.00 |100.00 | 50.00 |
        ---------+-------+-------+-------+
        male     |    1  |    0  |    1  |    2
                 | 20.00 |  0.00 | 20.00 | 40.00
                 | 50.00 |  0.00 | 50.00 |
                 | 50.00 |  0.00 | 50.00 |
        ---------+-------+-------+-------+
        Total         2       1       2       5
                   40.00   20.00   40.00  100.00
```

Getting SPSS system files into SAS   SAS can read SPSS system files and portable files. To do this you use a LIBNAME statement with this form:

```
LIBNAME libref SPSS 'filename';
```

After the keyword LIBNAME, you put the libref (similar to an SPSS file handle), then put the option SPSS followed by the name of your SPSS system or portable file. The option SPSS tells SAS to use the SPSS engine (instead of the default SAS data set engine) to read your data set. On some operating systems, SAS can read only SPSS portable files; on others it can read SPSS and SPSS-X compressed and uncompressed system files too. To find out what you can do, check the SAS Companion manual for your operating system.

When SAS reads SPSS system files, SAS preserves as much as possible. Variable names, variable labels, print formats, and the data remain the same. SPSS system missing values become SAS missing values. SPSS value labels are not copied because the SAS equivalent, user-defined formats, are not stored in SAS data sets. If you want value labels, you can create user-defined formats with PROC FORMAT and then use them with FORMAT statements. See section 5.7 for an explanation of how to do this.

Example   The following SAS program reads the SPSS system file SURVEY.SAV, created by the SPSS program in the preceding example. Here two LIBNAME statements are needed, one for the SPSS system file SURVEY.SAV and one for the permanent SAS data set that will be created in the MYDIR directory.

First, SAS prints a copy of the SPSS system file with PROC PRINT. Then, SAS prints a report describing the system file with PROC CONTENTS. Last, the DATA step copies the SPSS system file into a permanent SAS data set named MYDIR.SPSSSURV:

```
LIBNAME myspss SPSS 'survey.sav';
LIBNAME mydir '[]';

PROC PRINT DATA = myspss._FIRST_;

PROC CONTENTS DATA = myspss._FIRST_;

DATA mydir.spsssurv;
   SET myspss._FIRST_;

RUN;
```

In this example, the name SAS uses for the SPSS system file is MYSPSS._FIRST_. MYSPSS is the libref assigned to the SPSS system file in the LIBNAME statement. You can use any name you wish for the libref as long as it follows the rules for valid SAS names (eight characters or shorter; start with a letter or underscore; and contain only letters, numerals, or underscores). Since SPSS system files don't have internal names, you can also use any name for the member name. _FIRST_ is a common member name used for reading external files, but you could use any valid SAS name.

Here is the output:

```
                        The SAS System                              1

   OBS    NAME      AGE   SEX    SONG1    SONG2    SONG3    SONG4    SONG5

    1     Gail       14    1      5        3        1        3        5
    2     Jim        56    2      3        2        2        3        2
    3     Susan      34    1      4        2        1        1        5
    4     Barbara    45    1      3        3        1        2        4
    5     Steve      13    2      5        4        1        4        5



                        The SAS System                              2

                     CONTENTS PROCEDURE

Data Set Name: MYSPSS._FIRST_          Observations:          .
Member Type:   DATA                    Variables:             8
Engine:        SPSS                    Indexes:               0
Created:       11:20 Thurs, June 12, 1994 Observation Length: 64
Last Modified: 13:56 Sat, June 11, 1994   Deleted Observations: 0
Protection:                            Compressed:            NO
Data Set Type: DATA                    Sorted:                NO
Label:

              -----Engine/Host Dependent Information-----

     SPSSINFO: SPSS SYSTEM FILE.  SPSS RELEASE 4.1 FOR VAX/VMS
     COMPRESS: YES
     SPSSTYPE: SPSSX

          --------Alphabetic List of Variables and Attributes--------

     #    Variable   Type   Len   Pos    Label
     ------------------------------------------------------------
     2    AGE        Num     8     8
     1    NAME       Char    8     0
     3    SEX        Num     8    16
     4    SONG1      Num     8    24     Black Water/DB
     5    SONG2      Num     8    32     Bennie and the Jets/EJ
     6    SONG3      Num     8    40     Stayin Alive/BG
     7    SONG4      Num     8    48     Fire and Rain/JT
     8    SONG5      Num     8    56     Country Roads/JD
```

Appendix D   Coming to SAS from a Programming Language

You can write SAS programs that do many of the tasks that traditional programming languages like C, FORTRAN, and BASIC can do. There are many similarities between SAS and these languages, but there are some important differences. If you are used to programming with these types of languages, learning SAS will be easier if you remember the differences.

Built-in loop   The major difference is that SAS has a built-in loop for data handling. If you read data from a file, or process SAS data sets in the DATA step, SAS automatically loops through all the data. In a programming language, you typically need to set up an array to hold the data, then use a loop (DO, WHILE, or FOR) to process the array. You may need to know how many data elements are in the file, or check for end-of-file markers. The DATA step in SAS automates this.

While SAS processes all the data, it only *sees* one observation at a time. All the statements in a DATA step operate on only one observation at a time. In a programming language, you can *see* all the observations at once, by referencing the appropriate array subscript. In SAS you can simulate this using LAG functions or other techniques, but you will find that it is seldom necessary.

Loops   DO loops are present in SAS, but you must keep in mind that a DO loop in SAS is executed with each pass through the DATA step. So if your loop has 6 iterations, and you have 10 observations in your data set, the statements inside your loop will be executed 60 times—6 times for each of the 10 observations (assuming the INPUT or SET statement is not inside the loop). The built-in loop in SAS, in essence, puts a loop around your entire DATA step. Because of the built-in loop, arrays and DO loops are not used nearly as often in SAS programs as they are in other languages.

Arrays   SAS does have arrays, but they are used in different ways than in programming languages. An array in SAS consists of variables. You use arrays when you want to do the same thing to each variable in the array, and you don't want to write a separate statement for each variable. Arrays are temporary in SAS, existing only for the duration of the DATA step in which they are defined. Arrays provide ways to shorten and simplify your SAS programs.

Functions   SAS has many functions available that help simplify your programming tasks. Functions in SAS are used in DATA steps and, therefore, operate within an observation. If you want to find the minimum value for an observation across a group of variables, for example, you would use the MIN function. SAS has many functions available in the following categories: arithmetic, array, character, date and time, financial, mathematical, probability, quantile, random number, sample statistics, state and ZIP code, trigonometric and hyperbolic, and truncation.

Procedures   While functions operate across variables, SAS procedures operate across observations. If you want to find the minimum value for a variable across all observations, then use PROC MEANS. SAS procedures can do a lot in just a few statements. Results from procedures are nicely formatted and you don't have to worry about how many decimal places to print, or where to put the results on the page. A simple PROC PRINT statement, for example, will print all the data in your SAS data set, fit as many variables as it can on a page, decide on the best format for each variable, and label each variable at the top of every page. But, SAS is flexible, so if you don't like the way SAS printed your results, you can change it.

Data types   Another difference between SAS and most other languages, is that SAS has only two types of data: numeric and character. All numbers in SAS are assumed to be double-precision floating-point values. You don't have to declare what type of numbers you are using. You can, however, change the number of bytes used to store data using the LENGTH statement. The default length is 8 bytes, which safely stores all numbers. If you are using small integer values, you might be able to use a length of 4 or less depending on the computer and operating system you are using. The SAS Companion documentation or your operating system will tell you which numbers you can safely store in how many bytes.

Program structure   Many programming languages are particular about the layout of programs. In FORTRAN, for example, any character in column 6 indicates that the line is a continuation of the previous line. SAS has no restrictions on program layout. A statement can be indented, split on many lines, or on the same line as other statements. SAS simply reads a statement from one semicolon to another. In addition, SAS statements are not case sensitive.

Compilation and execution   Most programming languages have separate compile and execute phases. SAS does have separate phases, but when you submit a SAS program it automatically compiles and executes. You can however save compiled SAS DATA steps using the Stored Program Facility in SAS. This facility is most useful for production type jobs with long, compute-intensive, DATA steps.

Comparison of a SAS program to a C program   The following compares a SAS program to a C program. Each program reads the following data from a file and prints it. The data file has three columns for the students' names, ages and grade point averages:

```
Mary    19 3.45
Bob     20 3.12
Scott   22 2.89
Marie   18 3.75
Ruth    20 2.67
```

The SAS Program

```
DATA grades;
   INFILE 'gpa.dat';
   INPUT name $ age gpa;
PROC PRINT;
RUN;
```

The C Program

```c
#include <stdio.h>
#include <stdlib.h>
#define N 1000

void main(void)
{
        FILE *input_fp;
        int i=0,num;

        struct student
        {
                char name[16];
                int age;
                float gpa;
        } grades[N];

        if((input_fp=fopen("gpa.dat","r"))==NULL)
                exit(-1);
        while(fscanf(input_fp,"%s %d %f",\
        grades[i].name,&grades[i].age,&grades[i].gpa)!=EOF)
                ++i;

        for (num=i, i=0; i<num; ++i)
                printf("%s %2d %.2f\n",\
                grades[i].name,grades[i].age,grades[i].gpa);
}
```

In the C program, the variables *name* (character array), *age* (integer), and *gpa* (float) are grouped in a data structure called student. Then, an array of these structures named grades is declared with an arbitrary dimension of N. Each variable in the program must be declared both in type and dimension (if an array). The SAS program has no such section. The variables are defined as either character ($) or numeric in the INPUT statement.

Next, the C program opens the file and uses a while statement to read the data into *grades*, stopping when the end of the file marker (EOF) is returned by *fscanf*. In the SAS program, the DATA step sets up the built-in loop which reads all the data in the file. The INFILE statement specifies which file to read, and the INPUT statement defines the variables. The data are stored in a SAS data set named GRADES.

The final part of the C program uses a *for* statement to print the contents of grades to the standard output device. In the SAS program, a simple PROC PRINT prints the contents of the GRADES data set.

Stored Program Facility

Appendix E   Coming to SAS from SQL

If you already know Structured Query Language (SQL), then you will be pleased to know that you can use SQL statements in SAS programs to create, read, and modify SAS data sets. There are two ways to use SQL with SAS:

▶ You can embed complete SQL statements in the SQL procedure.
▶ You can use WHERE statements to select observations in standard SAS DATA and PROC steps.

Both of these features are available with Base SAS, so you don't have to license any other SAS software to use SQL.

Differences between SQL and SAS   Some vocabulary differences exist between standard SQL and standard SAS. To help you translate between the two, here is a brief dictionary of analogous terms:

SQL term	Analogous standard SAS term
column	variable
row	observation
table	data set
join	merge, set, or update
NULL value	missing value
alias	alias
view	view
no analogous term	DATA step
no analogous term	PROC step

Now that PROC SQL is part of SAS, all SQL terms are technically part of the SAS language too. In the table above, the SQL and SAS terms are separated to clarify differences, but please remember that SQL is part of SAS too.

SQL does not contain structures like SAS DATA and PROC steps. Basically, DATA steps read and modify data while PROC (short for procedure) steps perform specific analyses or functions such as sorting, writing reports, or statistical analyses. In SQL, reports are written automatically whenever you use a SELECT statement; sorting is performed by the ORDER BY clause; and the operations performed by most other SAS procedures don't exist.

SAS has fewer data types than standard SQL. The character data type is the same in both languages. All other SQL data types (numeric, decimal, integer, smallint, float, real, double precision, and date) map to the SAS numeric data type.

PROC SQL   The SQL procedure in SAS follows all but a few of the guidelines set by the American National Standards Institute (ANSI) for implementations of SQL. The work performed by SQL, and therefore by PROC SQL, can also be done in SAS by DATA steps, PROC PRINT, PROC SORT, and PROC MEANS. The basic form of the SQL procedure is:

```
PROC SQL;
   sql-statement;
```

The *sql-statement* in PROC SQL may be any SQL statement—ALTER, CREATE, DELETE, DESCRIBE, DROP, INSERT, SELECT, UPDATE, or VALIDATE—with a semicolon stuck on the end. You can have any number of SQL statements in a single PROC SQL.

You can use PROC SQL interactively or in batch jobs. Unlike most other SAS procedures, PROC SQL will run interactively without a RUN statement. You just need to submit the program statements. Any results from SELECT statements are displayed automatically unless you specify the NOPRINT option on the PROC statement like this:

```
PROC SQL NOPRINT;
```

An SQL view is a stored SELECT statement that is executed at run time. PROC SQL can create views, and other procedures can read views created via PROC SQL.

Example To show how PROC SQL works and to provide a comparison of SQL and SAS, here are programs using PROC SQL and standard SAS to perform the same function.

Creating a data set The first program uses PROC SQL to create and print a simple data set with three variables. This program uses CREATE, INSERT, and SELECT statements in a single PROC SQL step:

```
LIBNAME sports 'c:\mysaslib';
PROC SQL;
   CREATE TABLE sports.customer
      (custno  num,
       name    char(17),
       address char(20));

   INSERT INTO sports.customer
      VALUES (101, 'Murphy''s Sports ', '115 Main St.        ')
      VALUES (102, 'Sun N Ski        ', '2106 Newberry Ave. ')
      VALUES (103, 'Sports Outfitters', '19 Cary Way         ')
      VALUES (104, 'Cramer & Johnson ', '4106 Arlington Blvd.')
      VALUES (105, 'Sports Savers    ', '2708 Broadway       ');

   TITLE 'The SPORTS.CUSTOMER Data';
   SELECT *
      FROM sports.customer;
```

Notice that the LIBNAME statement sets up a libref named SPORTS, pointing to a subdirectory named MYSASLIB on the C drive (DOS, OS/2, Windows). The LIBNAME statement may be different for your operating system. See sections 3.12 and 3.13 for more information about LIBNAME statements. This program creates a permanent SAS data set named SPORTS.CUSTOMER in the MYSASLIB subdirectory. No RUN statement is needed; to run this program you simply submit it to SAS. Here is the output:

```
                    The SPORTS.CUSTOMER Data                    1

          CUSTNO  NAME              ADDRESS
          -------------------------------------------------
             101  Murphy's Sports   115 Main St.
             102  Sun N Ski         2106 Newberry Ave.
             103  Sports Outfitters 19 Cary Way
             104  Cramer & Johnson  4106 Arlington Blvd.
             105  Sports Savers     2708 Broadway
```

The next program uses standard SAS statements to create the same data set. Notice that the LIBNAME statement, the data set name, and the TITLE statement are identical in both programs. LIBNAME statements stay in effect for the duration of a session or job. So, if you ran these programs in a single session or job, you will not have to repeat the LIBNAME statement. It is repeated here only for the sake of completeness:

```
LIBNAME sports 'c:\mysaslib';
DATA sports.customer;
   INPUT custno name $ 5-21 address $ 23-42;
   CARDS;
101 Murphy's Sports   115 Main St.
102 Sun N Ski         2106 Newberry Ave.
103 Sports Outfitters 19 Cary Way
104 Cramer & Johnson  4106 Arlington Blvd.
105 Sports Savers     2708 Broadway
   ;
PROC PRINT;
TITLE 'The SPORTS.CUSTOMER Data';
RUN;
```

Here is the output from the standard SAS program. It looks a little different from the previous report, but it contains the same information:

```
              The SPORTS.CUSTOMER Data                    2

        OBS    CUSTNO    NAME                ADDRESS

         1      101      Murphy's Sports     115 Main St.
         2      102      Sun N Ski           2106 Newberry Ave.
         3      103      Sports Outfitters   19 Cary Way
         4      104      Cramer & Johnson    4106 Arlington Blvd.
         5      105      Sports Savers       2708 Broadway
```

Reading an existing data set The next two programs read the SPORTS.CUSTOMER data set (or table) and select one observation (or row). Here is the PROC SQL version of this program:

```
LIBNAME sports 'c:\mysaslib';
PROC SQL;
   TITLE 'Customer Number 102';
   SELECT *
      FROM sports.customer
      WHERE custno = 102;
```

The PROC SQL output looks like this:

```
                 Customer Number 102                   3

        CUSTNO  NAME              ADDRESS
        ----------------------------------------------------
          102   Sun N Ski         2106 Newberry Ave.
```

The following program uses SAS DATA and PROC steps to select the same observation from the SPORTS.CUSTOMER data set:

```
LIBNAME sports 'c:\mysaslib';
DATA sunnski;
   SET sports.customer;
   IF custno = 102;
PROC PRINT;
   TITLE 'Customer Number 102';
RUN;
```

Here is the PROC PRINT output:

```
                        Customer Number 102                     4

          OBS     CUSTNO     NAME          ADDRESS

           1       102      Sun N Ski    2106 Newberry Ave.
```

WHERE statement   The WHERE statement in SAS is modeled after the WHERE clause of SQL and can be used in DATA or PROC steps to select observations. The subsetting IF statement in SAS, which you can only use in DATA steps, is similar but there are some differences in how it works. When SAS processes a DATA step, it applies WHERE statements earlier than IF statements. This has several repercussions:

▶ The WHERE statement is more efficient than a subsetting IF because it avoids reading unwanted observations.

▶ The WHERE statement can only select observations from existing SAS data sets. The IF statement, however, can select observations from SAS data sets or from raw data files being read with INPUT statements.

▶ With a WHERE statement, you can only select observations based on the values of variables being read. With a subsetting IF statement, you can select observations based on the value of a variable created in the current DATA step.

▶ The WHERE and IF statements may produce different results when two data sets are combined in a MERGE, SET, or UPDATE statement. Operations that occur after SAS applies WHERE statements but before SAS applies IF statements may cause them to select different observations.

Examples   To show how the WHERE statement works and to provide a comparison with the IF statement, here are programs using WHERE and IF statements to perform the same functions. All three of these programs read the SPORTS.CUSTOMER SAS data set created by the previous programs. The goal of these programs is to select and print one observation from an existing SAS data set:

Subsetting IF   This program uses a subsetting IF statement to select one observation:

```
LIBNAME sports 'c:\mysaslib';
DATA sport;
   SET sports.customer;
   IF name = 'Sports Outfitters';
PROC PRINT DATA = sport;
RUN;
```

Here is the output:

```
                        The SAS System                    5

        OBS    CUSTNO        NAME            ADDRESS
         1      103      Sports Outfitters   19 Cary Way
```

WHERE statement in a DATA step

WHERE statement in a DATA step   The next program uses a WHERE statement in the DATA step and then prints the results with PROC PRINT:

```
LIBNAME sports 'c:\mysaslib';
DATA sport;
   SET sports.customer;
   WHERE name = 'Sports Outfitters';
PROC PRINT DATA = sport;
RUN;
```

The output looks like this:

```
                        The SAS System                    6

        OBS    CUSTNO        NAME            ADDRESS

         1      103      Sports Outfitters   19 Cary Way
```

WHERE statement in a PROC step

WHERE statement in a PROC step   The last program uses a WHERE statement directly in the PROC PRINT:

```
LIBNAME sports 'c:\mysaslib';
PROC PRINT DATA = sports.customer;
   WHERE name = 'Sports Outfitters';
RUN;
```

Here is the output:

```
                        The SAS System                    7

        OBS    CUSTNO        NAME            ADDRESS

         3      103      Sports Outfitters   19 Cary Way
```

Notice that the observation number for the first two reports is 1 while the observation number for the last report is 3. This happens because the first two programs create a data set with one observation and then print it. In contrast, the last program never creates a data set, it simply reads the existing data set searching for the right observation, which happens to be number 3.

Efficiency   Although the three previous programs create almost identical reports, they use different amounts of CPU time. The following table compares the amount of time that each program used when being run for this book. Keep in mind that if you started with a raw data file, the results would be different. This comparison is based on programs that read an existing SAS data set:

Type of program	CPU seconds
DATA step with subsetting IF statement and PROC PRINT	5.50
DATA step with WHERE statement and PROC PRINT	2.46
PROC PRINT with WHERE statement	0.55

The amount of time used on your computer will differ, but the conclusion should be the same. WHERE statements can be more efficient, especially when they allow you to avoid DATA steps.

Documentation   The SQL procedure has its own manual, *SAS Guide to the SQL Procedure: Usage and Reference, Version 6, First Edition.*

Index

INPUT reached past end of line
    message in log 35, 166-167, 169
INPUT statement
    column-style 36-37
    data with embedded blanks 36-37
    formatted-style 38-41
    free format 34-35
    list-style 34-35
    mixing input styles 42-43
    multiple INPUT statements 48-49, 138-139
    multiple lines per observation 44-45
    multiple observations per line 46-47
    reading blanks as missing 36-37
    reading non-standard data 38-39
    reading part of a raw data file 48-49
    skipping lines of raw data 44-45
    skipping over variables 36-37
    space delimited 34-35
INSERT statement in SQL procedure 205
inserting text in PROGRAM EDITOR 24-25
INT function 70-71
integer binary informat 40-41
integer data
    data types 12-13
    truncating decimal places 70-71
interactive line mode 19
interactive SAS 19
interleaving SAS data sets 120-121
internal data 32
invalid data message in log 170-171
    lost card note 168-169
invalid option message in log 178-179
inverting data sets 140-141
IS NOT MISSING operator 92
italics, explanation of usage 4-5
iterative logic 84-85

J

jobs, SAS
    executing 18-19
    stop in middle 184-185
Julian dates
    format 80-81, 100-101
    function 70-71, 80-81
    informat 40-41, 80-81
JULIAN*w.* format 80-81, 100-101
JULIAN*w.* informat 40-41, 80-81

justification
    character variables 70-71
    output 29

K

KEEP= data set option 132-133
    to save disk space 187
KENDALL option in CORR procedure 148
KEYS display manager command 23
KEYS window in display manager 22-23
kurtosis
    MEANS procedure 106
    UNIVARIATE procedure 146-147
KURTOSIS option in MEANS procedure 106

L

L95 keyword in REG procedure 150-151
LABEL option in PRINT procedure 96-97
LABEL statement 52-53 ,91
labels
    ATTRIB statement 182
    LABEL statement 52-53, 91
    value 102-103
    variable 52-53
LAST.*byvariable* 142-143
LEFT function 70-71
length of a variable 53, 182-183, 186-187
LENGTH statement
    character data 182-183, 186-187
    numeric data 186-187
LIBNAME statement 56-57
    CC= option 61
    examples by operating system 56-57
    SPSS system files 198
    transport data sets 60-61
    versus other methods for librefs 55
    XPORT engine 60-61
library, SAS data 54-55
libref
    default 54-55
    definition 54-55
    permanent SAS data sets 56-57
licensing SAS software ix
line commands in PROGRAM EDITOR 24-25
line numbers in PROGRAM EDITOR 24-25

variance with MEANS procedure   106
views with SQL procedure   204-205
VMS
    INFILE statement   33
    INFILE statement for transport   61
    LIBNAME statement   56

W

$w. format   100-101
$w. informat   40-41
w.d format   100-101
w.d informat   40-41
warnings in SAS log   162-163
WEEKDATEw. format   80-81, 100-101
WHERE statement
    compared to subsetting IF   207-209
    DATA steps   207-209
    efficiency   209
    procedures   92-93, 207-209
windows in display manager   22-23
Windows operating system
    INFILE statement   33
    LIBNAME statement   56
    LIBNAME statement for transport   61
WITH statement in CORR procedure   148-149
WORDDATEw. format   80-81, 100-101
WORK library   54-55
writing SAS data sets
    DATA step   14-15
    multiple data sets   136-137
    permanent data sets   54-57, 92-93, 116-117
writing raw data files   62-63
writing reports
    custom reports   104-105
    DATA _NULL_   104-105
    PRINT procedure   96-97

X

X display manager command   23
XPORT data engine   60-61

Y

YEARCUTOFF= system option   78
YYQw. format   80-81, 100-101

Z

ZDw.d informat   40-41
ZONE, invalid data message   170-171
zoned decimal data informat   40-41
ZOOM display manager command   23

Special Characters

! comparison operator   73, 92
#n line pointer   44-45, 62-63
& comparison operator   73, 92
¦ comparison operator   73, 92
* ; comments   6-7
+n column pointer   39
/ line pointer   44-45, 62-63
/* */ comments   6-7
    in MVS   185
; semicolon   10
    missing   164-165
< comparison operator   72-73, 92
<= comparison operator   72, 92
= comparison operator   72-73, 92-93
> comparison operator   72-73, 92
>= comparison operator   72, 92
@ line-hold specifier   48-49, 62-63
    compared to @@   49
@@ line-hold specifier   46-47
    compared to @   49
@n column pointer   42-43, 62-63
^= comparison operator   72, 92
| comparison operator   73, 92
|| concatenation operator   71
~= comparison operator   72, 92
¬ = comparison operator   72, 92